Catherine N
A Remarkable Convict Woman

# Catherine McMahon

# A Remarkable Convict Woman

Damian King and Liz Schroeder

ROSENBERG

First published in Australia in 2012
by Rosenberg Publishing Pty Ltd
PO Box 6125, Dural Delivery Centre NSW 2158
Phone: 61 2 9654 1502  Fax: 61 2 9654 1338
Email: rosenbergpub@smartchat.net.au
Web: www.rosenbergpub.com.au

Copyright © Damian King and Liz Schroeder 2012

All rights reserved. No part of this publication may be reproduced, stored in a retrieval system, or transmitted, in any form or by any means, electronic, mechanical, photocopying, recording or otherwise, without the prior permission of the publisher in writing

National Library of Australia Cataloguing-in-Publication entry

Author: King, Damian

Title: Catherine McMahon: a remarkable convict woman / Damian King and Liz Schroeder.

ISBN: 9781921719509 (pbk.)

Notes: Includes index.

Subjects: McMahon, Catherine
Women convicts--Australia--Biography
Irish--Australia--Biography.
Australia--History--19th century.

Other Authors:
Schroeder, Liz.

Dewey Number: 994.402082

Photograph on front cover reproduced with the permission of Tom Banfield, Grampians Paradise Camping and Caravan Parkland.

Printed in China by Everbest Printing Co Limited

# CONTENTS

Preface   7
**Part One: Catherine McMahon**   9
1    Cappabane 1827   9
2    The Potato Famine   12
3    Feeding the Starving   20
4    Transportation to Van Diemen's Land   28
**Part Two: John Copley**   43
5    South Yorkshire   43
6    Crime and Conviction   50
7    A Van Diemen's Land Convict   57
8    A House Burglary in Hobart Town   63
9    Norfolk Island   69
10   New Opportunities in Van Diemen's Land   82
**Part Three: Catherine and John**   87
11   A Convict Relationship   87
12   Establishing a Family and a Business   93
13   Business Troubles   101
14   The Insolvency Court   108
15   Opportunities and Risks   117
16   Seeking Gold   124
**Part Four: Thomas May**   139
17   Growing up in a Royal Seaside Resort   139
18   Rabbit Pie   146
19   A Boy Convict   152
20   A Second Chance   160
**Part Five: Jallukar Selectors**   163
21   Obtaining Land   163
22   The Farmer From Redman Bluff   174

| 23 | Catherine's Battle Begins | 182 |
|---|---|---|
| 24 | Catherine and the Squatters | 198 |
| 25 | A Struggling Widow | 202 |
| 26 | The Upright Thing | 211 |
| 27 | Working the Land | 216 |

**Part Six: Catherine and Thomas**  225
| 28 | Thomas Secures his Selection | 225 |
|---|---|---|
| 29 | Married Life in Stawell | 232 |
| 30 | Rather a Peculiar Will | 240 |

**Part Seven: Catherine's Final Years**  254
| 31 | A Difficult Decision | 254 |
|---|---|---|
| 32 | The Heat of Summer | 263 |

**Epilogue: What Happened to …**  267
Acknowledgments   286
List of Illustrations   287
Bibliography   290
Notes   295
Index   313

# Preface

I do not recall my parents ever discussing the history of their respective families. The present and the future occupied all their attention. However, when I studied Australian history as a teenager, I do remember asking them whether or not we had any convict ancestors. Mother was horrified by my suggestion and both parents assured me that it was not a possibility. I gathered from their response that convict ancestors were definitely not something any respectable family would wish for and my interest in ancestry was quashed. It did not re-emerge until 2002 when, while driving through South Yorkshire, I noticed my maiden name Copley displayed on several business premises and I speculated that maybe this was where my ancestors came from.

After returning to Australia, my friend Damian King used some spare time, a computer and his curiosity to see if he could find out whether or not my family could be traced back to Yorkshire. This was the beginning of five years of research—a process that rewards, excites and at times disappoints. It took remarkably little time to find a Yorkshire connection but this simply gave rise to more questions. Countless visits to libraries and archive centres, travel to England, Ireland, Norfolk Island, Western Australia and Tasmania, letter writing and the expenditure of quite a bit of money gave us some of the answers to our questions and introduced us to three very interesting people, born more than 175 years ago, who did not come to this country by choice. These three people were John Copley and Catherine McMahon, my great-great-grandparents, and Thomas May. As question led to answer and then again to question, Catherine, John and Thomas became alive to us and their stories and the times they lived in obsessed us in a very rewarding and enriching way.

This is their story.

Liz Schroeder (née Copley)

1. Places of significance in the story of Catherine McMahon. (This map taken from: d-maps.com/carte.php?lib=ireland_map&num_car=2295&lang=en)

# PART ONE
# CATHERINE McMAHON

# 1     Cappabane 1827

There is no record of the precise date of Catherine McMahon's birth, although we do know that she was born in early 1827 in the east of County Clare, Ireland.[1] Her family lived in a hilly area known today as Cappabane but identified on maps as Cappaghabaun Mountain.[2] The nearest town of any size is Scarriff, four kilometres to the south on the shores of Lough Derg—part of the Shannon river that runs roughly north-east to south-west through Ireland. Catherine, as a member of a good Catholic family, would have been baptized soon after her birth but again we have no record of the details of her baptism.

This lack of records documenting Catherine's entry into the world is explained by the situation of her family in 1827. English, if they spoke it at all, would have been the second language for the McMahons. The first language of Catherine's parents, James and Margaret ('Peggy'),[3] was the native Irish language.[4] At this time, English law actively discriminated against the Catholic religion and the Catholic Church was not in the position to formally record the cornerstone events of life such as births, marriages and deaths.

The place of Catherine's birth was rural and isolated. In the Scarriff region there was no manufacturing industry of any consequence and virtually all the land was owned by absentee landlords. Most of the local residents rented small allotments and survived on subsistence agriculture.

The main crop they grew was the potato and it was normally a tremendously productive crop.

In November 1825, a little more than a year before Catherine's birth, her father rented seven acres of land on the side of a mountain at Cappabane. This was recorded in a land occupancy record for the townland of Sheean that covered Cappabane and which stated that James 'Priest' McMahon was leasing two acres of second quality land, three acres of third quality land and two acres of fourth quality land. This record was taken to determine the tithe (tax) that land occupiers had to pay towards the upkeep of the Anglican Church in Ireland. This tax was paid by people of all religions and understandably it was the cause of considerable resentment amongst the overwhelmingly Catholic population. In 1825, James 'Priest' McMahon is recorded as paying five shillings towards the upkeep of the Anglican church.[5] While it is very difficult to equate the value of money in Ireland in 1825 to money today, this payment of five shillings would be roughly the equivalent of $500.

We can't be certain why James was identified as 'Priest' McMahon in this tithe land occupancy record, but it was most likely because of the Mass Rock, located at Cappabane very near to his home. From the early eighteenth century onwards, when the English authorities were trying to suppress the Catholic religion in Ireland, people congregated around this large rock to celebrate mass. It was in such an isolated location that Catholic services could be conducted there with little fear of discovery by the authorities. Maybe James McMahon had some sort of custodial role for this very significant site and the name 'Priest' was a shorthand way of recognizing this.

The McMahon house on the eastern side of the mountain was made of grey slate rock[6] with a thatched roof. Today there is a stunning view to the east from where this home was located. Small, lush green paddocks bordered by stone fences, hedges and trees follow the increasingly gradual slope of the land down to the shore of Lough Derg. The lough appears as a

2. The view today from the site of Catherine McMahon's childhood home.

winding ribbon of water that runs as far as the eye can see to both the north and the south. On the far shoreline are the hills of northern Tipperary. Little has changed since Catherine's childhood, except that in 1820s Ireland there were very few trees.

In the 1820s, the McMahon family actually lived in a community known as a clachan—a cluster of houses where there were close ties between the families. The Collins, Hart, Bolen, McNamara, Black and Minogue households were included in this clachan and they supported each other through the challenges and problems of life.[7] Notwithstanding this supportive environment, James McMahon, as a renter, had only a tenuous hold on his land. He did not have the vote in parliamentary elections and, without fluent English, he had at best a limited understanding of the language of law and business. As a Catholic, his rights were further restricted and indeed, at the time of Catherine's birth, it was illegal for a Catholic to sit in the British parliament. As a married woman, his wife, Peggy, had no property rights whatsoever. Catherine was born into a family where she would be loved, into a community where she should find plenty of support and into a land that was beautiful and fertile. It had to be hoped that this would be enough to ensure a smooth journey through life.

# 2   The Potato Famine

By the beginning of 1845, the family of Peggy and James McMahon had increased to six sons—Denis, William, Michael, Patrick, James and John.[8] Catherine was their only daughter. Now seventeen years of age, the red-haired, freckle-faced Catherine[9] would have been very familiar with the world around her home. She no doubt knew the story of the Mass Rock, where occasionally mass was still celebrated, and understood the importance of Lough Derg and the Shannon River as a vital transport route. She almost certainly appreciated the importance of the nearby Holy Island where more than 1200 years earlier monks had established a monastery. Holy Island, in Lough Derg, is one of the most significant religious sites in Ireland, considered a holy place by the people of East Clare. By now she would have known the members of all the families at Cappabane because she was growing up in an environment where you relied on the support of your local community.

There is anecdotal evidence to suggest that the amount of land the McMahons rented may have increased from seven acres in 1825 to around ten acres by this time.[10] With the significant growth in the size of his family, it is easy to understand why James would have been interested in increasing the amount of land he worked.

Neither James nor any of the other men who farmed at Cappabane owned any of the land. It was owned by absentee English landlords, Sir Arthur B. Brooke and Lady Franklin. These two landlords engaged an Irish land agent, John Sampson, and it was from Sampson that James and the other small farmers rented their holdings.[11] Their rental payments had increased significantly since Catherine was born. In that period the rent paid for the McMahon holding had increased by at least 500 percent.[12] This increase had been propelled by substantial growth in the Irish population and in the export markets that had opened up for grains and livestock. This meant that the owners of agricultural land could extract higher rents from land that was used to service export markets than from small allotments rented to families who had to survive on subsistence agriculture. To add to the tenant farmers' problems, they still had no security of tenure and no recognition or reward for improvements they made to the land. Their security rested almost totally on the success that was experienced with the annual potato harvest.

In September 1845, a disaster hit Ireland that was to kill hundreds of thousands of people and totally change the direction and circumstances of Catherine's life. This disaster was the Irish potato famine.

Prior to July 1845, the weather in Ireland had been good and there had been every indication that they were in for a bumper potato crop in early October. However, in August there was heavy rain throughout the country, accompanied by humid conditions and it was well known that this was not favourable for the potato. Far worse was to come when on 16 September 1845 the eminent English botanist Dr John Lindley announced that 'the potato murrain has unequivocally declared itself in Ireland'.[13] The potato murrain or blight that was at this time spreading across Ireland was later found to be caused by a fungus *Phytophthora infestans* that initially attacked the leaves on the potato plant and then spread throughout the plant to the potatoes themselves.

The impact of the blight on the McMahons' 1845 potato harvest was not recorded but it was estimated that around half of that year's potato harvest in Ireland was lost to the blight. At this time potatoes were the main crop of most small land-holders, although part of the land was often planted with another crop such as oats. A ten acre holding was far larger than that of many families, so if the McMahons had been able to extract some sound potatoes from their holding and get another crop from the land they would have experienced hardship in the latter part of 1845 and into 1846, but it would not have been a disaster. Some families rented as little as a quarter of an acre and if the potato crop failed on such a small holding the family immediately faced a desperate situation. However, at this time the Irish people still had real hope for some support from the government authorities to get them through the major food shortage caused by the potato blight.

In 1845, the British Government did provide some assistance to mitigate this food shortage. Lead by the Conservative Prime Minister Robert Peel, they intervened in the market and made Indian corn available at cost price. This corn was of poor quality but at least the corn merchants were not given a totally free hand to exploit the situation. Also some employment relief schemes were initiated in late 1845. Nevertheless, the main factor that enabled the Irish people to get through the period to mid-1846 was hope—hope that the blight would not strike again and that this season would produce a good potato harvest.

*\*\**

Sadly, hopes and prayers were not fulfilled and the 1846 potato harvest was a disaster. There were no potatoes to harvest. Accounts of the failure of this crop are quite stark. One night, small land-holders went to bed with an apparently vigorous and healthy potato crop on their land and woke the next day to find the same potato plants withered and dead. Catherine and her family would have shared this experience. Like virtually all other small holders they would have hastily dug up the withered plants to find out the condition of the tubers. The blight was so potent that in most cases the tubers had already started to rot. The prospects for the McMahon family were dire.

The effect of the failure of the 1846 potato crop in Ireland was like a dam bursting. People had placed everything on the hope of a good crop. With this hope gone, all people had was hunger, depression and panic. The Work House at Scarriff had been built in 1841 to hold a maximum of 600 paupers,[14] but by November 1846 it had 700 inmates.[15] There was vigorous competition for the limited employment places on the government relief schemes. Groups of men engaged in standover tactics and threatened government officials in an attempt to obtain employment which would give them the ability to purchase some food.

Inevitably the number of potato famine deaths and burials in the Scarriff area began to increase. The local graveyard started to fill rapidly. Unfortunately at this time wood was in short supply throughout Ireland, so on occasions the dead were taken to their burial in a recycled coffin. When the coffin was laid above the grave and the burial was due to take place, a lever was pulled on the side of the coffin, the hinged bottom swung open and the body dropped into the bottom of the grave. The coffin was then used again and again for other burials.

While the conditions were rapidly deteriorating, changes in the British Government meant that even less support was now going to be provided. Robert Peel and his Conservative Government were defeated in a general election and replaced by the Whig Free Market Government led by Lord John Russell. The new government strongly believed that the Irish alone should meet all the costs associated with the failure of the potato crop and that the market should be responsible for organizing and providing replacement food. This included the market setting the price for corn.

Although the potato harvest failed completely, there was still plenty of food grown in Ireland that year. Scarriff was a good area for growing grain and in 1846 excellent oat and wheat crops were harvested[16] and sold to local merchants. Despite large numbers of people now starving in the district, most of this grain was exported and not sold for local consumption. The same fate awaited most of the livestock in the fields around Scarriff, with large land-holders selling cattle and sheep to export markets. By October

1846, the McMahons and all the small land-holders in the region faced a very uncertain future. The stark question to be answered was how would they survive the coming winter?

\*\*\*

The winter of 1846/1847 was one of the worst in memory. One of the only pluses of the terrible weather was that with snow lying on the ground at Cappabane, the McMahons would have been able to track hares and rabbits through the snow to catch and eat.[17] In early 1847, the public works program that provided some income for men to purchase food for their hungry families ceased. The British Government was withdrawing most of the limited support it had been giving and now the Irish were supposed to live on free market ideology.

It should not be inferred from this that these public works programs provided either reasonable or generous support for the hungry men who worked on them. Workers were paid between eight pence and ten pence a day. At the free market corn prices that applied in January 1847, this would have enabled a man to purchase around fifteen kilograms of corn with one week's wage. This was not enough to feed himself, much less a wife and other family members.[18]

When we compare the British Government's treatment of the starving Irish to their treatment of British army horses at this time, we get a clear picture of its priorities. In 1847, each British army horse in Ireland was fed 4.5 kilos of oats and 5.4 kilos of hay daily and this cost the government one shilling and nine pence.[19] Yet in early 1847, the British government decided it was no longer prepared to pay eight pence a day to give starving Irish labourers some ability to purchase food for their families.

Through 1846 and 1847 the death rate in the Scarriff area continued to grow. There was now no ceremony associated with death. There was no coffin, not even a recycled one. Individual carts carrying five or six bodies travelled through the town and no mourners followed them. These bodies were buried anonymously in mass graves. By early 1847, the Scarriff graveyard was full and people did not even try to observe any of the rituals of death.[20]

When it withdrew employment relief programs, the British Government decided to support the provision of soup in areas where people were desperate for food and famine relief. However, as often occurs with the implementation of new government policies, it took longer to establish the soup kitchens than the authorities envisaged. This meant more people starved to death waiting for the kitchens to be established. A soup kitchen was eventually established at Cappabane and was run by a person with the name of Alison.[21]

The soup in these kitchens was cooked in a boiler provided by the government and contained a variety of ingredients such as meat, fish, vegetables, grain or meal. Along with the soup, each person received a daily issue of either one and a half pounds of bread, or one pound of biscuit, flour grain or meal. A person under nine years of age was given a half issue. This soup issue was not the equivalent of the normal diet for the people at Cappabane. In fact, it was the bare minimum to sustain health. At this time, some deaths went unreported so that the family could continue to collect the dead person's issue. Hiding a death in the family was sometimes the means by which other family members survived.

\*\*\*

The 1847 potato crop in Ireland was the first crop in three years that had not been affected by blight but, unfortunately, at the start of the season only a small amount of ground had been planted out with potatoes. We do not know the amount of potatoes harvested from the McMahon land-holding that year, but even land-holders who did harvest a good potato crop were still under considerable pressure. Landowners were pressing them for overdue rent and the government authorities were pressing for the payment of taxes.

The new British Government policy of offering virtually no support for famine victims caused major economic problems in Ireland. Very heavy rates of taxation had to be applied to the land to pay the costs associated with the operation of the Irish work houses. At this time, the work houses were given full responsibility for providing famine relief within their regions.

The new British Government policy also contained two key provisions that were designed to bring about a dramatic restructure in land occupation in Ireland. The first of these provisions involved the landlords becoming responsible for paying the land tax on land rented by small land-holders. As the land tax in the Scarriff area almost doubled to seven shillings and six pence per pound of land value,[22] this created a strong incentive for landlords to throw small land-holders off their land. The second provision required that in order for a person or family to be eligible to receive famine relief from a work house, they must not rent or hold any land or other assets. Prior to September 1847, people could receive famine relief, yet in the next year return to their land and a normal livelihood. Under this new provision, this could no longer happen. These two provisions were designed to remove the small land-holders in Ireland from their land in a very short period of time. In introducing these provisions, the British Government was inviting disaster for hundreds of thousands of families.

The one positive for the small Irish land-holders in late 1847 into 1848 was the hope that the potato blight had in fact disappeared from the land. Many people took the view that all they had to do was to plant out as much acreage as they could in early 1848 and then survive until a large crop was harvested in September/October. However, by August it was apparent that this strategy was going to fail dismally. In the Scarriff region and throughout County Clare, the blight struck as strongly as it had in 1846.

Catherine's brother, Denis, his wife Julia and their young child went into the Scarriff work house at around this time,[23] but there was very little support for them there. In June 1848, there were 900 people in the work house and it was providing support to many more people outside its walls. Its weekly expenditure was £700 and no rates were being paid to the authority that ran it. It was £15,000 in debt and had no credit anywhere. Denis and his family soon returned to Cappabane. On Christmas Eve the sheriff took possession of the work house and its effects were sold off in an effort to raise some money for the creditors. Blankets and bedding were taken from the starving inmates and auctioned. A riot followed, but with the intervention of the police the successful bidders were able to strip the work house of its goods.[24]

By late 1848, the Scarriff region and much of County Clare was in a state of economic and social collapse. A large number of families were now being thrown off their land or were leaving it voluntarily. There was no support available from the government for many thousands of hungry and destitute people. There was widespread famine and death and people were now so desperate that they were prepared to do virtually anything to survive.

# 3   Feeding the Starving

By February 1849, the McMahon family and others at Cappabane were starving. Catherine's father James was dead.[25] We do not know when or how he died but most likely death was caused by starvation or an associated disease. The last option available to the McMahons to obtain some meat—by tracking and catching hares and rabbits through the winter snows—was not available at this time. In early February, a period of mild weather set in and there was no snow on the ground.[26]

In desperation, the McMahons focused on a large supply of meat that was available close to Cappabane—the flock of sheep owned by a local farmer, Darby Rogers. Darby farmed in the Aughrim townland, on the western side of the Cappabane mountain ridge, and he was one of the largest farmers in the Scarriff region.[27] He would have produced grain, livestock and wool for export markets. Darby had significant problems of his own with the high rents that applied to his land and the very heavy taxes charged by the authorities that ran the Scarriff work house. He also had a growing problem with hundreds of starving people in the vicinity looking enviously at his livestock and at the produce grown on his land. By early February 1849, one cow had already been stolen from his farm. Nevertheless, the McMahons and their neighbours had more serious problems and the McMahons decided that Darby should, on an involuntary basis, contribute one of his sheep to the starving people on the eastern side of the mountain.

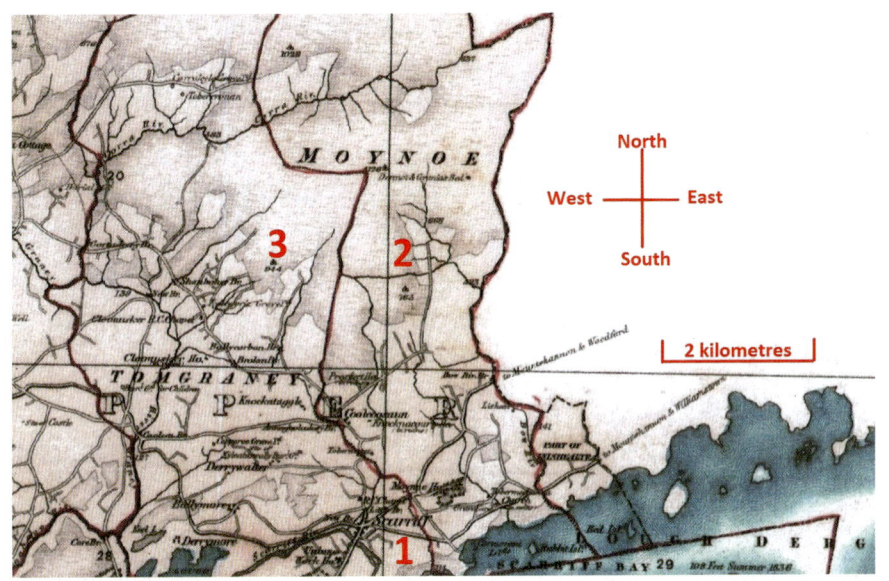

3. 1842 Ordnance Survey map covering the Scarriff and Cappabane region with places of significance highlighted: 1. Scarriff; 2. The location of the McMahon home; and 3. The location of Darby Rogers' farm.

On the night of Sunday, 4 February 1849, at least a couple of hours before midnight, Denis, William and Catherine left their home and headed west, taking with them a knife that was used by the family for slaughtering and cutting up livestock.[28] They would have known the surrounding countryside like the back of their hands. After they crossed the ridge, they walked down the western slope, entered one of Darby Rogers' fields and caught and slaughtered one of his sheep. This was the depth of winter and the warm blood of the slaughtered sheep would have created a large steam plume as it drained from the carcass and made contact with the freezing winter air. The three siblings would have worried that the steam plume might draw attention to their presence in Darby's field. By moonlight, they roughly carved up the sheep into four quarters.

Carrying the four quarters of the slaughtered sheep and their knife, they then headed back to the eastern side of the Cappabane mountain. On their way, they called in at the house of the widow Hart and gave her two forequarters and one rear quarter of mutton.[29] The widow Hart's domestic situation is not known, but we do know that she was almost certainly a friend of the McMahons. In 1825, two families with the surname Hart lived near the Mass Rock in close proximity to the McMahons.[30] In this community, people supported each other and this is what Catherine, Denis and William were doing when they shared the slaughtered sheep with the widow and her family at the worst of times during the potato famine.

Denis, William and Catherine then headed for home. It had been a big night and they must have been looking forward to giving the remaining rear quarter of mutton to their mother and going to bed.

At around midnight, and not far from their home, they were confronted by a police patrol.[31] No doubt the police were immediately suspicious of anyone walking around outside at this hour in the depth of winter, and they already knew the McMahons and were later to describe them as a family of the 'worst character'.[32] Because of stock losses in the area, the Scarriff police were undertaking night patrols. Apparently by chance, this patrol consisting of Constable Colleary and Sub-Constables Dwane and Gibson had stumbled upon the three siblings. Although the McMahons tried to hide the evidence, the police found the quarter of sheep and the knife that was still covered in blood. At this, they took the three into custody.[33] Catherine, Denis and William were never to return to the family home at Cappabane.

The next morning, Darby Rogers found the remains of the slaughtered sheep in his field. No doubt, he also heard that the police had arrested three of the McMahon siblings with a hind quarter of mutton in their possession. What was needed was evidence that showed that the mutton came from his slaughtered sheep. Patrick Dwyer, his servant, provided this evidence. Dwyer came forward and told him that the widow Hart had the remaining three quarters of the sheep and that the McMahons had given it to her. Dwyer added that on the previous night he had seen the three McMahons in Darby's field, killing, skinning and carrying away the carcass of the sheep.[34]

Darby promptly notified the police, and Constable Thomas Taylor attended the house of the widow Hart. Taylor was later to report that the widow 'immediately gave up two fore quarters and one hind quarter of mutton and without hesitation stated that it had been left the previous night by the McMahons and that they had told her that it was one of Darby Rogers sheep they had killed'.[35] The widow Hart had clearly decided that she was going to cooperate with the police in the hope that she could avoid facing a charge with the McMahons.

The Scarriff police now had all the evidence they needed. Denis, William and Catherine were each charged with killing and stealing a sheep from Darby Rogers and continued to be held in custody. The charges were to be heard at the Clare Spring Assizes in Ennis, the largest city in the county.

\*\*\*

On 5 February 1849, which was the first full day in custody for Catherine, William and Denis, an article under the headline 'REPEAL OF THE CORN LAWS AND IRISH DISTRESS' appeared in the *Clare Journal*.[36] The *Journal*, which was the main newspaper that circulated throughout County Clare, was primarily a newspaper for businesspeople, professionals and farmers of large land-holdings. This article referred to the abolition of the British parliament's Corn Laws that up until only a few days earlier had placed a government tax on the importation of food into Ireland. It warned the nation that the present parlous state of affairs could not be allowed to continue and it noted that 'an anomalous condition of society exists around us! While one portion of the community are crying out against the superabundance of food which the country contains, another portion pines away and dies for want of the common necessaries of life!' It predicted rising discontent among the people that would auger ill for 'order and good government in Ireland'. It observed that 'Of provisions, the country now, it seems, contains "enough to spare"—and yet, even now, gaunt famine desolates the land around us. Thousands of the people willing to labour for their bread, are daily pining away under the half sustenance doled out to them; and gradually dropping into their graves; while they are debarred from the culture of that fertile soil which invites their labour, and would furnish them with an ample reward.'

It urged that people had to be given gainful employment on the land and strongly advised the landlord class to sacrifice 'all narrow selfish views to the advancement of the public good'. It demanded that 'In the name of the starving and—we regret to add—now deeply demoralized people— some decisive measure for ameliorating the physical and moral condition of the country' needed to be taken. It clearly stated that the landlord class was responsible for solving these problems and that they must put an end to the situation of 'people starving in the midst of plenty'. This was the Ireland that had left Catherine, Denis and William McMahon believing they had no option but to steal and kill a sheep.

\*\*\*

Soon after the three siblings were charged, they were taken on a forty kilometre journey from Scarriff to Ennis for their trial at the Clare Spring Assizes. The McMahon family was probably aware that it was unusual in County Clare for people to receive a long prison sentence or a sentence of transportation if they were convicted of sheep stealing for the first time. At the 1848 Clare Spring Assizes, men convicted of sheep stealing offences received twelve to eighteen months imprisonment, and some women received as little as one month in gaol.[37] With famine rife in County Clare, it would have been reasonable to believe that the punishment for stealing food would have been no greater in 1849 than it had been in 1848.

Catherine and her two brothers were taken to the county gaol in Ennis. Catherine was held in the women's area of the prison that was separate from the main area where Denis and William were held. This gaol was originally constructed to hold 115 prisoners, but in February 1849 it held 740.[38] In the three and half years since the first failure of the potato harvest, a crime wave had occurred as people became more desperate in the fight for survival. This was not unique to Clare, and the gaols of the neighbouring counties of Galway, Limerick and Tipperary (south riding) were equally overcrowded.[39] For Catherine, who had lived all her life in the country, the close confinement of the Ennis gaol would have been a dramatic and horrific contrast to everything she had previously known.

The Clare Spring Assizes opened on Wednesday, 28 February, and were conducted at the Ennis Courthouse in the very centre of the city.

In 1849, this courthouse was in a poor state of repair and in fact it was knocked down in the following year. It was located where, today, a column supporting a statue of the great Irish Liberator Daniel O'Connell is to be found. There were 327 people to be tried on criminal matters at these Assizes.[40] The criminal cases were dealt with before Baron Richards, who was a large landowner in County Clare. In the month prior to these Assizes, Richards' estate agent was throwing people off lands they had rented for years and levelling their houses and cabins.[41] Baron Richards was

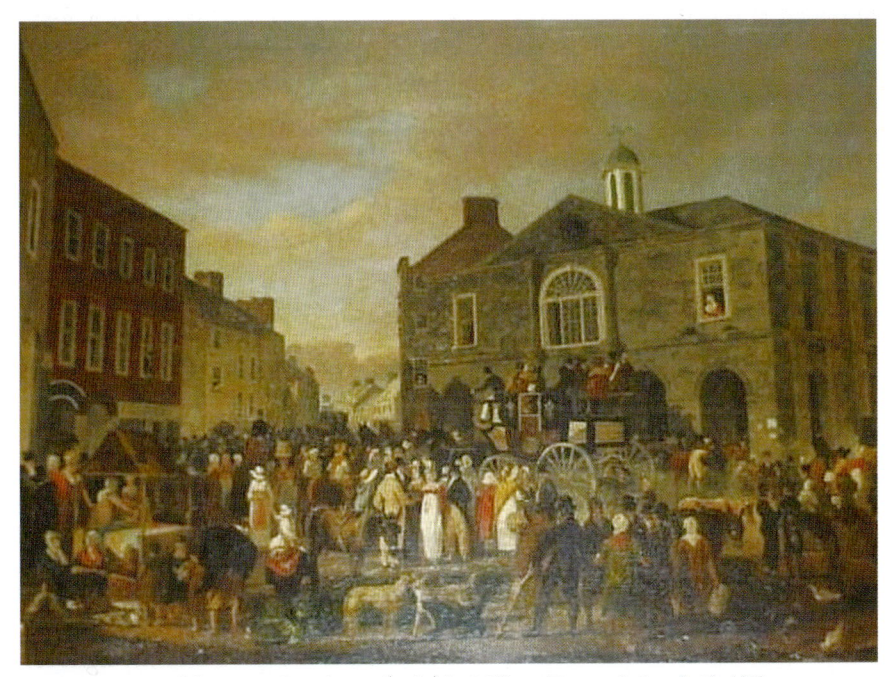

4. 1820 painting of the Ennis Courthouse (right) by William Turner de Lond titled 'The marketplace and court-house, Ennis, Co. Clare'.

implementing the British Government policy in relation to restructuring land occupation in Ireland and he was clearly determined that he was not going to pay land taxes on behalf of impoverished small land-holders. At the opening of the proceedings, Richards expressed concern at the large number of cases involving cattle stealing and larceny.[42] This was the first indication of the approach he was to take to such cases.

The sheep stealing charges against Catherine, Denis and William were all dealt with at the same time. Catherine and Denis also faced charges of stealing potatoes. There were three witnesses for the prosecution.

The first witness was Constable Colleary. He gave evidence about the police's encounter with the three McMahons at around midnight on the night of 4 February and about the bloody knife and the rear quarter of mutton that was found in their possession.[43]

The next witness was Patrick Dwyer. He told the court that he had seen the McMahons killing, skinning and carrying away Darby Rogers' sheep and leaving the mutton at the widow Hart's house.[44]

The widow Hart also gave evidence and confirmed that the three accused had given her the mutton and told her that it was from one of Darby Roger's sheep.[45] Once the police arrived at her house on 5 February, she would have had little option but to cooperate. Not to do so would be a death sentence for her family. She could not afford to be sentenced to gaol and she was doing what she believed she had to do in order to survive.

The McMahons do not appear to have had a 'legal' defence to present to the court. They may well have told the court that they were starving, their family was starving and most of the community of Cappabane was starving. It would have been reasonable for them to point out that they had in fact given most of the mutton away to others in the community. This sheep stealing offence appears to have been the most justifiable of crimes in the most extraordinary of times.

The jury found the three siblings guilty of all charges. Denis and

Catherine were found guilty of sheep stealing and stealing potatoes and William of sheep stealing.[46]

The severity of the sentences brought down by Judge Baron Richards must have horrified the McMahons. Catherine was sentenced to be transported for seven years for the sheep stealing conviction, and she received a further one month sentence for stealing potatoes. Denis was sentenced to be transported for ten years for the sheep stealing conviction and a further three months for stealing potatoes. William was sentenced to be transported for ten years for the sheep stealing conviction.[47]

While it was no consolation to Catherine and her brothers, Baron Richards had sentenced most who came before him in the same harsh manner. He had given 120 persons transportation sentences of varying terms. Most of these people had been convicted of livestock or other stealing offences. For the full calendar year of 1849, 341 persons received transportation sentences at the Clare Assizes. This compares to 104 persons sentenced to transportation in 1848. In fact, in the eight years prior to the commencement of the potato famine in 1845, only 161 persons were sentenced to transportation at the Clare Assizes.[48]

The priorities of Baron Richards can best be seen in his treatment of the McMahons compared to his treatment of John Fox. Fox was convicted of rape but was only given a seven year transportation sentence.[49] The large land-owning Baron Richards was clearly far more concerned with the security of livestock than the treatment of people.

In less than a month, Catherine had gone from freely roaming the beautiful land on the mountain side at Cappabane to being a convicted felon held in Ennis gaol. All her life, she had watched the waters of the Shannon River run from the north to the south through Lough Derg heading for the oceans of the world. She was now going to see where all that water went.

# 4 Transportation to Van Diemen's Land

On the morning of Tuesday, 27 March 1849, Catherine was one of twenty-nine women prisoners at the Ennis gaol who were loaded into horse-drawn prison vans and taken to the city of Limerick, forty kilometres away.[50] All of these women had been convicted at the recent Clare Spring Assizes and had received sentences of transportation.

By now Catherine would have heard that she was to be sent to Van Diemen's Land, as it was then the only transportation destination for women convicts. She would have known that it was highly unlikely she would ever see her mother Margaret again, or her four brothers, James, Patrick, Michael and John. At this time there was also no guarantee that she would ever be reunited with Denis and William, as in the late 1840s male convicts could be transported to either Van Diemen's Land or Bermuda in the West Indies. For all her life Catherine had lived in a large and close family but now she faced being totally cut off from them.

At Limerick, Catherine and the other female prisoners from Clare were loaded on the 2 pm train bound for Dublin.[51] She was about to be taken to the Grangegorman Depot, where women awaiting transportation were held. In due course, William was taken to Kilmainham prison in Dublin[52] and Denis to Spike Island in Cork Harbour. After spending time at Kilmainham prison, William joined his brother on Spike Island where they both awaited transportation.[53]

Since her arrest, Catherine had been confronted by many new and challenging experiences. Prior to her arrest, she had almost certainly never been to the busy centre of Ennis. The Ennis gaol was another new experience and very definitely an unpleasant one. Now she was to travel by train from Limerick to Dublin. This train line and service had only been established a few years earlier and it was one of the first in Ireland. This would have been a day of mixed emotions for Catherine. She would have felt deep grief for the loss of her family and an intense fear of the unknown but perhaps, despite her grief and fear, she would have experienced a thrill of excitement when she boarded this very new form of transport.

By ten that night, eight hours after boarding the Limerick train, Catherine had not only arrived in Dublin but she was logged in at the Grangegorman Depot to the north-west of the city centre.[54] At this time, the Grangegorman Depot was the only female prison in the United Kingdom. It housed both women awaiting transportation and women serving their sentences in Ireland.

An important function of Grangegorman was to train women bound for Van Diemen's Land in work skills such as sewing, knitting, cooking and cleaning. The women also received two hours training a day in reading and writing. This was meant to make them suitable for employment as hired servants. Having lived in a household with her mother and six brothers, Catherine would already have gained a sound knowledge of domestic skills, but she was illiterate and had the added disadvantage that her first language was the native Irish and therefore she was a long way behind women whose first and often only language was English. When Catherine grew up at Cappabane in the 1830s, the education of children was limited to a hedge school where a very basic curriculum was provided in informal classes in the open air or, if they were lucky, in a farmer's barn. Because she was girl, it was unlikely that her parents thought it necessary to give her even this rudimentary education, and the Grangegorman Depot almost certainly provided her first experience of any formal learning.

The diet at the Grangegorman Depot was limited but it was an improvement on what had been available at home prior to her arrest. For breakfast, she had seven ounces (about ¾ cup) of oat and Indian corn meal porridge and a pint (about two cups) of milk. For dinner, she had one pound (about half a loaf) of wholemeal bread and a pint of buttermilk. Potatoes and meat were not features of the diet at the Grangegorman Depot.[55]

Catherine spent a little less than three months at Grangegorman. Her gaol report described her as 'never been convicted before and quiet'.[56] This was not a surprising report for a young woman from the country who was a long way from home in an environment that was totally and frighteningly unfamiliar.

Catherine left Grangegorman Depot as one of 200 female convicts who were taken under police escort to the Victoria Wharf, Kingston, eleven kilometres south of Dublin. At Victoria Wharf, the women boarded the barque *Australasia* that was to transport them to Van Diemen's Land. Prior to departure, Catherine was given a set of rosary beads. Rosary beads were given to all the women who could not read, while the minority who could read were given prayer books.[57]

On Tuesday, 26 June 1849, the *Australasia* left Dublin bound for Hobart Town, Van Diemen's Land.[58] As well as leaving Dublin, Catherine and the other female convicts were also leaving behind the Irish potato famine. This was undoubtedly a positive feature of their transportation. It is estimated that by 1852 around one million people had died in Ireland as a result of the potato famine and the highest proportion of famine deaths were in the western counties, which included County Clare.

*\*\*\**

As the *Australasia* sailed down the east coast of Ireland and into the Atlantic Ocean, there were more than just the 200 women convicts on board. There were 28 children, 26 of them offspring of the female convicts, a ship's crew of 33 led by Captain James Connell, and 5 free settlers including Alexander Kilroy, the Surgeon Superintendent, and Miss Lambert, the matron. The

Surgeon Superintendent was responsible for the health of the women and their discipline on the voyage. Miss Lambert was responsible for their religious instruction and she also supervised the schooling and work classes. The *Australasia* also carried a cargo that included wool and oil.[59]

Alexander Kilroy initially observed that on leaving Kingston the health of the women convicts seemed 'excellent'. He later observed in his journal that 'in reality' their health was not excellent, 'for most of them had suffered from insufficient and bad food before their conviction and in Grangegorman Depot had been fed a good deal on bread and milk which gave them a healthy appearance, but very soon after the change from that diet to the salt provisions of the ship they suffered considerably in health, labouring under obstipation with indigestion and gastric irritation'. Kilroy recorded that this change to ship salt provisions 'was felt the more suddenly from the want of the usual supply of potatoes which are generally given to fresh convict ships and which could not be procured at the time the *Australasia* sailed from Kingston.'[60]

On board the ship, the convict women were formed into messes of around eight women. Each mess slept and ate together and one woman acted as the mess captain. The mess captain was responsible for distributing rations to the women in her mess and making sure they kept their area clean. The diet of Catherine and the other convicts consisted of bread, salt pork or beef, and peas and they were also given lemon juice with sugar to help prevent scurvy. In the last week of the voyage the convict diet improved, with preserved potatoes served every second day and rice substituted for peas.[61]

On the voyage three convict women died—all of dysentery. Three convict children also died but one baby was born. Unfortunately he was born prematurely and died eighteen days later. Alexander Kilroy recorded sixty-one cases of obstipation (severe and obstinate constipation) in his journal of the voyage and dysentery became more prevalent on the ship after it passed the Cape of Good Hope and the weather became colder. Interestingly, Alexander Kilroy put this down to the thinness of the shoes worn by the women whose feet became cold and damp whenever they were on deck.[62]

The *Australasia* made good time on its voyage and arrived in Sullivan's Cove, Hobart Town, on 29 September 1849,[63] ninety-five days after its departure from Ireland. Kilroy described Catherine's conduct during the voyage as 'quiet'.[64] The women were kept on board for a further five days and during this time they attended an address given by Father William Hall, the Catholic Vicar-General of Van Diemen's Land. In this address, Father Hall covered the need for the women to put their days of crime behind them and he outlined the opportunities for a good woman in Van Diemen's Land.[65]

There was another visitor to the barque while they were awaiting permission to disembark; the convict muster master came on board to obtain the convict records. The record he received for Catherine contained the following information. She was twenty-two years of age and five feet and half an inch in height. Her complexion was described as ruddy and freckled, and she had a round head with a medium forehead, red eyebrows and grey eyes. Her hair was red. Her nose, mouth and chin were described as medium.[66] The record listed her religion as Roman Catholic, reported that she was illiterate and described her occupation as farm servant.

\*\*\*

When Catherine disembarked from the *Australasia*, the Hobart Town she saw spread out before her was a city with a population of more than 20,000. At this time, the total population of the island colony of Van Diemen's Land was more than 70,000. Although there was starting to be a significant push amongst the people of the colony for the abolition of transportation, there was an imbalance in the population with a ratio of two males to every female. The British authorities did not consider such an imbalance desirable for good order and they saw a need to increase the female population. Catherine and the other Irish women from the *Australasia* answered this need. They were not only in the colony to serve their sentence of punishment but to assist with a serious social problem.

The recognition by the authorities of the need for convict women in the colony is evident when we compare Catherine's situation in early October 1849 to that of her two brothers who were convicted at the same time. Seven months after her conviction, Catherine was already in Van Diemen's Land, whereas Denis and William were still in Ireland at the Spike Island prison near Cork. In fact, it was September 1850, nearly twelve months later, before Denis and William started their voyage on the transportation ship *Hyderabad*.[67]

\*\*\*

On leaving the *Australasia* in early October 1849, Catherine was transferred to the hulk *Anson*, a former British naval warship that had served as a hulk for convict women since 1844. It was moored in the Derwent River off Queen's Domain. Most female convicts at this time spent a six month probationary period on the *Anson*. During Catherine's time on board, she undertook work that was considered good training for domestic service such as sewing, spinning, knitting and dressmaking. She was also given regular

5. The *Anson* moored at Queen's Domain near Hobart Town.

religious instruction by Sarah Troy, the Roman Catholic Catechist, and she attended rudimentary schooling in reading and writing. Sarah Troy also helped interpret for those convicts who only spoke Irish. Catherine and the other women exercised by walking on the deck twice a day for up to an hour, and during this time they were allowed to engage in quiet conversation. The women slept in hammocks and were provided with three meals a day.[68]

In April 1850, Catherine was transferred to the Brickfield Hiring Depot in New Town. From this depot, convict women were hired out for domestic service in the Hobart Town area. The Brickfield Depot did not operate as a gaol but the women held there were subject to a set of rules. They were not allowed to communicate with people outside the depot, restrictions applied on the property they could keep in their possession and they could not smoke or drink. Punishments for breaches of the rules were carried out at the Cascades Female Factory in Hobart Town.

For the twelve months from April 1850 to the start of April 1851, Catherine spent her time either at the Brickfields Depot or working in hired domestic service. In many ways she was now far better off than she had been at Cappabane. In Ireland she had been forced to exist on a government soup kitchen diet whereas at the Brickfield Depot or in hired service she was provided with shelter and adequate food. The rules for female convicts in hired service stipulated that they had to be provided with suitable lodgings and bedding and that, as a minimum, they had to be given a daily ration that consisted of 1 pound of meat, 1½ pounds of bread or 1 pound of bread and 2 pounds of vegetables, an ounce of roast wheat or ¼ ounce of tea, 1 ounce of sugar and ½ ounce of salt.[69] On the other side of the ledger, Catherine was living as a convict under convict discipline, in a new and unfamiliar country, in a city rather than the countryside, and she had no family support. She committed no offences against the rules of the convict system in this period, but it was still to be seen how she would react when she became more familiar with her environment.

\*\*\*

By April 1851, Catherine appeared to have adjusted to her new life. She had moved in and out of hired domestic service and was no doubt aware that if she continued to observe all rules and regulations, her good conduct would be rewarded. Subject to a clean record, she should be eligible to receive a ticket-of-leave within a year and a half and within three years she could receive a conditional pardon.

On Thursday, 1 May 1851, apparently after the conclusion of a period in hired service, Catherine entered the Cascades Female Factory that was about three kilometres to the west of the city centre. The Cascades Factory was the main establishment for female convicts in Van Diemen's Land. At this time, it held more than 1,000 convict women along with 170 young children who had convict mothers.[70] Catherine's entry was not prompted by misconduct but appears to have occurred because the Brickfields Hiring Depot was full to capacity. Both facilities hired female convicts out for domestic service but there was an important difference between them. While the Brickfields Depot had rules and regulations that the female

6. The Cascades Female Factory in 1880. Reproduced with permission from the Tasmanian Archive and Heritage Office (NS1013/1/46).

convicts had to obey, it was not a gaol. The Cascades Factory was a gaol and all areas, including the one that held the female convicts available for hire, operated under a tighter and stronger system of discipline.

Like all new arrivals at the facility, Catherine would have been informed of the rules that applied to female convicts. One of these was 'that the utmost cleanliness, the greatest quietness, perfect regularity, and entire submission, are laid down as fundamental Laws of the Establishment; and accordingly to the degree of offending against any of them, punishment of some kind is invariably to follow'.[71] Such a ruling would surely be almost impossible for any woman of spirit to obey in its entirety for any length of time.

Almost inevitably, on 2 May Catherine was found guilty by the Superintendent of disobedience of regulations. For this offence she was admonished.[72] We do not know the details of this disobedience but it could have been something as simple as not curtseying or not curtseying properly to an official she encountered.

Shortly after this, Catherine was moved back to the Brickfields Hiring Depot. It appears that either her attitude had changed or her luck had run out, because ten days after her first admonishment she was charged with falsely representing that she had no shoes.[73] No detailed account of this offence has survived, but perhaps she had been involved in a trading scheme with other female inmates. A pair of shoes would have been a valuable article to trade.

The following day Catherine was brought before Algernon Burdett Jones Esq, who was visiting Magistrate to the female convict establishments in and around Hobart Town. She was found guilty of the charge and sentenced to three months hard labour at the Cascades Female Factory.[74] She was now to go into the 3rd class or criminal class, and she was about to find out that life could be far tougher in the Factory than her first brief incarceration there would have indicated.

The Cascades Female Factory carried out a number of very different roles within the Van Diemen's Land convict system. By May 1851, it was the place where newly arrived female convicts were processed and inducted because the *Anson* hulk had been abandoned in mid-1850. It held women who were awaiting assignment to settlers and householders in the southern part of the island. It was the place where pregnant female convicts delivered their babies and where the new mothers and their babies stayed at least until the child had been weaned. It was also the place where female convicts, such as Catherine, served their punishment. In carrying out these different roles it had the overall objective of reforming the women through hard work and discipline.

However, the Factory was very poorly sited and it was a totally unsuitable environment in which to keep hundreds of women, much less a large number of infants and very young children. It was located in a valley alongside a stream with Mount Wellington (over 1200 metres above sea level) immediately to the west, and other high hills to the north-west. In winter, this reduced its exposure to sunlight and maximized its exposure to cold, wet and freezing conditions. It was a large prison complex whose high walls encouraged the retention of damp and further deprived the inmates of the limited available sun. In May 1851, Catherine was about to spend a winter in this miserable environment as a criminal class convict.

Soon after her arrival at the Factory to begin her sentence of three months hard labour, an overseer cut Catherine's thick red hair with scissors as close as it could be cut to the scalp. After this, she would have looked a completely different woman, retaining only isolated tufts of red hair on her virtually bald head. She was then dressed in a jacket that had a large yellow C on its back with another on its right sleeve, and her petticoat also had a large C on the back. This uniform was designed to make it immediately obvious that she was a criminal class convict, which was the lowest category of inmate. During her earlier short stay at the Factory, Catherine had been a 1st class convict and her clothing had not been marked.

As a 3rd class convict, Catherine worked from 7 am to sunset. There were two breaks for meals: breakfast at 8 am and dinner (lunch) at noon.[75]

There were two main types of hard labour that female convicts undertook—picking oakum and working in the Cascades laundry. If assigned to picking oakum, the women had to pick apart old, tough, tar and salt encrusted ropes from ships with their bare and often bleeding hands. The picked fibres were then used to make matting or for caulking the seams of wooden ships. Each female convict had a daily minimum quota of oakum she was required to pick. Picking oakum was considered far harder work for women convicts than domestic service and Catherine would have gained little sustenance or energy from the criminal class diet that was limited to bread and weak soup. Each day of hard labour in the criminal class ended with prayers at 7 pm.[76]

The laundry work performed by criminal class convicts was as arduous as picking oakum. The women worked in the cold and wet laundry doing the heavy manual work of scrubbing, washing and attempting to wring dry heavy items of linen and clothing from the Cascades Factory and other government institutions. As Catherine shivered over a large stone wash trough in the middle of winter she would not have needed anyone to tell her that this punishment was far worse than any benefit she had hoped to obtain from an extra pair of shoes.

On 13 August 1851, Catherine finished her three months of hard labour. At the end of this sentence, she became a 2nd class convict. With this change in her convict class, she had a change in her attire. She now had only one large yellow C on the left sleeve of her jacket and no C at all on her petticoat. She was now allocated lighter work such as folding linen after it had been washed and dried by the 3rd class convicts.

In early September, Catherine attended chapel at the Factory for the Sunday service. The only noise the female convicts were permitted to make during the service was to recite prayers. In fact, throughout the Factory the women were only supposed to engage in conversations that were directly relevant to work functions or to other official requirements. This rule was broken by all the women but they were very careful to check that the overseers were not present or that their conversations would not be detected by anyone in authority. Catherine was not careful enough. Two days after this Sunday church service, she was brought before the Superintendent, Mr May, and found guilty of a charge of talking in chapel. Mr May said he was satisfied the charge was proven and he sentenced her to two days in solitary confinement.[77]

We can't say exactly where in the Factory Catherine served her sentence. We don't know whether she was placed in the solitary working cell in Yard 2 where she would be required to undertake work such as picking oakum, or whether she was incarcerated in a dark cell in Yard 1 where she would have been left in total darkness.

However, we do know that solitary confinement was the punishment that the women at the Cascades Factory hated most. Sentences of hard labour picking oakum or scrubbing at the laundry trough were very hard work, but many of the female convicts had had tough lives in England or Ireland before their conviction and transportation. To some women these jobs could be considered just another tough break in life. No one said that about solitary confinement. In Yard 1 and Yard 2, you were locked in a cell measuring 1.4 metres by 2.75 metres, surrounded by brick or stone walls and a thick door. The cruellest aspect was that the prisoner had no human contact at all. If Catherine could not be silent when required, the system decreed that she would be put in a place where she was surrounded by silence. For someone who had grown up in a large family and had always lived with people around her, the two days in the solitary cell would have been a tough punishment indeed. Nevertheless, it could have been tougher. At the Cascades Factory, sentences of solitary confinement in the pitch black cells in Yard 1 could last for up to twenty-eight days.

By the beginning of October, Catherine was no doubt hoping that her winter of punishment would soon come to an end. Nearly three weeks earlier, she had completed her two days in solitary confinement. The Cascades Factory operated under a system of piece work where every job had a productivity target that the convicts were expected to meet. If a convict exceeded these productivity targets, then she was given credits that helped her improve her convict class and her position within the Factory. By this time Catherine had achieved the classification of 1st class convict, which made her eligible to be hired out into the community. She could now see a future without the repressive discipline she had experienced inside the high walls of the Cascades Factory.

However, Catherine's hopes experienced a setback when she was charged and found guilty of 'disorderly conduct at mess table'.[78] We do not know the precise circumstances of this 'disorderly conduct'. It could be that her table manners were deemed not to be up to standard. It could be that she inadvertently did something like knock over a bowl. In the Female Factory, where silence was the golden rule, this would have been considered disorderly. For this offence, she was sentenced to be kept in a separate apartment from her mess group when not at work.[79] Catherine's convict record shows no duration for the application of this punishment, but fortunately it did not make her ineligible to be hired out into domestic service.

\*\*\*

On 10 October 1851, Catherine was taken to the room in the Cascades Factory where 1st class convicts stood waiting to be viewed by prospective employers. That day, a red-haired man in his early thirties entered the room to inspect the women who were available to be hired. This man was John Goss, a stonemason who lived in Macquarie Street in Hobart Town. On what proved to be a lucky day for Catherine, Goss hired her as a domestic servant on the basis of paying her £7 for twelve months of service.[80] He also committed to the authorities to provide her with proper lodgings and to meet the minimum dietary requirements that had to be provided for female convicts in domestic service. On leaving the Cascades, Catherine was given whatever property she owned that had been held in store for her and her cold, hard winter of punishment was finally over.

There is no record of when Catherine became aware of who John Goss actually was, but it would not have been long before she realized that she had been hired by the husband of Bridget Crotty, a fellow convict on the *Australasia*.[81] We get a better idea of why John Goss hired Catherine when we learn that following his marriage to Bridget, he had hired four other female convicts transported on the *Australasia* for periods of domestic service.[82] With a well paid stonemason husband, Bridget was apparently doing everything she could to help out friends who had been transported with her. Periods of domestic service got her friends out of the convict system, and gave them comfortable lodgings and a good reference that they could then use to assist with getting another suitable position. Bridget knew Catherine not only from the *Australasia* but also from their time on the hulk *Anson* and they had been in the Grangegorman Depot near Dublin at the same time.

Catherine must have been impressed with Bridget's situation. While Catherine had been working hard in domestic service and putting up with the stern discipline of Brickfields Depot and the Cascades Factory, Bridget had lived comfortably as a housewife with one of the highest paid tradesmen in Hobart Town. Catherine undoubtedly thought that this was a great way to be serving a sentence of transportation.

Soon after Catherine started her period of service with John and Bridget Goss, she met John Copley, an acquaintance maybe even a friend of Bridget's husband John. This meeting almost certainly took place at the Goss house in Macquarie Street. The John Copley that Catherine first met was thirty-nine years of age and slightly taller than the average male at that time. He had light brown eyes that matched his light brown hair that may well have been showing signs of grey.[83] As a blacksmith who had been well fed for the previous few months, he was almost certainly a strong, well-developed man.

So, who was John Copley?

7. Map of England showing places of significance in the story of John Copley. (This map taken from: d-maps.com/carte.php?lib=england_map&num_car=5579&lang=en)

# PART TWO
# JOHN COPLEY

# 5   South Yorkshire

John Copley was born on Friday, 12 June 1812,[84] in a cottage that was attached to his father's nail making workshop in Thorpe Hesley, South Yorkshire. It was a normal working day for the baby's twenty-three-year-old father,[85] who also went by the name of John. It is quite possible that the first sound the newborn child heard was that of his father hammering away on an anvil at hot metal rods that he was shaping and forming into nails. Time would show this to have been an appropriate introduction to life for young John.

June 1812 was the best of times for John Copley, the nailor. The nail making trade and the metal trades generally in South Yorkshire were enjoying a period of great prosperity fuelled by the war economy that had been created by England's decade-long war with France. England had to support both its navy that commanded the world's oceans and its massive armies in Europe that were fighting Napoleon. South Yorkshire with its abundant resources of coal, iron ore, water and engineering skills provided much of the engineering might to support this military machine and war economy.

In 1812, Thorpe Hesley was a major centre for nail making. At this time, nail making did not take place in a factory. Rather, individual nailors had a workshop alongside their cottage. They purchased iron bars from middlemen known as nail manufacturers, that they then shaped and formed into a wide range of nails to be used in the building trades and manufacturing industries. They then sold the manufactured nails back to the nail manufacturers who in turn sold them on to the building trades and industry. There is evidence to suggest that the nailors in Thorpe Hesley acted collectively in seeking to negotiate the best prices for their finished nails.[86] In 1812, with the booming war economy, these nailors were very well positioned to extract a top price from the middlemen.

The Thorpe Hesley nailors did not just live on the payments they received from the nail manufacturers. Typically, they had a few acres of land near their workshops where they ran livestock such as a cow, sheep and pigs and they also grew fruit and vegetables. The livestock and produce grown on these few acres helped sustain the nailors and their families and they were also able to sell and trade any surpluses.

While these nailors were living comfortably in 1812, they had no real power or position of consequence in South Yorkshire. Most of the land, mines, iron ore and manufacturing capability in the surrounding area were owned by Earl Fitzwilliam. The Earl lived in a massive Palladian mansion at Wentworth two kilometres to the north of Thorpe Hesley. Every day John Copley senior and his fellow nailors would have been reminded of the presence, power and wealth of Earl Fitzwilliam by a 115 foot high stone column that a predecessor of the Earl had constructed in the small village of Scholes, a few hundred metres to the east of their homes. This column served no practical purpose whatsoever but it was a strong statement as to who owned the key resources and called the shots in the local area.

On Sunday, 6 September 1812, baby John Copley was christened at St Mary's Anglican church at Ecclesfield, three kilometres to the south of his home.[87] The christening of their first son was no doubt a great occasion for John and his wife Hannah. However, at this time more than 2000 kilometres to the east, Napoleon Bonaparte was just about to experience a catastrophic setback with his failed invasion of Russia. This failed invasion was to be the pivotal event in his eventual defeat. With this defeat came the end of the war economy in Britain and in turn the end of the booming demand for manufactured goods, including the nails produced in Thorpe Hesley. Many years were to pass before the future for baby John would be as secure and prosperous as his family's situation had been when the baptismal water was sprinkled on his head at St Mary's in Ecclesfield.

After Napoleon was defeated at Waterloo in 1815, Great Britain experienced a severe recession. Most of the British Navy was mothballed and the Army put off tens of thousands of soldiers. The war economy evaporated and there was a substantial reduction in demand for metal trades work and the products manufactured in South Yorkshire. This resulted in reduced prices for the nails that the nailors of Thorpe Hesley were able to sell. From the time of John Copley's birth, it became progressively harder for his family to make ends meet.

\*\*\*

In March 1822, when young John was nine years old, a police search was undertaken of the Copley family home. The local police constable, Charles Butcher, and John Fletcher, a butcher from nearby Ecclesfield, suspected that John Copley senior had been involved in stealing two of Fletcher's sheep.[88] At this time, to be under suspicion of sheep stealing was a very serious matter. Courts had the power to sentence convicted sheep stealers to death. Nothing was found in this search and no action was taken.

It was around this time that Thorpe Hesley assumed the nickname of Mutton Town. This was prompted by the large number of sheep that 'disappeared' on the outskirts of town from flocks that were being driven from the Rotherham sheep markets to Manchester, forty kilometres away. Manchester was a major industrial city and consequentially had a very strong demand for mutton. The shepherds herding these flocks often stopped at The Gate pub at Thorpe Hesley for a refreshment break and it was known that sometimes a sheep or two became permanently 'separated' from the flock at this time.[89] There is no doubt that while John was growing up, he, like everyone else in the community, was familiar with stories of sheep stealing occurring in and around the town.

As a young adult John identified himself as a nailor and by 1822 he would have been hard at work in his father's nail making workshop. His introduction to work would have involved learning how to heat metal in a blacksmith's forge, working white hot and red hot metal to shape and learning how to work with the various tools of the nail making trade. While there are no historical records to specifically confirm that John started work at this early age, census records in 1841 show children at this age or even younger working full time. John Copley senior, would have been keen to get young John working in the nail making shop as soon as possible.

In February 1826, John's mother Hannah died, apparently soon after giving birth. The registry of St Mary's Church at Ecclesfield records that forty-two-year-old Hannah Copley was buried on 13 February,[90] and that on the same day her baby daughter was christened and given the name Hannah.[91] This was the seventh christening recorded at St Mary's for children of John and Hannah. The survival of Hannah after the death of her mother may have provided some consolation for the Copley family, but if so it was short lived. Baby Hannah died a few weeks later and was buried alongside her mother on 6 March.[9] No doubt the then thirteen-year-old John was deeply saddened.

In October of the following year, in All Saints Church of England in nearby Rotherham, John's father married local widow, Sarah Bagnall.[93] The fifteen-year-old John who witnessed his father's second marriage had by now been substantially shaped into the man he was soon to become. He had worked as a nailor for around five years and at the same time he must have acquired some knowledge of farming from the few acres of land adjoining his father's workshop. He had grown up in a large family in hard economic times and he undoubtedly knew that life could be tough and that you had to be tough to survive.

\*\*\*

The mid-1830s saw the development of the Chartist movement throughout Britain. Its objective was to give working men full rights, standing and a significant voice in the British political system. At this time, only one in five adult males had a vote in parliamentary elections.[94] The main qualification that men had to meet to obtain the vote was the possession of wealth and/or property. In 1838, the Chartists launched the People's Charter that called for six fundamental changes to the British parliamentary system. They wanted universal male suffrage, annual parliaments, vote by ballot, abolition of the property qualification for members of parliament, payment of MPs and equal size of electoral constituencies.

However, by September 1839 the Chartist movement was starting to move away from the 'constitutionalist' approach of petitioning and requesting rights for working people. In June 1839, the Chartists had presented a petition with over a million signatures to the British parliament calling for the Charter to be adopted, but it was overwhelmingly rejected. Significant figures in the Chartist movement believed they needed to adopt new strategies and some of its leaders were speaking of a general strike. Even insurrection was being spoken of in some quarters.

On 22 September 1839, 20,000 people attended a chartist Camp Meeting on Hood Hill near Wentworth in South Yorkshire.[95] John Copley was now twenty-seven years old and he lived in the village of Scholes, only two kilometres from Wentworth. We cannot be certain that he attended this meeting but we can be sure that the meeting, and what it was about, would have had an impact on him.

The people at the Camp Meeting came from Sheffield, Rotherham, Barnsley and the villages around Wentworth and they were eager for the opportunity to support and fight for the Chartist cause.[96] They listened to rousing speeches and sang songs in support of the cause. Massed voices singing

'Brothers and sisters now unite,
And contend for your just rights;

Then soon the poor will happy be,
Glorious times we all shall see.
And the Chartist's song shall be,
My country and sweet liberty'

must have stirred some very powerful emotions.[97]

Not everyone at the Hood Hill Camp Meeting was a Chartist supporter. Standing on a rise overlooking the large gathering was local lord of the manor, Earl Fitzwilliam.[98] No doubt he was interested to hear what the rabble-rousing Chartists were up to, but his main purpose was to impress upon those working in his collieries, on his lands and in his industrial businesses that they would be risking their jobs by attending this meeting. Many of the working people in the Wentworth and Thorpe Hesley area would have found a powerful attraction in the agenda for change the Chartists presented. The Chartists offered them a say in the political process that at this time offered no support for working people. Their agenda also supported the challenge to the Corn Laws that had been passed by the British parliament in 1818. These laws placed a high tariff on imported corn that inflated the price of food and they were strongly supported by landed interests such as Earl Fitzwilliam but despised by working people.

By this time John was a husband and the father of three children. There is no surviving record of where his marriage took place and all we know of his wife is that she was called Mary.[99] John identified his religion as Wesleyan,[100] which suggests that he was a strong-minded man who did not curry favour with the local establishment. The local lord, the Earl Fitzwilliam, and all the leading members of the local community were Anglicans. Indeed, John's own father was an Anglican. The Wesleyan Church had been created in the early nineteenth century as a result of the crusading campaign by the eighteenth-century English theologian, John Wesley, who challenged the Anglican establishment. Wesleyans were attracted to the belief of John Wesley that people should have a direct relationship with God through knowledge of the scriptures and a church without the hierarchy of the Anglican Church. Typically, Wesleyans were inclined to challenge authority in English society; the type to support the people's charter of political reform.

When the Hood Hill Camp meeting took place, John was working as a labourer.[101] This situation was almost certainly caused by the poor economic environment of the late 1830s. At this time, working as a labourer almost certainly meant that he was not employed full time and that he was earning considerably less than the income earned by a nailor in full-time employment. These circumstances would have made the Chartist cause look very attractive to John.

In many ways, by September 1839 John seems to have been living at the edge of society. He was a member of a minority religion that challenged the established church and he was not able to work in his trade. The Chartists were moving towards a direct challenge to the British authorities and John appears to have been the sort of person to be attracted to this challenge.

# 6 Crime and Conviction

On the night of Saturday, 11 January 1840, events occurred in nearby Rotherham and Sheffield that meant that the prospects of any success for the Chartist campaign were lost for the foreseeable future. A group known as the Physical Force Chartists had planned to initiate an armed uprising to take control of the area from the government authorities. The plan involved activists in Rotherham and a number of other places in South Yorkshire initiating diversions such as setting fire to police stations and the isolated houses of magistrates. The Physical Force Chartists believed that this would result in units of police and soldiers being drawn out of Sheffield to put down these violent actions. This would enable their leader, Samuel Holberry, and his supporters to take over Sheffield—the largest city in South Yorkshire. Following such a success, they would be able to build the uprising elsewhere in the country. The plan fell apart because James Allen, a Rotherham Chartist and publican, betrayed them to the authorities. Before any significant moves could be initiated, Holberry and others in leadership positions were arrested and the plan did not even get off the ground, much less enjoy any measure of success.[102] However, this incident gives a clear indication of the depths of discontent that existed among many people in South Yorkshire.

Two days after the failed uprising, John Copley walked down Scholes Lane towards his home in Scholes that he shared with his wife Mary and their children. It was 11 pm.[103] What happened next was about to dramatically alter the course of John's life.

The only detailed account of what happened to John that night is contained in the 18 January 1840 edition of the *Sheffield and Rotherham Independent* newspaper when it reported on proceedings that took place three days earlier in the Rotherham Courthouse.

John was not the only person outdoors on this cold mid-winter Yorkshire night. He was being observed by Charles Murfin, a local labourer. Murfin, who was hiding behind a hedge on the other side of the lane opposite John's cottage, was acting as a lookout on behalf of John Cutt, one of the largest land-holders in the area. In the moonlight Murfin saw John walk down the hill towards his cottage, enter it and lock the door. There was no suggestion he was carrying anything with him at that time.

Soon after John had locked his front door, three other men joined Murfin to keep watch. These men were William Burgin, a neighbour of John Cutt, Thomas Butcher, a local nail manufacturer who lived next door to Cutt, and Cutt's son also called John.[104] No doubt Butcher and the Copleys had a history of disagreements about a fair price for nails. These four men behind the hedge were awaiting the arrival of John Cutt senior and of Constable Bennett, the local part-time police constable, before undertaking a search of John's cottage.

When the two men arrived, the constable took the lead and knocked on the front door. In response to the vigorous knocking, John shouted, 'Who's there?' Constable Bennett identified himself and demanded that John open the door. John asked the men what they wanted and Cutt senior replied, 'I have a sheep gone, and we want to search thy house.' John did not refuse them entry or act as if he had anything to hide. Instead he replied that he had nothing in his house that he cared for and the men could search where they liked. At this, all the men entered the house and commenced their search.

During this search, Constable Bennett found an apron smeared with blood and he later told the court that on being shown this apron, John ran out of the house with Burgin and Murfin in pursuit. John was caught and brought back to the house, whereupon Bennett sent for Constable Henry Womack, the full-time police constable based in Rotherham.

The threat of the Chartist uprising had ensured that there were hundreds of additional police officers and soldiers in the Rotherham area at this time, so Constable Womack was able to respond without delay. Upon his arrival at the Copley house he started his own search. He later told the court that he looked under one of the beds and dragged out a bag which contained a quantity of mutton in a mangled state. At this, he took John into custody under suspicion of stealing and killing one of Cutt senior's sheep.

On Wednesday, 15 January, John stood in the dock in one of the courtrooms at the Rotherham Courthouse. This was a committal hearing before a local magistrate, Colonel Fullerton, to consider a charge of sheep stealing laid by John Cutt.[105] In the time since his arrest in the early hours of the morning of 14 January, John had been held in one of the ten prison cells located at the back of the court building.[106]

John Cutt senior was the first person to give evidence. He told the court that at 6 pm on Monday, 13 January, he had inspected the sheep in one of his fields at Scholes and found that all twenty-eight sheep were accounted for. However, as a consequence of some information he had received, he went back to the field at 10 pm and found one sheep had been taken.[107]

Charles Murfin's evidence connected John to the theft. Murfin told the court that on the night in question he was walking down Scholes Lane when he saw a man in John Cutt's field peeping over a hedge. In the moonlight, he was able to recognize the man as John Copley. Murfin stated that he then had a five-minute conversation with Copley, during which he 'observed two men in the field at a short distance'. When he asked Copley who these men were, Copley said he did not know. The conversation concluded with him asking Copley whether he was going to go down Scholes Lane to which Copley replied, 'No, not yet'. Murfin said that as he found this behaviour to be suspicious, he reported it to John Cutt and then went on to observe events outside the Copley house.[108]

Thomas Butcher's evidence covered more than the events that transpired after Constable Bennett knocked on the door of John's cottage that night. He told the court that on 6 January, one week before the theft, John Copley entered his nail manufacturer shop and told his workers that he, Copley, would give five shillings to anyone who would steal one of John Cutt's sheep.[109]

The newspaper account of this court hearing contains no record of any comment made by John. He may have felt that there was no value in making any comment at this time, because this was a committal hearing and all that had to be shown was that he had a case to answer. What we do know is that Colonel Fullerton had no trouble concluding that there was indeed such a case and he determined to commit John for trial at the forthcoming Lent (March) Assizes to be conducted in York.

Shortly after the committal hearing, John was moved to York and held in the Castle prison. Since medieval times, a prison had existed on this site near the centre of the city. While John's whole future was on the line with the serious criminal charge he faced, the Assizes Court session was a major social event. Assize balls were held and wealthy people actually came to town for the social life associated with these court proceedings.

On 5 March, John's trial began.[110] He stood in the dock and was charged with stealing a sheep owned by John Cutt of Thorpe Hesley. This courthouse, constructed in 1777, is still used to hear criminal cases. Beautifully restored and maintained, it is little different today from the building that John would have entered.  It is both impressive and intimidating and certainly would have seemed so to a nailor from Thorpe Hesley.

We have not been able to find a detailed account of the York Assizes proceedings against John Copley. The newspaper reports of the March 1840 Assizes were, not surprisingly, dominated by accounts of the proceedings against the ring leaders of the threatened rebellion in Rotherham, Sheffield

8. York Court House where in 1840 John Copley was convicted and sentenced.

and throughout South Yorkshire. The *Rotherham and Sheffield Independent* simply reported that John Copley was found guilty of sheep stealing and was given a sentence of transportation for ten years.[111] This meant he could be sent to either the Australian colonies of New South Wales or Van Diemen's Land or perhaps to Bermuda in the West Indies.

We can only assume that the evidence presented at the trial was based on that presented at the committal hearing and that it painted John as not only a sheep stealer but as a very inept and not particularly bright one.

If, as Thomas Butcher stated, John offered Butcher's workers five shillings for stealing one of Cutt's sheep just one week before he himself allegedly stole a sheep, it was incredibly stupid behaviour. In 1840, a conviction for sheep stealing carried severe punishment including transportation. Also, when we remember that Butcher the nail manufacturer was a neighbour of John Cutt, we realize that John Copley would have known that any attempt to incite Butcher's men would almost certainly be reported back to Cutt.

On top of that, the time chosen by John to commit this offence was the worst possible time for anyone to engage in serious criminal conduct. Two days prior to the theft of John Cutt's sheep, South Yorkshire had been on the brink of an armed rebellion involving thousands of men. As a result of this, there were hundreds of additional policemen and soldiers on active duty in South Yorkshire. By the night of 13 January it was known that this attempted rebellion had failed, but the authorities were still in a heightened state of alert. Surely any criminal of sense would have been lying low at such a time.

The evidence of Charles Murfin at the Rotherham committal compounds the apparent stupidity of John's behaviour. It is hard to believe that John would have stolen one of John Cutt's sheep straight after he had been found in Cutt's paddock by Murfin and they had engaged in a five minute conversation.

Unfortunately for John, one fact seems to have been overlooked during his trial. No one questioned how he smuggled that parcel of meat and a bloodied apron into his cottage under the watchful eyes of Murfin. It should be remembered too that no one saw John handling a sheep or a carcass and at no time was it suggested that he carried anything with him as he walked home that night down Scholes Lane.

Obviously no one can accurately say what really happened in John Cutt's field in Scholes on that January night. Criminals do act stupidly and this is often why they are caught and convicted, but the evidence presented at the Rotherham committal hearing suggests that John committed multiple acts of gross stupidity and does leave scope for further speculation.

We do not know the nature of the relationship between John Cutt and Charles Murfin prior to John Copley's arrest and conviction. As a large landowner in the Thorpe Hesley area, no doubt Cutt was able to chose whether or not he offered work to labourers such as Murfin. We do know that life improved for Murfin after January 1840, and in the 1851 census he was listed as a nailor, not a labourer[112].

A couple of weeks after John's conviction, all the cases at the York Lent Assizes against the Physical Force Chartists had been completed. Samuel Holberry, the leader of the group, was given a prison sentence of four years.

The other leaders of the Sheffield/Rotherham uprising were given prison sentences of between one and three years.[113] Meanwhile John received a ten year sentence of transportation for stealing a sheep that was worth twenty shillings.[114] He was to be sent halfway around the world and would never see his family again.

# 7  A Van Diemen's Land Convict

At the start of April 1840, John Copley and other York Castle prisoners who had been sentenced to transportation were loaded on top of a public coach and transferred under guard to Woolwich, just outside London. It took several days to reach their destination—the prison hulks located on the Thames River.

At Woolwich, John was handed over to the convict authorities who directed that he be taken aboard the hulk *Justitia*.[115] From 1804 to 1811, during the war with France, this ship had been the fifty-gun British warship HMS *Hindostan* but since 1830, as the *Justitia*, it had been used as a convict hulk.[116] Before going on board, John was stripped naked and scrubbed with a hard scrubbing brush. His hair was cropped with scissors as close as it could be to his scalp. He was given a new convict 'magpie' suit with one side blue or black and the other side yellow and then was taken to the blacksmith shop where an iron ring was riveted around both ankles.[117] Finally, John was given his hulk convict number: 5881 called five, eight, eighty-one.[118] From then on this was what he would be known as on the hulks. Names were not used.[119]

For the next six and a half months, the hulk was home for John. We do not know precisely what work he did during this time but we do know that convicts from these hulks undertook a variety of jobs at the Woolwich Arsenal. They repaired the large mounds of earth into which practice shots from guns were directed, emptied barges, cleaned shot, moved gun carriages and weeded lanes. At the Woolwich naval dockyard, convicts from the hulks loaded and unloaded a wide range of materials including iron, stone, wood, copper and bricks.[120] At this time a 120-gun Royal Navy ship, *Trafalgar*, was being built[121] and convicts worked on its construction. While working at the arsenal or at the naval dockyard, John would have become accustomed to wearing leg irons weighing about twelve pounds.[122]

The main meal of the day for convicts on the hulk was served at noon. This often consisted of broth, beef and potatoes, but sometimes of bread or biscuit and cheese and half a pint of ale.[123] At the end of his time on the *Justitia*, John's physical condition was described as 'healthy' and his behaviour as 'good'.[124]

Around 28 October, John had his leg irons removed and he was taken off the hulk for the last time.[125] In late October and early November, 250 male convicts were boarded on the vessel *Lady Raffles*, to be transported to Hobart Town in Van Diemen's Land. On boarding, John and the other convicts were given their cooking, eating and drinking utensils along with a small keg for water.

Before leaving England, the convict transport headed for Portsmouth. After leaving Woolwich, she headed south-west down the English Channel and struck severe weather which damaged the main and fore yards in her rigging. This necessitated a return to the port of Deal, near Dover, for repairs.[126] This delay to the voyage was described by the ship's Surgeon Superintendent, Robert Wylie, as being caused by 'the inefficiency of the crew'.[127]

Eventually, the *Lady Raffles* made it into Portsmouth harbour,[128] where she took on another eighty male convicts. She also stocked up with final provisions for the start of the voyage to Van Diemen's Land. On 30 November 1840, she departed Portsmouth with 330 convicts, thirty soldiers from the 96th Regiment, five women and eight children on board[129].

On that night, John slept in a bunk with three other convicts. He was to do so for another 107 nights before the ship arrived in Hobart Town. The trip was considered 'a favourable passage' by Robert Wylie[130] and at no time during the voyage was the name John Copley entered into his sick book. Not all the men were so lucky. There was an outbreak of ringworm among those who had come off the hulk *Justitia* and three convicts, a sailor and a soldier died. Towards the end of the voyage scurvy began to appear. However, on their arrival in Hobart Town on 17 March 1841, Robert Wylie stated that 'the appearance of the men, on the whole, was as good on their debarkation as on their embarkation.'[131]

After disembarking, John and his fellow prisoners walked from the docks in Sullivan Cove up the hill to the Prisoners Barracks on Campbell Street where they were processed. This is near where the old Penitentiary Chapel and Criminal Courts are now located. The convict records carried by the *Lady Raffles* were consulted in the processing of John and they contained the following information.

John Copley was a twenty-eight-year-old man who was five feet six and a half inches in height. His complexion was dark, his head was large and he had dark brown hair and thin, dark brown whiskers. His face was oval, with a high forehead and light brown eyes and eyebrows. His nose was very sharp and his mouth was small, but his chin was broad and he had a puckpitted scar on the left side of his nose that indicated previous exposure to smallpox. His religion was Protestant and Wesleyan. He could not read or write and his trade was listed as nailor.[132]

On the following Sunday, John attended his first church service in the colony at the Trinity Church located on the Prisoners Barracks site. This building, which was constructed in 1833, had the rare distinction of combining a place to worship God with a place for the punishment of convicts. Under the church floor, thirty-six solitary confinement cells had been constructed in the foundations.[133] The church authorities had not been consulted about these cells prior to the construction of the building and the Anglican Bishop of Australia, William Broughton, determined that they made it unacceptable for consecration. Nevertheless, the building was still used as a church and the presence of convicts in these cells would have been a memorable introduction to convict life in Van Diemen's Land for John. Four years later, James Boyd, the Superintendent of the Penitentiary, described the cells under the church as 'without exception, the most objectionable places of confinement, I have ever seen'.[134]

After his arrival in Hobart Town and processing into the convict system, John served a fifteen month probation term. At this time, this was required of all new convicts and it involved working in large gangs of up to 300 men. John spent his probation period at the Jerusalem Probation Station,[135] forty kilometres north of the city. When walking to Jerusalem, he may well have stayed overnight at the Richmond gaol, conveniently located at approximately the halfway point on the walk. The work undertaken by convicts at Jerusalem included road construction, timber harvesting and agricultural work, but in 1841 the convicts were still working on further construction of the Probation Station. John may have undertaken nailor and blacksmithing work associated with this construction. Jerusalem is today the township of Colebrook and very little remains of its convict past.

John's fifteen month probationary term expired on 17 June 1842 and his behaviour at Jerusalem was described both as 'orderly' and 'good'.[136]

From November of that year until the beginning of March 1844, John was located at Campbell Town in the centre of Van Diemen's Land. At this time, he was a 1st class PPH (probation pass holder)[137] which meant he could be hired for wages or serve in a government gang.

On 29 January 1844 a Convict Department Notice in the *Launceston Examiner* newspaper advertised that John Copley and a number of other convicts were available for hiring. From 25 March to 4 July, John worked for a Mr Shaw at Perth in the north of the colony. On 5 July he started work for a person identified as F. Jones at Campbell Town. On 12 September, while working for Jones, John appeared in the Campbell Town court on a charge of misconduct for 'hawking nails in the township'.[138] He had apparently been using his old trade skills and then showing some entrepreneurial flair by directly selling the product to the customers around town. The town builders may have liked this arrangement, but no doubt the town merchants were not impressed. The Police Magistrate found John guilty and he was sentenced to one month hard labour. Such a sentence usually involved the convict being placed on a punishment treadmill and/or being shackled in leg irons while working in a government gang on tough physical work for extended work days with reduced rations. However, it appears John did not experience such punishment as his convict record indicates that this sentence was 'remitted'.[139]

Unlike many convicts in Van Diemen's Land, John had trade skills which would have been in demand within the convict system. By December 1844 he was back working in Perth, after which he went to work for an extended period for a person identified as B. Jones at Franklin Village near Launceston. In September 1845 he was working at Spring Bay, fifty kilometres north-east of Hobart. He then moved back to near Launceston working at Patterson Plains for a time. In December of that year he was working for John Kelsey at Kings Meadows, just to the south of Launceston.[140] At this time, the Van Diemen's Land economy was in recession, with the government unable to hire out thousands of convicts for service. John, however, was a person with skills and the convict authorities had no problem hiring him out.

On 17 April 1846, John made a major step towards moving out of the convict system. On this day, he obtained his ticket-of-leave.[141] Convicts were entitled to receive a ticket-of-leave based on the length of their service and good behaviour. With his ticket, John was free from government supervision and was able to move anywhere in the colony. The ticket also enabled him to obtain work for himself and to be independent. All he now had to do was to report to the police once a week.

At this time, a system existed whereby convicts could apply for families to be given passage to the colony. John was now eligible to take advantage of this. He could have applied for his wife Mary and their three children to be given passage to Van Diemen's Land, but there is no record of him making such an application. We have been unable to find any record of Mary or the children living in South Yorkshire in either the 1841 or 1851 census.

After obtaining his ticket-of-leave John moved to Hobart Town and lived in Goulburn Street,[142] either alone or in shared accommodation. In the city, he worked as a blacksmith. His wage would have been around five shillings and five pence a day, which was considerably more than the three shillings a day paid to labourers.[143]

On 3 April 1847, J.S. Hampton, the Comptroller-General of the Convict Department, signed off on a recommendation that John be given a conditional pardon.[144] The granting of a conditional pardon meant that he was free to leave Van Diemen's Land and move to the British colonies on the Australian mainland or to New Zealand and live as a free man. The only condition that applied to him was that for the balance of his ten year term he could not return to England. It is not clear when John became aware of this recommendation. He had not been involved in any serious incidents during his time in the colony and he had now served seven years of his sentence. Undoubtedly, by this time, he would have been aware that he should soon be free from his convict transportation sentence. With the receipt of a conditional pardon, John would be able to plan a new life.

# 8  A House Burglary in Hobart Town

At around 9.30 pm in the evening on 8 April 1847, James Fraser, a former convict, was walking quickly down Warwick Street to the west of the centre of Hobart Town, carrying a bundle of goods wrapped inside a blanket.[145] The street was quiet. It was the week after Easter and the city was recovering from its annual three day horse racing carnival. Suddenly Fraser was confronted by Constable Clarkson, an on-duty police constable.[146]

The forty-year-old Fraser was well known to Constable Clarkson and the Hobart Town police generally. He was an easy person to identify with a large 'D' brand on the left side of his face that he received as a young man when he had been convicted of deserting his army regiment. He had been transported from Scotland in 1836 for house breaking and since his arrival in Van Diemen's Land he had been convicted twice for stealing offences. In October 1839, he was convicted of stealing a double-barrelled shot gun and served a three year sentence at the Port Arthur penal settlement. In April 1841, he was convicted of breaking and entering into a house and for this he received a further two year sentence at Port Arthur. He also had a long list of convictions for lesser offences including drunkenness, representing himself to be a police constable, being out after hours, absconding from Port Arthur convict settlement, idleness, misconduct and disorderly conduct.[147]

Constable Clarkson asked Fraser to explain what he was carrying in the blanket and Fraser replied that he was carrying his bed. The constable was not satisfied with this answer and told Fraser he wanted to look inside the blanket. Fraser put the blanket down on the ground and as soon as the constable bent down to check out the contents Fraser ran off. Clarkson pursued him and within five minutes he had captured Fraser and they returned to the bundle of goods that they had abandoned in Warwick Street. The constable picked up the bundle and Fraser was taken to the police watch-house on Bathurst Street.[148]

At the watch-house, Constable Clarkson searched the bundle and found its contents to include a number of fashionable ladies dresses, a gold chain, silver spoons and some jewellery.[149] The constable was certain that these goods had not been obtained by honest means, so he took Fraser into custody. Fraser knew that he was in deep trouble and that it would only be a matter of time before the owners of this property reported its theft to the police. Aware that he would be facing a serious charge in the Supreme Court, he decided to 'cooperate'.

Fraser told Constable Clarkson that the blanket and the goods had been taken from the house of Christopher and Mary Horwood, who lived on Bathurst Street. Christopher Horwood was a thirty two-year-old publican. Fraser insisted that he had not broken into the house and that only half of the goods taken were contained inside the blanket.[150]

At this, Constable Clarkson went to the Horwood house and he found that there were no marks on the back door to indicate that a forced entry had been made.[151] At around 11 pm, Christopher and Mary Horwood returned home from a night at the theatre.[152] The Horwoods inspected their house and Christopher told the police that the property stolen included some of his wife's dresses, bedding, jewellery, silver spoons, brooches and a gold chain.[153]

The next morning Detective Chief Symonds and Detective Constables Brown and Daley interviewed Fraser.[154] Experience would have taught Fraser that he needed to appear to fully cooperate with the police and that he should do everything he could to minimize the seriousness of the conviction and punishment he would receive. At this interview Fraser told the police that he was just one of two people who had been involved in the theft. He reiterated that he had not broken into the house and explained that entry had been gained via the open back door. A few days later the *Colonial Times* reported that during this interview James Fraser gave the police 'a clue to his confederate'.[155] Fraser told the detectives that John Copley, who lived in Goulburn Street, had also been involved. Goulburn Street ran parallel with Bathurst Street and bordered the same blocks of land.

Detective Constables Brown and Daley then visited the house where John was living where they found blankets from the Horwood house on his bed and other goods from the house under his bed.[156] No record survives to tell us what goods were found. The detectives then placed John under arrest and took him down to the watch-house.

Ironically, on this very day, 9 April 1847, a public notice was included in the evening edition[157] of the *Colonial Times* that would have made John, if guilty of house burglary, deeply regret the utter stupidity of his actions, or if innocent feel a burning hatred for James Fraser. In this edition, J.S. Hampton, the Comptroller General in charge of the Convict Department, announced: 'It is hereby notified to the under-mentioned individuals, that it is the intention of His Excellency the Lieutenant-Governor to recommend them to the gracious consideration of Her Majesty the Queen for Conditional Pardons'. One of the individuals listed in this notice was the newly arrested 'John Copley, *Lady Raffles*'.[158]

On the morning of Monday, 12 April, both James Fraser and John Copley were committed for trial in the Van Diemen's Land Supreme Court on charges of 'burglary in the dwelling of Christopher Horwood'.[159] John no doubt realized that, if convicted, he faced an abysmal future. A conviction for stealing property from a house in Hobart Town would bring a considerably longer sentence than the ten year transportation sentence he received for stealing a sheep and almost certainly it would be served at Norfolk Island—to convicts, a place worse than death.

9. The Hobart Town Supreme Court (left) where John Copley was convicted of house burglary in April 1847.

The trial occurred on Tuesday, April 20,[160] in the Supreme Court building that was located on the corner of Macquarie and Murray Streets, opposite the old Hobart Town gaol. It was conducted before Justice Algernon Montague who was dismissed from office later in the year by Governor Denison because of longstanding debts and misbehaviour in office.[161] Both Fraser and John pleaded not guilty to the charge. Fraser was represented in the court by Mr W. Brewer,[162] but John had no legal representation. It is not surprising that John lacked the savings or assets to obtain representation, because he had only received his ticket-of-leave twelve months earlier. The foreman of the jury was Edward Abbott, a justice of the peace and a pastoralist who owned 1100 acres on the Derwent River.[163]

Fraser pleaded not guilty to the house burglary charge on the basis that John had entered the Horwood house and actually taken the stolen property. He told the court that the back door of the Horwood house had been unlocked and that the theft had occurred prior to sunset. Mr Brewer explained that a theft in these circumstances was larceny rather than house burglary.[164] In law, larceny was a less serious offence. Fraser and his lawyer were in effect telling the court that he should only be found guilty of receiving stolen goods and that at the very worst he could only be found guilty of larceny.

John told the court that he was not guilty because he had no involvement in the theft. In relation to the goods found on and under his bed he said that 'A man had left them at his house' and he did not know 'the things were stolen'.[165] While there is no record to confirm it, John almost certainly told the court that he had no track record whatsoever of being involved with house burglary and that during more than six years in Van Diemen's Land he had at no time been suspected of committing any criminal offence.

The evidence presented by Fraser that the theft occurred before sunset and that the back door of the Horwood house was unlocked was contradicted by Mary Horwood in her evidence. She told the court that she and her husband 'secured the house' and left at 'about 7.00 pm'.[166] This was well after sunset. She also stated that 'about three months' prior to the theft 'one of the prisoners was at my house' and stayed 'there all night'. She told the court 'I gave him supper and a bed'.[167] While there are no records that identify this person, it appears highly probable that it was James Fraser. John lived in Goulburn Street, which backed onto Bathurst Street, and it is difficult to see why he would have had any reason to stay overnight at the Horwood house.

In retiring to consider its verdict, the jury had a number of issues to consider. They had to decide whether it was James Fraser or John Copley who was responsible for the theft or whether it was both of them as submitted by the prosecution. They also had to determine whether the offence was house burglary or the lesser offence of larceny. After the jury had retired for a short time, Edward Abbott, the foreman of the jury, told the court that both of the accused had been found guilty of the house burglary charge.[168]

In considering the sentences to be imposed, Justice Montague stated that 'this was Fraser's third trial for housebreaking'. The judge noted that

James Fraser 'obtained his freedom in 1846 and was now again before him'. Justice Montague went on to state that he believed 'There was no doubt about Copley's guilt'.[169] He then sentenced both Fraser and John to 'transportation beyond the seas for the term of their natural lives'.[170]

On 23 April the *Colonial Times* congratulated the police on the convictions of James Fraser and John Copley, stating: 'The case was clearly proved against both the prisoners who were respectively sentenced to transportation for life. The apprehension of the thieves and the recovery of the property was owing to the vigilance and activity of the police, who deserve due credit accordingly.'[171]

Later that month, Lieutenant Governor Denison received the details of Justice Montague's sentences and he determined that John would be sent to Norfolk Island for four years, while Fraser would serve a four year sentence of labour at an unspecified location.[172] This was the first indication that James Fraser was going to be treated much more leniently than John.

# 9   Norfolk Island

In late May 1847 John Copley was taken aboard the brig *Lady Franklin* for transportation to Norfolk Island. Thirty-eight other convicts, who had been convicted of second offences in the Australian colonies, were transported along with John.[173] James Fraser did not join him on the ship and instead he remained in the Hobart Town gaol.

Norfolk Island lies more than 2300 kilometres to the north-east of Hobart Town. It is a small island measuring at its widest points roughly five kilometres north to south and eight kilometres west to east. It has a semi-tropical climate. It was first established by the British as a convict settlement in 1788, only a few months after they settled at Sydney Cove in New South Wales, but for ten years between 1815 and 1825 it lay abandoned. In 1825 the second penal settlement was established on the island.

In mid-1847, there were around 500 convicts on Norfolk Island, the vast majority of whom had been convicted on more than one occasion for serious crimes.[174] At this time, it had the reputation of being one of the harshest gaols in the British Empire and it was said that prisoners sentenced to the island were not meant to return. In fact, when the second penal settlement was being established in 1825 Governor Darling declared that the island was intended to be 'a place of the extremest punishment short of death'.[175]

The Commandant in 1847 was John Price and he had the most formidable reputation of all the commandants for imposing harsh treatment and oppressive discipline. In the well-known Australian novel that was written in the 1870s, *For the Term of His Natural Life*, Marcus Clarke used John Price as the basis for the tyrannical character, Maurice Freer, a military officer who spent time as the Commandant of Norfolk Island. In John Price's first sixteen months as commandant, the convicts on the island received more than 20,000 lashes with the cat-o'-nine-tails.[176] Whippings were ordered for the most trivial of reasons. One convict received thirty-six lashes for losing his shoe laces.[177] Convicts received sentences of four to fourteen days in solitary confinement for arriving a minute late to muster, for not touching their hat in deference to a superior, for not walking fast enough or for having a pipe.[178] Solitary confinement was not what the name suggests but was spent in hot, airless, cramped, overcrowded cells that were full of gut-wrenchingly fetid smells. While in solitary confinement, prisoners were on a near starvation diet.

Another person in a position of authority who was hated by the convicts was Alfred Essex Baldock, the chief constable of the island and a close

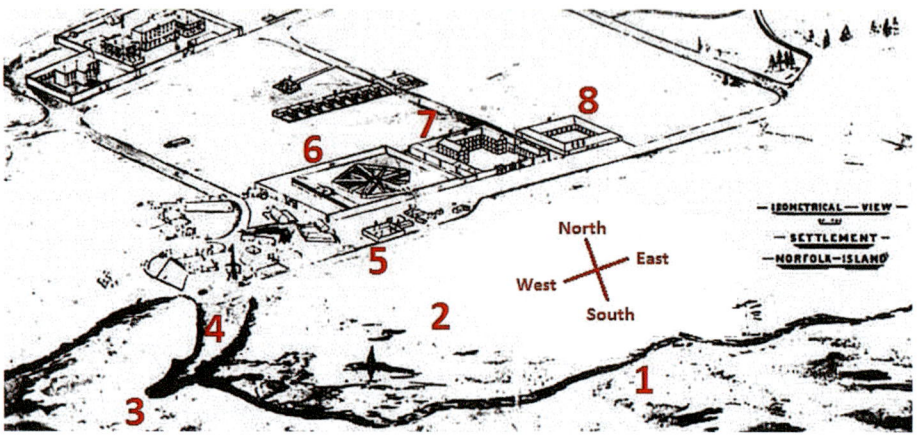

10. Part of a sketch of the convict establishment at Kingston on the south coast of Norfolk Island with significant features marked: 1. Sydney Bay outside the line of reefs; 2. Slaughter Bay inside the line of reefs with the Kingston convict establishment on the shoreline; 3. The bar area of sea where whale boats coming into Kingston crossed the bar; 4. Kingston jetty where the whale boats landed; 5. The small rectangular nailors' and blacksmiths' workshop; 6. The pentagonal prison where convicts served punishment sentences; 7. The main convict barracks; and 8. The timber yard where convicts received their meals.

confidant of John Price. The position of chief constable was normally held by a free man, but Baldock had been transported from England in 1841 with a fifteen year transportation sentence for a stealing conviction. He had only received a conditional pardon in 1845.[179]

John arrived at Norfolk Island on 24 June 1847[180] and, like all the convicts serving a sentence for a serious conviction in the Australian colonies, he was based at Kingston on the south coast. The area of sea just off Kingston was known as Sydney Bay. The main convict barracks in Kingston was located on Bay Road that ran parallel with the shore line just back from the beach. As a nailor with blacksmithing skills, John would have worked in the nail making and blacksmith workshop that was also located on Bay Road. This workshop was on the opposite side of the road to the main convict barracks and was not far from the Kingston wharf.

Soon after John arrived, he began to attend school. He was now thirty-five years old and this was possibly the first formal schooling he had ever received. The provision of education is hard to reconcile with such a violent and oppressive penal regime, but documentation exists that shows he attended school from late June 1847 to the end of September.[181] The school was located in a corner of the yard that housed the main convict barracks and attendance was optional. Instruction was available between 6 and 8 pm, after the completion of a full day's work. During this time, around twenty-five other convicts also attended the school. Over a little more than three months, John studied reading and writing and his school reports said he was attentive, regular and improving.[182] We could find no record of the school operating after September.

John kept out of trouble during his first nine months on Norfolk Island. He did nothing to attract the attention of the prison authorities. However, this situation changed on 12 April 1848. On that day, the brig *Governor Phillip* was anchored at least a kilometre off the coast from Kingston, preparing to leave for Sydney and Hobart Town. Late in the afternoon, a whale boat went out from Kingston Pier to the *Governor Phillip* taking a final group of passengers to board the brig before its departure. A number of senior convict authority officials had accompanied these passengers to see them off. John was one of the convicts who rowed this whale boat out to the brig. It is not surprising that John would have been selected for this task because the blacksmith workshop was located close to Kingston Pier and John would have been a physically strong man because he was involved in heavy metal trades work. Considerable strength was a prerequisite for anyone rowing a whale boat well out to sea through the often rough and always treacherous surf off the coast. The power of the sea was dramatically demonstrated soon after the establishment of the first convict settlement, when the First Fleet supply vessel, *Sirius*, was wrecked on the reef just off the coast.

For some reason, the government officials were held up on the brig and it was after dark before the whale boat with the officials on board headed back to Kingston Pier. The convict authority officials in the whale boat were Alfred Essex Baldock, the notorious Chief Constable, Mr Padbury, the official in charge of stores, Mr Simmons, another government employee, and Mr Matthew Walker, the Senior Assistant Superintendent of Convicts.[183]

Matthew Walker was an experienced government official on Norfolk Island who came up through the ranks. He first came to the island in late 1831 as a corporal in the King's Own 4th Army Regiment and returned in 1841 as a sergeant major of police. In 1843, he was appointed as an assistant superintendent of convicts.[184] By April 1848, Mr Walker was thirty-nine years of age and he lived on the island with his wife Jane and three young children.[185]

All John and the other convicts had to guide them as they rowed the kilometre back to shore was moonlight from a half moon[186] and light from beacons that were lit on a small hill behind Kingston Pier. Even in daylight, it was a testing manoeuvre to find and travel through the gap in the reef to the west of the pier that enabled whale boats to come alongside and land their cargo. Going though this gap was known as crossing the bar. At

11. The Norfolk Island jetty with, to the right, the area of sea where whale boats crossed the bar.

night, it was far more difficult. It was much harder to locate the pier and the landmarks in Kingston, and it was almost impossible for the officials and convicts on the whale boat to see and therefore be prepared to ride the rolling swells of the sea. When the whale boat was less than a hundred metres from the shore and just at the most crucial and difficult stage of the trip—the crossing of the bar—a sudden squall of rain hit them and obscured the moon.[187] The sea suddenly became very rough. The officials and convicts on board were blinded, and the rising and falling of the waves and surf upset the whale boat, throwing everyone into the water. The rough waves made it impossible to see either the shore or the overturned boat and they were in danger of being washed onto the rocky reef by the heavy rolling surf.

Mr Simmons was a strong swimmer and was able to make it to shore without assistance. Mr Padbury had the good fortune to be picked up by a boat that put out from the settlement after the whale boat was upset.[188]

John not only made it back to shore but in the surging sea he came across a struggling Matthew Walker and was able to bring him back to the shore alive.[189] John had saved the life of one of the most senior government officials on Norfolk Island.

Alfred Essex Baldock was not so fortunate. He was not able to swim to shore and he was not rescued from the rough surf. The whale boat was dashed to pieces on the reef in Sydney Bay and that night a watch was kept on the shore for Baldock. The next morning, his body was washed ashore in Sydney Bay.[190]

John had shown great courage in rescuing Mr Walker. On 14 April 1848, John Price made a 'good conduct' recommendation for him 'on the occasion of the whale boat upsetting'.[191] Very few convicts ever received such a recommendation from John Price. No doubt he would have been even more pleased if John had rescued his confidant and lieutenant, but given Baldock's unpopularity among the convict population it is perhaps not a surprise that he was the only man identified as having died on that night.

Today a headstone marks Baldock's grave in the Norfolk Island cemetery, the work of a convict stonemason. It is quite an impressive, traditionally inscribed stone that reads:

> Sacred to the Memory of Alfred Essex Baldock late Chief Constable of the Island, who was unfortunately drowned by the upsetting of a boat in crossing the bar on the 12th April 1848 AE27.
>
> Therefore be ye also ready for in such an hour as ye think not the Son of man cometh.
>
> MATT. XXIV. 11

However, the inscription contains its own little mystery. Matthew XXIV.11 is not accurately quoted. It actually reads: 'And Jesus said unto them, See ye not all these things? Verily I say unto you, There shall not be left here one stone upon another, that shall not be thrown down.'[192] It is interesting to speculate whether this was a simple error or whether someone was expressing an opinion of Baldock, the headstone itself or the penal settlement as a whole.

\*\*\*

By October 1848, John had been on Norfolk Island for sixteen months. Up to this time, his convict records show that no disciplinary measures had been taken against him. The only entry on his record was the good conduct recommendation for saving the life of Matthew Walker. However, in mid-October James Fraser finally arrived at Norfolk Island.

12. The headstone on the grave of Alfred Essex Baldock with its inaccurate and puzzling quotation from the book of Matthew.

From April 1847 until September 1848, Fraser had been held at Hobart Town gaol,[193] despite the fact that he had been sentenced to be transported for the term of his natural life and that during this time there had been regular transport ship voyages between Van Diemen's Land and Norfolk Island. Fraser had been treated more leniently than John, apparently for identifying his confederate in the burglary. John must have been both upset and annoyed by the leniency shown to Fraser.

John Price's approach to discipline was not based on the principle of being tough but fair; he wanted the convicts to be in a state of constant and deep fear. He believed that if the convicts were completely intimidated, they would cause the least possible trouble. As a matter of normal practice, Price appointed tough, devious, hardened and totally unprincipled convicts as police sub-constables. From the correspondence of the Reverend Thomas Rogers, an Anglican clergyman, we get a vivid picture of the role played by these sub-constables. Rogers was so critical of John Price's methods that Price ordered him to leave Norfolk Island in 1847, just prior to John

Copley's arrival. The Reverend Rogers did not approve of the use of convicts as overseers and sub-constables. He was very critical of sub-constables having the right to search a fellow prisoner at any time and at any place. He stated that these searches were often 'conducted in the most obscene and disgusting manner', and he noted that if a convict resisted he might be bludgeoned by the sub-constable and at risk of having limbs broken. He stated that 'Perjury on the part of the constables was rife'.[194] James Fraser, with a military deserter background, four serious criminal convictions and numerous other appearances before the court, was just the person who would do whatever John Price demanded he do to make life a little easier for himself on Norfolk Island. There is no record to show that Fraser was appointed to the position of police sub-constable but according to John Price's practice on Norfolk Island he was an ideal candidate.

On Tuesday, 14 November, John was searched by a sub-constable for tobacco.[195] Typically such a search involved the sub-constable looking down the mouth and throat of a convict. Finding very small traces of tobacco down a convict's throat was enough to deem that the convict had been found in possession. The regulations relating to the possession of tobacco by convicts were not straightforward. They stated that it was not an offence to possess tobacco if the convict had obtained it by honest means. This provided considerable scope for argument and it left each case open to the interpretation of the authorities. Nevertheless, after this search John was charged with having been found in the possession of tobacco.

Later that day, John was charged with another offence; that of 'inciting prisoners to bring a charge against a sub-constable'.[196] We do not know how John allegedly incited the prisoners or what his grievance against the sub-constable was, although it almost certainly related to the tobacco charge. What we do know is that a convict was taking an incredible risk by advocating in any way that a charge should be brought against anyone in a position of authority in the convict system. If such a charge was not proved to the satisfaction of the convict authorities, then the convict advocating such a charge was guilty of an offence. Even with a fair and objective commandant running Norfolk Island, it would have been very difficult to get the convict authorities to accept that one of its sub-constables was in the wrong. To do so with John Price as commandant appears to be both brave and foolhardy and very definitely a move doomed to failure. At the very least, John must have been extremely upset and angry with the sub-constable in question, and one cannot help but wonder if James Fraser had been that sub-constable.

On Norfolk Island, John Price had the power of an absolute dictator. He was the head of the police force and also the judge on the island for all

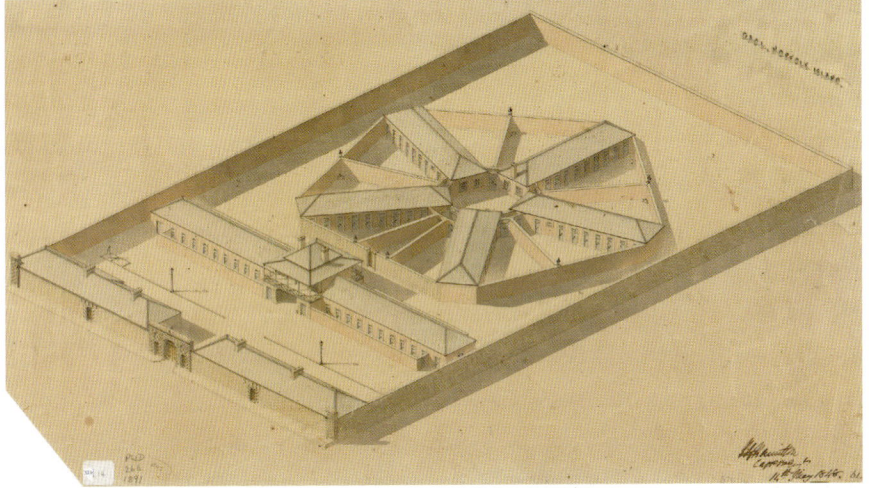

13. The pentagonal gaol at Kingston, Norfolk Island (the new gaol) where convicts served punishment sentences for breaches of discipline.

matters concerning alleged breaches of convict discipline. He found John guilty of both charges. Price determined that as punishment, John would serve a sentence of seven days hard labour in chains for having tobacco in his possession and a further one month hard labour in chains for inciting prisoners to bring a charge against a sub-constable.[197] Straight after Price brought down these punishments, John was taken to the new gaol that had been constructed alongside the large prison barracks. It was almost directly opposite the nail making and blacksmith workshop where he usually worked.

During John Price's time as commandant only very limited records were kept in relation to the punishments given to convicts and John's convict record contains no evidence to show that he was flogged with the cat-o'-nine-tails. Nevertheless, these were typical of the offences which resulted in the convict offender being flogged with the cat.

Assuming John was flogged for these offences, it would have occurred on the morning after the conviction. Typically, a convict was escorted into the yard of the New Gaol, his shirt was removed and his arms and legs were tied to the whipping triangle. This wooden frame was designed to ensure that the prisoner could not move while receiving the lash. A contemporary description tells us that around the triangle there was a rough circle of blood and human gore that was about a metre in diameter. Out from this circle were streaks of blood that ran for a further half to a full metre.[198] This residue of blood and gore left by the prisoners who had been flogged earlier was a horrific sight for a convict awaiting punishment. The cat-o'-nine-tails was embedded with metal thorns in the leather straps that ripped and tore at the flesh of the back. After only a few strokes of the cat, most convicts yelled and screamed in pain. These floggings were not only designed to punish the individual. Any flogging was a public relations exercise, with a group of other convicts witnessing the event. It was meant to send a powerful message illustrating John Price's strength, control and authority but, most importantly, it was to engender fear into the convict population.

Prior to Price's time as commandant, the practice after a convict was flogged with the cat was that he was taken to a gaol cell and the cooling leaves of the banana tree were applied to his bloodied and mangled flesh. The leaves had been found to take away some of the intensity of the pain from the flogging. When Price became commandant he stopped this practice.[199] This was indicative of his approach to punishment. He apparently considered intense pain a deterrent to bad behaviour. If banana leaves reduced the intensity of the pain, then they lessened the effectiveness of the flogging. He was not going to allow this to happen.

John's more than five weeks of hard labour involved doing the heaviest manual work on the island from sunrise to sunset, weighed down by heavy ankle chains. Jobs like breaking and carrying rocks and pushing and pulling carts qualified as the heaviest work, and although the temperature did not exceed 25°C during this time, the high humidity of a sub-tropical location made it extremely strenuous and exhausting. In the weeks leading up to Christmas 1848, John had his first real experience of why Norfolk Island had such a fearsome reputation.

On Saturday, 10 February 1849, John was again in trouble with the authorities and John Price found him guilty of 'disobedience of orders'. His punishment for this offence was fourteen days hard labour in chains.[200] We do not know the details of the alleged 'disobedience of orders' but we do know that for two weeks, at the height of summer, John was forced to do hard manual labour in chains from sunrise to sunset with a minimum of food to sustain him.

This charge in February was not the last time that John fell foul of John Price's rules and authority. In September that year, he appeared before Price on a charge of 'loitering on the road'.[201] The road where this offence occurred was almost certainly Bay Road in Kingston that was just back from the beach on Slaughter Bay. On several occasions during the normal working day John would have walked along Bay Road. It led to the timberyard and mess where the convicts were fed and also to the nail making and blacksmith workshop opposite the new gaol. The details of the loitering offence do not survive. It could have been something as simple as walking too slowly or stopping for a brief word with another convict. Maybe he paused as people do today to appreciate the beauty of the ocean. Nepean and Phillip Islands lie offshore and the usually calm, aqua blue water of the bay contrasts strikingly with the rough sea beyond the reef. As a punishment for this offence Price sentenced John to one month of hard labour in chains.[202] This was the brutal regime of crime and punishment while John Price was commandant of the Norfolk Island penal settlement.

\*\*\*

James Fraser only remained on Norfolk Island for eighteen months. He left the island on the barque *Lady Franklin* in mid-April 1850 and by mid-May he was back on Van Diemen's Land. Straight after his return, he was given a 3rd class pass,[203] and after serving just eighteen months of a life sentence of transportation he was available to be hired out to settlers. During his time on Norfolk Island, no accounts of any offence or punishment were entered into his convict record.[204] Compare this with the early 1840s, when Fraser served two punishment sentences at the Port Arthur settlement and on both occasions received several additional sentences. Also, when free to move about the colony, he was repeatedly subject to other disciplinary sentences and punishments.[205] Fraser's convict record on Norfolk Island was significantly different to the rest of his record and it was typical of the record for a convict who acted as a sub-constable during John Price's time as commandant.

\*\*\*

Not only had no disciplinary charges been recorded against John Copley prior to Fraser's arrival on Norfolk Island, but after Fraser returned to Van Diemen's Land John was never again put on a charge or punished.

Although John had been subjected to brutal discipline and punishment on the island, it appears that during this time he was able to develop and expand his trade skills. A convict establishment generated a considerable amount of metal trades work. The most obvious example of this is the need for chains to shackle the convicts. There are accounts that tell us that during John's time on Norfolk more than half the convicts at one time were shackled in chains.[206] These chains had to be maintained, and shackled and unshackled to individual convicts. When John was undertaking hard labour in chains, he may well have been struck by the irony that he could have repaired and maintained the very same heavy chains that bound his legs and ankles.

Norfolk Island required far more complex metal trades work to be undertaken than other convict establishments. Not only was there considerable building work going on, but it was also necessary to manufacture and maintain a wide range of agricultural implements. As was shown with the whale boat incident in 1848, it was very difficult to land people and goods on the island. Indeed, there were considerable limits on the weight and shape of goods that could be transferred by whale boats from offshore vessels to the pier at Kingston. Consequently the carriages and drays that were used to transport both the non-convict population and goods would have had to be fabricated and assembled on the island and there was no one else around but the convict tradesmen to build and maintain these vehicles. John could not have avoided exposure to a wide range of new work and skills.

It was March 1851 before John boarded the *Lady Franklin* for the trip back to Van Diemen's Land. He arrived there in early April.[207] By this time, the animosity between John Copley and James Fraser appears to have been well known to the convict authorities. Because Fraser was working at the Hobart Town Hospital,[208] John was ordered to stay at the Launceston convict depot and he was not to enter Hobart Town.[209] Despite this restriction on his movements, John was finally free of Norfolk Island and the harsh punishments he had experienced there.

# 10  New Opportunities in Van Diemen's Land

When he arrived at the Launceston depot, John Copley had to adapt to life in a work gang. This tough gang work was normally given to recently convicted prisoners who had just arrived in Van Diemen's Land and it aimed to instil discipline into them. This work would have seemed easy to John when compared with what he had gone through over the previous four years.

While John was no doubt appreciating this change from Norfolk Island, he would have been aware that as things stood, he still faced a long time in the convict system. Soon after his arrival in Launceston, he was given the required pass holder status[210] that allowed him to be hired out to settlers in the area. He was now back where he had been in the system in June 1842, after his initial fifteen months at the Jerusalem probation station. Under the rules that normally applied to a convict serving a life sentence, he now faced at least another six years before he would be eligible for a ticket-of-leave and at least ten years before he would be eligible for a conditional pardon that would enable him to live as a free man. At this time, John was thirty-eight years of age and he had already been in the convict system for more than ten years.

The future did not look very promising. As things stood, John faced the prospect of spending much of the next ten years in the Launceston depot or, if he was lucky, working for settlers in the surrounding area. Although he was available to be hired out, no one was willing to take him. It appears that his convict pedigree on Norfolk Island did not make him attractive to prospective employers.

In early June 1851, John first heard news that was to change his life and his status in the colony. Word had got out that in the previous month, one Edward Hargreaves had discovered gold near Bathurst west of Sydney in the colony of New South Wales.[211] When this news hit Launceston, John must have cursed his 1847 burglary conviction. Without it he would have been able to join the rush, travel to the goldfields and start digging. Even convicts like John would have heard reports of large numbers of men boarding ships in Launceston and Hobart Town and heading north to make their fortune.

By July, the gold rush had spread from New South Wales to the colony of Victoria. Victoria was only a few days sailing from Launceston across Bass Strait. This latest discovery had occurred at Clunes in central Victoria where two men, James Esmond and Dr George Brahn, picked up £50 worth of gold with little effort.

While John must have been frustrated by his inability to join the gold rushes, the discovery of gold was causing major problems for the government of Van Diemen's Land. By mid-July, only a month after the first news of the discovery had reached the island, a large number of men had already left, seeking their fortune on the mainland. Many of these men were skilled tradesmen such as blacksmiths. There was a great demand for blacksmiths on the goldfields because their trade had a key role in manufacturing and maintaining both mining equipment and the infrastructure that moved men and materials to the fields. In Hobart Town, the convict authorities were being pressed to supply labour to replace the departing blacksmiths. Their records would have included the name John Copley, but they had banned him from entering Hobart Town while James Fraser was residing there.

Although the key reason for the convict authorities reviewing the order that banned John from entering the city was the shortage of labour caused by the gold rushes, they may have been starting to change their view of Fraser. Since returning to Van Diemen's Land in May 1850, Fraser had spent some time in prisoners' barracks and from there he had been hired out to work for a number of masters. He had spent most of his time working at the Hobart Town hospital. His main skills were his ability to read and write and to work as a gardener. In March 1851 he was convicted by a police magistrate of 'being absent from his Master's premises without leave and contrary to express orders' and was sentenced to 'seven days solitary' and to be moved to prisoners' barracks.[212] In May, the authorities determined that he had to serve four more years colonial service as a convict.[213] This decision meant that he would not be fast tracked to ticket-of-leave status as had initially appeared likely after his return from Norfolk Island. In June, he sought permission from Lieutenant Governor Denison to marry.[214] Although Denison was the man who had approved the more lenient treatment of Fraser compared to John after their house burglary convictions, his application was rejected.[215] His attitude and behaviour during his time in Hobart Town appears to have made the convict authorities feel less inclined to look upon him favourably.

As more men left for the goldfields, the shortage of blacksmiths continued to grow, and in July 1851 the convict authorities made two decisions. The first was that James Fraser was not to reside in the Hobart district any longer. As a consequence of this decision, Fraser was sent to work at Lake River, an isolated settlement in the centre of Van Diemen's Land.[216] The second decision was to lift the order that John Copley was not to enter Hobart Town. Following this, John was engaged to work for a Mr John Ball on New Town Road.[217] John was now back in the city working as a blacksmith, four years and three months after he left to serve a transportation sentence for the term of his natural life.[218] While he was still a pass holder convict, his skills were in great demand and although he had not left Van Diemen's Land, the gold rushes had brought about a major change in his status and position.

In August, John changed his master and started to work for John Wilmot, a farrier, who lived at 140 Murray Street in the centre of Hobart Town.[219] John would have been well fed by his employers and, almost certainly, living comfortably. He was clearly well on the way to fully recovering from the privations and trauma of Norfolk Island. As a pass holder convict, he was not supposed to be directly receiving any money for his work, but with a shortage of blacksmiths he may well have been able to earn a few shillings.

Soon after his return to Hobart Town, John made contact with John Goss, the stonemason who lived in Macquarie Street. Goss was a convict with a colourful past who had been convicted at the York Assizes in 1839 of poaching and shooting a man with intent. For these offences, he had received a fifteen year transportation sentence. In Van Diemen's Land, he had further convictions and in the 1840s he served sentences in the coal mines near Port Arthur, where he worked in chains.[220] Due to these further convictions, Goss had only just received a conditional pardon. Since both men were tradesmen, it is possible they first met on a building site after John's return to the city, but more likely that they met during the 1840s, either in convict gangs or in isolated settlements. The two men had their convict experiences in common and Goss, too, was a native of South Yorkshire. The thirty-two-year-old Goss came from the town of Wombell,[221] only four kilometres from John's birth place of Thorpe Hesley.

John Goss had also benefited from the gold rushes in Victoria and New South Wales. Gold had prompted a substantial exodus of stonemasons from Van Diemen's Land so Goss's skills were in great demand, and as a conditional pardon convict he was free to charge a high price for his services. It would soon have been apparent to John that Goss was now doing very well for himself and it would not have been long before he learned that Goss had a young Irish wife. News of this marriage could well have surprised John because he would have known of the substantial imbalance between men and women in the colony, and convict men were at the bottom of the pecking order in terms of being seen by women as potential marriage partners.

Some time after meeting in Hobart Town, John Goss introduced John to his new wife Bridgett Goss (nee Crotty). Bridgett was a small twenty-eight-year-old with hazel eyes and black-brown hair. She had been convicted at the County Waterford Assizes in December 1848 for stealing three geese.[222] For this conviction, she had received a sentence of transportation and she arrived in Van Diemen's Land on the barque *Australasia*, as did Catherine McMahon, who was at this time in service to the Gosses. When Bridgett married John Goss in 1850[223] she was one of the very first of the 200 women who arrived on the *Australasia* to marry. She had encountered no disciplinary problems at all in the convict system.

It is likely that John Goss's domestic situation held considerable appeal for John and no doubt it made him think about what he wanted to do with his own life. It was at this time that John met the Goss's domestic servant, Catherine McMahon.

# PART THREE
# CATHERINE AND JOHN

# 11 A Convict Relationship

The Catherine McMahon that John Copley met was twenty-four years old, and after five months in the Cascades Factory on a meagre diet she almost certainly had a trim figure. Obviously John liked this red-haired, freckle-faced Irish girl and Catherine must have reciprocated because a relationship very quickly developed between them.

It would have been more than physical attraction that cemented the relationship. Catherine was almost certainly impressed with Bridgett's situation. Bridgett had spent no punishment time in the Cascades Factory and since her marriage she had not worked for anyone in domestic service. Instead, she lived with a well-paid tradesman who provided her with plenty of food and considerable domestic comfort. To Catherine, John Copley would have appeared to have the potential to be her John Goss. He was a skilled tradesman whose skills were in demand and he was capable of providing the means to keep her out of the Cascades Factory, out of domestic service and in a comfortable situation out of the convict system. Perhaps, John's reputation as a tough convict who had survived Norfolk Island also had some attraction for Catherine.

Some may say that John's age of thirty-nine and Catherine's age of twenty-four is enough to explain why John was attracted to Catherine. Nevertheless, the domestic situation of his friend John Goss would have been a considerable contrast to the lot of a single male convict in Van

Diemen's Land and an incredible contrast to the brutal, masculine, single sex environment John had experienced for four years on Norfolk Island. Goss's domestic situation would have shown John what it was now possible to have as a skilled convict tradesman in Hobart Town, and since he was obviously attracted to this red-haired young woman a settled relationship would have been very appealing.

The relationship between Catherine and John developed at a whirlwind pace and within a month of leaving the Cascades Factory Catherine was pregnant.[224] Pregnancy raised a number of very difficult issues that they had to address.

The first issue was that John had already married another woman. He had left his wife Mary and his three children in Scholes. This raised the issue of whether John still had a wife and whether he was in any position to marry Catherine. We do not know whether Mary Copley was alive or dead in 1851. We can find no evidence of her or the children on the public record. Neither do we know whether, late in 1851, John had any idea what had happened to his Yorkshire wife.

The other difficult issue was whether both Catherine and John would receive the approval of the convict authorities to get married. A prerequisite for convicts receiving such approval to marry was that they be considered of good conduct. Catherine had some problems in this regard with her three month hard labour sentence in the Cascades in the winter of 1851 but it was John who was the real problem, having less than five years earlier received his life transportation sentence for house burglary.

The consequences of not being able to marry were far greater for Catherine than John. For an unmarried convict woman, giving birth to a child was an offence for which the standard punishment was six months hard labour at the Cascades Factory. Catherine had seen her relationship with John as the means to get her out of the convict system, but at the start of 1852 the pregnant Catherine had to face the fact that John could be the cause of her having to serve an extended period of punishment as a 3rd class convict.

John's marriage in Yorkshire in the 1830s appears to have been the lesser of the two problems. The last time John had seen Mary was eleven years earlier in 1840 at the time of his arrest and conviction for sheep stealing. Regardless of whether Mary was still alive, English common law at this time provided that if a man had not seen or heard from his wife for at least seven years then he was considered to be a widower and therefore able to marry again.[225] It was clearly not difficult for John to present himself as a widower under this law and the Church of England had to accept him as such.

This still left the issue of whether the convict authorities would give both parties the necessary approval to marry. Catherine and John did not do the predictable thing and submit their applications for approval to marry at the start of 1852. Instead they seemed to be trying to give themselves time to maximize their chances of being seen as suitable candidates and thus gain approval from the authorities.

In early January 1852 Catherine completed three months domestic service with Bridgett and John Goss. This provided her with the means to receive a good reference and to obtain a new position elsewhere. Armed with her reference, she left the Goss household and went into Brickfield Hiring Depot. On the next day, she was hired into domestic service by a J. Davis of Murray Street in Hobart Town.[226] The successful period of service with the Gosses and the start of another period of domestic service would have put Catherine in a strong position to meet the good conduct requirement for her application to be approved.

John seemed to believe that his best chances of gaining permission to marry would be by maximizing the time he worked as a skilled tradesman and by keeping out of trouble. With blacksmiths in short supply and with a good work and behaviour record, he clearly hoped that the authorities would be pleased with him and would approve his application.

On 3 February 1852, Catherine made an enquiry of the convict authorities that appears to indicate she was thinking of another major problem that was associated with her pregnancy. On this day, she asked when she would be due to obtain her ticket-of-leave. She was advised that she must serve three years and six months of her sentence before she could receive the ticket.[227] With her original conviction in Ennis occurring at the end of February 1849, this meant that she was not due for a ticket-of-leave until the end of August 1852, after she was due to give birth to her child. Therefore even if she was given permission to marry John, she still had a serious problem—as a pass holding convict as distinct from a ticket-of-leave convict, she would be required to give birth to the child in the Cascades Factory nursery, and that nursery was a death trap for infants.

From 1851 to 1855, 366 children under three years of age died in the Factory nursery. This was approximately 30 percent of the children born there during this period. In the same period, approximately 10 percent of the children born in Hobart Town died before they reached the age of three. Of those 366 children who died in the Cascade convict nursery, 51 percent died of dysentery, diarrhoea, or enteritis compared to 13 percent amongst those who died in Hobart Town. In the Factory, 13 percent of child deaths were caused by influenza, bronchitis or pneumonia compared to less than 5 percent of the child deaths in the city.[228]

The high infant death rate at the Cascades Factory was caused by a combination of factors. At the Factory, two and sometimes four babies were placed like sardines in a single wooden crib. This, along with the cold and damp, made it a very fertile environment for spreading disease and illness amongst young children. On top of this was the poor diet fed to the expectant and weaning mothers. The overall objective of the Cascades Factory was to punish and discipline the women convicts and the authorities were not prepared to compromise this objective, even though so many of the young children paid the ultimate price for their mothers' crimes.

This alarmingly high infant death rate at the Cascade Factory was widely known among the convicts and people of Hobart Town. Any concerned prospective parent would be prepared to do virtually anything to avoid giving birth there and leaving their newborn baby in the nursery. By delaying the submission of their applications to marry, Catherine and John not only improved the chances of these applications being approved but they also opened up a way for Catherine to avoid giving birth in the Factory.

By 23 February 1852, Catherine was around four months pregnant and she realized her pregnancy would soon start to show. She and John decided that they had delayed long enough and in the following two weeks both of them submitted their applications for approval to marry.[229]

The two people who would decide their future were Lieutenant Governor Denison and the Reverend William Bedford. The Lieutenant Governor had to approve or reject their applications after Reverend Bedford had made a recommendation in relation to their suitability for marriage. The convict women in Van Diemen's Land considered Bedford pompous and behind his back called him 'Holy Willie',[230] but Catherine and John needed to treat him with considerable respect.

By 1852 the Reverend Bedford had been involved with the Van Diemen's Land convict system for more than twenty years and he held that convict women had to be 'brought into habits of decency and industry' before they could be permitted to marry.[231] Catherine, with her good record of service since leaving the Cascades Factory in October 1851, met the criteria of decency and industry and her application to marry was approved.

John's application was more problematic, but since he had been in Hobart Town he had had no difficulties with the authorities and, with still more people leaving Van Diemen's Land for the gold rushes, he had skills that were in short supply. Also maybe his 'good conduct' on Norfolk Island[232] would work in his favour. Fortunately and perhaps surprisingly, John's application to marry was approved by Lieutenant Governor Denison; the same person who had sent him to Norfolk Island less than five years earlier.

On Monday, 15 March 1852, Catherine McMahon and John Copley were married by the Reverend William Bedford at St David's Church in Hobart.[233] As a Catholic, Catherine would no doubt have strongly preferred to be married in the Catholic church, but with John on the record as a

Wesleyan and with Reverend Bedford playing a key role in approving the marriage, this would not have been an option. Today St David's Church is the Anglican Cathedral in Hobart but in 1852 it was the Church of England and Ireland parish church. The marriage register identified Catherine as a spinster who was a pass holder convict and her age was given as twenty-seven years when in fact she was no more than twenty-five. John was identified as a widower who was a pass holder convict and his age was given as thirty-eight years when he was actually thirty-nine. Both Catherine and John signed the register with an X. The witnesses to the marriage were John and Bridget Goss, the couple who brought John and Catherine together.[234] On the day of her marriage, Catherine was nearly five months pregnant and she knew that there was at least one major matter that she still had to deal with before she could have any confidence that she was effectively out of the convict system.

14. St David's Church in Hobart Town where Catherine McMahon and John Copley married in March 1852.

# 12 Establishing a Family and a Business

With their marriage behind them, John and Catherine Copley faced up to the problems involved in having their baby in Hobart Town while they were pass holder convicts.

On 18 May, Catherine again approached the convict authorities seeking a precise date when she would be able to apply for a ticket-of-leave. Catherine was told that in three months she would be able to apply for the ticket.[235] Because she was married, Catherine understood that the granting of the ticket in mid-August 1852 would be a formality provided she stayed out of trouble with the authorities. It is obvious that by this stage, Catherine and John had definitely decided that their child must not be born in the Cascades Factory.

On Tuesday, 27 July, Catherine gave birth to a son in their home at Old Wharf.[236] They named the baby John after his father and his grandfather. Fortunately there were no complications associated with the delivery and the birth could be kept a closely guarded secret. John may have appreciated the coincidence that in March 1841 he started his life in Van Diemen's Land by landing at Old Wharf, and here was his son John also starting his life at Old Wharf.

Three weeks after the birth of her son, Catherine was granted a ticket-of-leave.[237] There could be no problem now if she 'officially' gave birth to her child. No doubt by the end of that week, Catherine and John would have let it be widely known that within the space of a couple of days they had been doubly blessed. On 17 August Catherine had received her ticket-of-leave and on 19 August she had given birth to their son John.[238]

On Sunday 5 September, Catherine attended mass at St Joseph's Roman Catholic church on the corner of Macquarie and Harrington Streets and after mass her son John was baptized.[239] Although Catherine had married in a protestant church, she remained a Catholic and she was determined that her son would be raised in her faith. In filling out the baptism records, the priest asked Catherine the date on which young John was born. This was not the place or the occasion when Catherine could tell a lie and she replied '27 July'.[240]

Three days later, John registered the birth of his son with the authorities in Hobart Town. John told the Deputy Registrar that his son had been born on 19 August 1852.[241] Catherine and John had achieved their objective—their son had been born away from the Cascades Factory and he was healthy.

\*\*\*

After receiving her ticket-of-leave and with the birth of a healthy son, Catherine settled down to life as a married woman with her time in the convict system effectively behind her. Some time after the birth of baby John, Catherine and John moved from Old Wharf to the New Wharf area,[242] which today is known as Salamanca Place. Life continued to go well for John. There was plenty of work available with good pay, because the gold rush activity in Victoria was reaching fever pitch and the shortage of skilled tradesmen in Hobart Town was now chronic.

Towards the end of 1852, Catherine found she was pregnant again, but this time there were no complications associated with the pregnancy or with her situation in the convict system. During this pregnancy, Catherine moved a step closer to total freedom from her convict status when in May 1853 she was recommended to receive a conditional pardon.[243]

On 31 July 1853, Catherine gave birth to her second child. This child, a girl, was born at New Wharf.[244] On 7 August the baby girl was baptized at

15. 1858 view from St David's Church looking down Murray Street, Hobart Town. The row of buildings (upper right) running parallel with the docked ships is the New Wharf area.

St Joseph's Catholic church in Hobart Town and given the name Catherine Copley.[245] This relatively early baptism only a week after the birth suggests that Catherine may have been concerned about the health of her baby, and as a Catholic felt it was important to expeditiously baptize her.

Two days later, John registered the birth of his daughter with the name Margaret Copley.[246] Margaret was the name of Catherine's mother and it would not have been surprising if Catherine had intended her first daughter to carry her mother's name. On this occasion, John did not mark the registry with an X but signed the registry as John Copley, a blacksmith living at New Wharf.[247] John's time in the convict school on Norfolk Island had given him the basics necessary to formally sign his daughter's arrival into the world.

We do not know why Catherine and John gave their baby daughter different names two days apart. Was there a change of mind about the name or was there a mix-up by the priest during the service which the parents felt unable to rectify at the time? The seemingly confused parents finally decided that Catherine was to be their daughter's name and a few days after the initial registration, John returned to the registry office and asked the registrar to change the baby's name. This the registrar did, noting in the register against the birth of the Copley daughter that 'This should be Catherine altered in the presence of informant'.[248]

By 11 August, baby Catherine had a fever and was experiencing difficulty in breathing. She had a barking cough that progressively became more intense and settled deeper in her chest. During the course of that day, tragedy struck and ten-day-old baby Catherine died of croup.[249]

Croup was a generic name for a number of respiratory diseases that often affected babies and infants. In the mid-nineteenth century there was no effective treatment for croup and babies and infants often died of the condition. Croup was generally more prevalent during winter, and early August was the depth of winter in Hobart Town.

That same day, almost straight after the death of baby Catherine, John again visited the office of the Registrar for Births and Deaths in Hobart Town and registered the death of his young daughter.[250]

After this tragedy, John and Catherine moved on with their lives and at the end of 1853 for the third year in a row, Catherine found that she was pregnant.

***

Since John's arrival in Van Diemen's Land in 1841, he had progressed from basic nail making and blacksmithing into quite advanced metal trades and fabrication work. By 1853 it appears he was starting to be involved in manufacturing a light open pleasure carriage that was used to carry one or two people. These carriages were known as chaise carts. The private ownership of carriages in the Australian colonies was just starting to become a statement of personal status and wealth. Manufacturers in Van Diemen's Land were tapping into a new and growing market and were looking to export chaise carts to the boom colony of Victoria. The manufacture of a chaise cart involved heavy metal trades blacksmithing work on the undercarriage and on the basic structure of the carriage. It also involved working with timber and upholstery, and finer more intricate metal work on the body of the cart. As a pass holder convict, John would have found it very frustrating to have to work as an employee and not be able to operate his own business. He appears to have had an entrepreneurial spirit. He grew up in a family where his father worked as a nailor on what we would call today a self-employed basis. In 1844, he had been sentenced to one month of hard labour later remitted when he was caught with a money making sideline of selling nails around Campbell Town in the north of the colony. In 1853, John would have been on good wages but it would have been hard to watch other people making big money when he was not able to pursue these opportunities himself.

While John was still locked into the convict system, major changes were occurring in Van Diemen's Land. In mid-1853, the last British ship carrying convicts arrived in Hobart Town. During the previous six years there had been a growing anti-transportation movement in the colony and public opinion was now strongly against transportation. While the British Government had finally appeared to concede to the demands of this movement, it was actually the great gold rushes in nearby Victoria that ensured the end of transportation. The close proximity of all the gold finds hardly made Van Diemen's Land a place you would send someone for a sentence of punishment.

In early 1854, Catherine's brother Denis McMahon took a major step out of the convict system when he received his ticket-of-leave.[251] However, at this time things were not going so well for her other brother, William. In March 1854, while working for Thomas Duggan at Westbury in the north of the island, he was charged with misconduct by representing himself as a free person and for resisting a constable and tearing his clothes. He was convicted of the misconduct offence and received a sentence of three months hard labour.[252] He served this sentence in the prison barracks at

Launceston and during this sentence he would have spent time on the punishment treadmill.

At around this time, John received some very good news. On 14 February 1854, the convict authorities determined that John Copley 'will be allowed a deduction of two years from the period he would have to serve for meritorious conduct'.[253] This deduction from his sentence was due to his actions nearly seven years earlier when he rescued Matthew Walker from the sea off Norfolk Island. The convict authorities' consideration of some reward for John's actions on that night in April 1848 was well overdue, but things had changed considerably by 1854. By this time, John Price and his brutal and inhuman regime on the island had finally been discredited. In January 1853, due to 'failing health', Price had vacated the post of Norfolk Island Commandant[254] and by early 1854 the convict authorities had started the process of closing down the convict settlement. At this time and in this environment, the authorities were finally prepared to recognize a convict who had risked his own life to save the life of a senior government official.

What this reduction of two years in John's sentence actually meant was clarified a month later when the convict authorities determined that he 'must serve twelve years from the date of conviction in 1847'.[255] With the two year reduction in sentence, this meant John was eligible to receive a conditional pardon in April 1859 and be free of the convict system. This decision also meant that in a short while he would be eligible to receive a ticket-of-leave. With the large amount of metal trades work available in Hobart Town, John would now have been starting to think about the business opportunities that would open up to him when he received his ticket.

On 4 April 1854, while her younger brother William McMahon was pushing the treadmill in Launceston prison, Catherine officially moved outside the convict system. On this day, she was granted a conditional pardon and a week later she attended the Hobart Town post office and picked up the conditional pardon documentation.[256] With her freedom gained and the recent good news concerning John's position in the convict system, Catherine would have had growing confidence in her family's future as free people in Hobart Town.

\*\*\*

August 1854 was a great month for Catherine and John. On the first day of the month, John was granted a ticket-of-leave.[257] He was now able to work for himself in Van Diemen's Land. On 11 August, Catherine gave birth to a son who was given the name James Copley. The baby was named after Catherine's father James McMahon, who had died at Cappabane prior to her transportation. On 20 August, baby James was baptized at St Joseph's Catholic church in Hobart Town. It was very much a family occasion as Catherine's older brother Denis was able to be one of the baptismal sponsors for her new son.[258]

Soon after receiving his ticket-of-leave, John approached George Rex, a businessman based in Liverpool Street,[259] with a proposal that would give him the necessary support to establish a blacksmith and coach building business. George Rex operated a grocery business in Hobart Town but he appears to have also dabbled in other activities where he thought he could make a profit. John proposed that he establish a blacksmith and coach building business based on a substantial loan from Rex. John would then pay the loan back over an agreed period. John was aware of the money that had been made in the previous few years from metal trades and coach building work and he had good reason, based on this experience, to believe that his proposal was financially sound and that he should be able to meet his obligations under the arrangement.

The two men then proceeded to talk terms and it was agreed that George Rex would lend £90 to John and this amount plus interest would be repaid within the next twelve months.[260] Catherine's reaction to John's plans is not known. It would not have been surprising if she had been worried about the extent of the financial burden John was taking on. After all, only three years earlier she had worked as domestic help for John Goss under a contract where her labour was only worth £1/15/- for three months work. Now

John was committing to repay £90 plus interest to George Rex over a twelve month period and also generate hundreds of pounds of additional earnings to meet the costs of establishing and running the business. Also, he had to provide the means to support his growing family.

By October 1854, John had commenced to operate a combined coach building general metal trades business in a rented workshop on Brooke Street in the Franklin Wharf area.[261] During the remaining months of 1854, the Copley business apparently operated successfully. As John had predicted, there was plenty of metal trades and coach building work around Hobart Town.

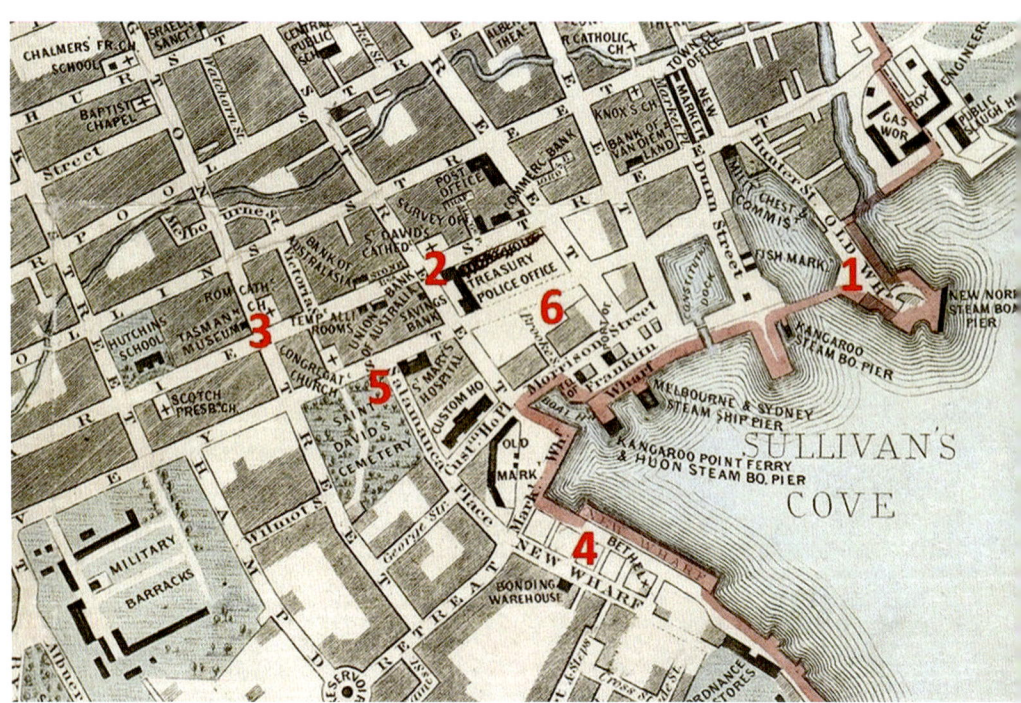

16. Section of the 1858 Jarman map of Hobart Town showing the area around Sullivan's Cove. The following significant locations are marked: 1. Old Wharf where John Copley disembarked in 1841; 2. Saint David's Church where Catherine and John were married; 3. Saint Joseph's Catholic Church where four Copley children were baptized; 4. New Wharf where Catherine and John lived between 1853 and 1855; 5. Saint David's Cemetery where baby Catherine Copley was buried in August 1853; and 6. Brooke Street where John Copley operated a metal trades workshop and business.

# 13  Business Troubles

The year 1855 started on a good note for the Copleys with Catherine's brother William McMahon receiving his ticket-of-leave in January.[262] Catherine was now able to enjoy periodic contact with both her brothers. Life in Hobart Town at this time must have provided the siblings with quite a contrast to their suffering during the potato famine. During this year Denis and William lent £27 to John[263] to assist in the further development of his business. This loan appears to have been entered into on an informal basis and it was left for Catherine and John to pay it back when they could.

In early 1855, John entered into an agreement with Mr Rupel to purchase a workshop on Sandy Bay Road, near the city.[264] John planned to move his engineering and coach building business into what almost certainly would have been larger premises, and owning the workshop would have provided significant savings in the medium to long term. He no longer had to pay rent on a workshop and he would hold increasing equity in the property. This deal also gave him the opportunity to construct a house on vacant land on the property, which would have enabled the family to live adjacent to the business and no longer pay rent for premises at New Wharf. John paid £200 to Mr Rupel to purchase the Sandy Bay Road property, and to do this he took out a mortgage of £250. This mortgage covered the cost of purchasing the property and helped cover costs associated with building a house and establishing the business. Soon after taking over ownership of the property,

John and the tradesmen he engaged commenced work on the new family home.

In early 1855, George Rex entered into a new contractual arrangement with John.[265] Apparently he appreciated the success John was having with the business and he was aware of the growing market for chaise carts. This new arrangement involved Rex providing a further £100 bank bill on the basis that over the following six months John would manufacture five chaise carts for him.[266] Rex obviously believed that he would be able to find buyers for the chaise carts at a good price and he was aware that John, as the owner of a new business, would find the prospect of having £100 immediately at hand a very attractive proposition. At this time, John was able to charge £25 for a chaise cart[267] and therefore Rex's proposition involved a 20 percent discount on the going rate, but because it was guaranteed money immediately in hand, John accepted the offer. Upon receiving the £100 bank bill, he used it to pay an outstanding £30 account he had with timber merchants Marsh & Chapman, and with the balance he purchased additional timber from them.[268]

It appears that up to June 1855, business was going well for John. By this time, he had already manufactured and was about to deliver the first of the five chaise carts for George Rex. Since opening the workshop eight months earlier, he had taken in an average of around £11 a week.[269] This was a good return but not a fortune. He had to pay for the materials and costs associated with running the business and he had payments to meet both on the mortgage and to Rex.

From the middle of 1855, the business climate for John and in Hobart Town generally began to deteriorate. While John had found his services in demand since July 1851, this demand had not been caused by great economic activity generated in Van Diemen's Land. Instead it had been caused by the shortage of skilled labour. Now, however, some new tradespersons were arriving in Van Diemen's Land from Britain and some tradespersons who had gone to the gold rushes in 1851–52 were returning to the island colony. Additionally, in the years immediately after the first gold rushes, some work had been created in Van Diemen's Land by the demand from the goldmining colonies for tools, equipment and consumer goods. Now, New South Wales and Victoria were getting tooled up to meet a higher proportion of this demand within their own borders. On top of this, while the vast majority of citizens supported the end of convict transportation, there was an economic consequence associated with it. By mid-1855, with no more transportation vessels arriving in Hobart Town, the economic activity generated by the convict system was in a steady decline.

When John started to see a reduction in new orders for work, he no doubt believed he was well positioned to ride out this dip in the economy. He had a significant amount of cash in hand and that should have enabled him to meet his mortgage repayments and cover his debt to George Rex.

John's confidence in this assessment of his financial situation was shaken around August 1855 when Rex notified him that he no longer wanted the five chaise carts and demanded the repayment in cash of the £100 bank bill.[270] Like all businesspeople in Van Diemen's Land, Rex was exposed to the new economic environment and he had apparently determined that the market was no longer there for him to make money out of the five chaise carts. Under the loan agreement reached in October 1854, John was already due to repay the £90 loan plus interest in October 1855. Now Rex wanted John to pay him another £100 as well as the £90 and he did not want to take any chaise carts. This demand combined with existing financial obligations took John to the brink of insolvency. John refused to pay the £100 to George Rex and the matter was headed for the courts.

The final court judgment concerning the financial dispute between George Rex and John Copley confirmed that John owed the £90 loan plus interest in accordance with their October 1854 agreement. There was never any dispute in the court concerning this matter. The court further determined that Rex should take the chaise cart already completed and that the cost of work already undertaken by John on the remaining four chaise carts should be deducted from the sum of £80 that was their nominal value. The result of the court decision was that in October 1855 John was due to pay £170 to Rex.[271]

John would have been very disappointed with this court decision. When the £100 five chaise carts agreement was entered into, it had considerable benefits for George Rex. Now Rex was trying to change the deal when circumstances outside the control of both of them reduced the attractiveness of the deal to Rex. After all, if the market price paid for chaise carts in Hobart Town had increased after the deal was entered into, there is no doubt Rex would have totally rejected any suggestion that the deal should be renegotiated in John's favour. Nevertheless, there was nothing John could do. Perhaps he gained some small consolation from the fact that the court determined Rex had to take the chaise cart that had already been manufactured.

John now had to review his total financial position to see if he could stay in business. His financial problems increased when the bank that held his mortgage became aware of his tight financial position and demanded that he pay out the mortgage. At the same time, other people he owed money to pressed him for prompt payment of his debts and accounts. While this was happening, the business situation in Hobart Town only worsened. There was less work available and the customers who were around were demanding significantly reduced prices. John could no longer sell chaise carts for £25 each. Instead, by October he was only able to get £17 for a chaise cart he sold to a Mr Poynton from Brown River, in the south of the island.[272]

On 17 October, John entered into a complex deal concerning the property on Sandy Bay Road. The end result of this deal was that he was no longer responsible for the mortgage and he lost the ownership of the workshop and the land on which it was located. William Milner, a local businessman, took over ownership of the workshop and the land. As a part of this deal, John made a £79 bill of exchange payment to Milner that enabled him to retain ownership of his newly constructed house.[273]

On the same day, John also paid £150 to George Rex. This was the time when he was due to pay back the original October 1854 loan of £90 plus interest.[274] This meant he still owed around £20 to Rex.

Following the completion of these financial arrangements, John continued to run his business in the Sandy Bay workshop on the basis that he would pay twenty shillings rent a week to William Milner.[275] As a result of making the payments associated with these deals, John had only limited cash in hand and he still had a significant number of creditors.

A number of these creditors were now vigorously pursuing John for the prompt payment of debts and it soon became clear to him that if these creditors started to take legal action, he would be on the verge of insolvency. If this happened, the only thing that could save him was a major improvement in the business environment, and that was not going to happen.

Amid all these business woes John received some totally unexpected but very good news. On 27 November 1855 he was notified that had been granted a conditional pardon.[276] John and Catherine would have been delighted because it had been understood that John would not receive a pardon until April 1859. As a person who in 1847 had received a sentence 'for the term of his natural life' he could not get better news than this. A conditional pardon meant that in Van Diemen's Land he was now no longer classed as a convict. When knowledge of John's conditional pardon spread, a number of businesspeople in Hobart Town would have been aghast. With such a pardon, John had the legal right to leave Van Diemen's Land and they no doubt feared that he would take up this option and never be held to account and made to pay his creditors. Representations appear to have been made to the convict authorities and on 4 December, a week after the pardon had been granted, it was cancelled.[277] This would have been a dreadful blow for John and Catherine. Nothing was going right for them. There is no evidence to suggest that John had planned to leave Van Diemen's Land but he was now back as a ticket-of-leave convict.

Around the time the conditional pardon was cancelled, Abel & Piggott, a firm of shopkeepers on New Wharf, commenced proceedings in the Court of Requests for an order for John Copley to pay a debt of £9/5/6.

By mid-December 1855, John had to have known that within the next month he would almost certainly be declared insolvent and he faced losing virtually everything. The strategy of two months ago to get George Rex and the bank off his back had not worked and he faced being back before a court of law again and, on this occasion, it would be the Van Diemen's Land Insolvency Court. He and his family were approaching crisis point.

John then proceeded to implement a plan he had formulated to deal with his affairs leading up to his inevitable insolvency. In broad terms his creditors could be divided into two categories. The first category consisted of businesspeople and shopkeepers around Hobart Town. These creditors included the ironmonger Joseph Moir, who was owed £33/11/- and who had supplied John with iron bars and other metal products. Twenty pounds was still owed to George Rex and £22 to John Risby and he had several other smaller creditors. In total, more than £130 was owed to businesspeople, including shopkeepers. The second category was made up of employees and tradespersons. More than £200 was owed to John's employees and to the carpenters and bricklayers who had worked on his house and enlarged and upgraded his workshop. Some of the payments owed to the bricklayers were for bricks used in constructing the house.[278]

At this time the assets John possessed were limited to the house on Sandy Bay Road, his tools of trade and a horse. Before the end of the year, he had sold the house for £153, virtually all his tools of trade for £30 and the horse for £20.[279] With the funds raised from these sales and some cash in hand, he paid all money owed to the employees and tradesmen in category two.[280] John apparently felt the greatest obligation to these workers and he gave them priority over the businesspeople and shopkeepers. The one exception to this was William Milner, from whom he had rented the Sandy Bay Road workshop since mid-October 1855. On 7 January 1856 John made his last payment to a creditor when he paid William Milner £13 to cover the rent up until the end of the calendar year 1855.[281]

In early 1856, the business of Abel and Piggott obtained an order in the Court of Requests against John for the payment of £9/5/6. John determined that he was unable to make the payment required by this court order. Two other creditors were also suing him. On 23 January he filed a petition in the Court of Insolvency to be declared insolvent.[282] John was now headed back to court to appear before a judge who had the power to send him back to gaol.

# 14 The Insolvency Court

John Copley's 23 January petition to be declared insolvent was lodged with Commissioner Fielding Browne, the Tasmanian Commissioner of Insolvent Estates.[283] He was the Tasmanian Commissioner because at the start of 1856 the name of the colony had been changed from Van Diemen's Land to Tasmania. No one wanted to retain a name that served as a reminder of the convict past.

In the late 1840s, Fielding Browne had been the visiting judge dealing with criminal matters on Norfolk Island. He had been a supporter of the Reverend Thomas Rogers who was then the strongest critic of the cruel and inhumane way John Price performed his duties as Commandant. At that time, providing such support was not considered to be a positive move in terms of improving Fielding Browne's position and prospects but it was widely seen as testament to his courage and integrity. If John had been aware of Fielding Browne's reputation, he would no doubt have derived some comfort from it.

In his petition, John identified himself as a blacksmith living on Sandy Bay Road. He told the Commissioner that he was 'ready and willing to produce such proof' as required 'that he may be declared insolvent'. His petition went on to request that Commissioner Browne appoint a provisional assignee to manage his estate. John did not sign this petition with his signature but instead with an X.[284]

Attached to his petition, John provided a list of the 'persons to whom the petitioner is indebted' and 'the nature and amount of such debts'. This list had fourteen names and John assessed that his debts amount to £180/7/10. Virtually all the creditors listed were businesspeople and shopkeepers in Hobart Town. The standout exceptions were his brothers-in-law, Denis and William McMahon, who jointly were the second largest creditors with £27 owed.[285]

He also provided a 'full list and particular account of all the Estate and effects both real and personal' that he now owned. This list made miserable reading with the estate and effects having a total value of £10/10/-. This was made up of £6 worth of 'Household Furniture and effects at Dwelling House Sandy Bay Road' and 'Working implements in Blacksmith's Shop' worth £4/10/-. A note on this list indicated that John also had a further book debt of £4.[286]

As part of the process of dealing with this insolvency petition, Fielding Browne had to establish whether John was insolvent, who his creditors were and the amounts that were owed to the creditors. When this process was completed, the Commissioner was charged with distributing to the creditors any assets in the insolvent estate. In this process, John was legally required to divulge all his estate and assets. If he did not do this, then Fielding Browne had the power to send him to gaol. Further, under the Insolvency Act of the Tasmanian parliament, the Commissioner had the power to send him to gaol if he believed that debts to creditors had been contracted without a reasonable expectation of them being paid. In going through this process, the creditors were entitled to attend and/or be represented at meetings with the Commissioner. The creditors and their representatives were entitled to ask questions concerning any matter related to the insolvency application and to make submissions to the Commissioner concerning what should be done in relation to the application.

Commissioner Fielding Browne's first meeting to deal with the John Copley insolvency application occurred on Wednesday, 6 February. It did not get off to a good start, with Fielding Browne opening the meeting by stating that the preliminary arrangements for a meeting of creditors, such as advertising, serving of notices, etc. had not been complied with, and consequently the meeting could not take place.[287]

This was not a good situation for John because, as the petitioner for insolvency, it was his responsibility to organize and pay for advertising the meeting and providing written notice to the creditors of the meeting. Mr Tonkin, the representative for one of the creditors, was given permission by the Commissioner to question John in relation to his failure to make these necessary arrangements. In reply to Mr Tonkin's questions, John stated that he had asked Mr Armitage, a legal clerk, what he would charge to make the necessary arrangements. John told the court that Armitage informed him 'he could do them for £2'. He went on to explain: 'I had not £2 but gave him 30 shillings to do all the writing that was necessary. I saw him again and gave him seven shillings to pay for the advertising. There have not been any notices served, nor has there been any advertisement.'[288]

After John had answered Mr Tonkin's questions, Commissioner Browne took up the matters raised in the John's answers. He condemned 'in the strongest terms' the actions of Mr Armitage 'in obtaining money from persons in the condition of insolvency and not carrying out the agreement'. He went on to say that 'he hoped the exposure of the case would act as a warning to others not to trust their affairs in the hands of individuals of so unprincipled a character.'[289] The meeting was then adjourned to a later date.

This statement by the Commissioner was a positive one for John and a good start to the process of dealing with the insolvency application. Fielding Browne could have attacked him for not carrying out his obligations in relation to the meeting but his evidence had been accepted and Mr Armitage had received a rebuke from the bench. Nevertheless, at the end of the day this was only a procedural matter and there were some very substantial financial and business matters that still had to be dealt with before the court.

Following the preliminary hearing, Commissioner Browne declared John Copley insolvent.[290] A fortnight later, John applied to be discharged from insolvency.[291] If such an order was granted he would be legally free of the debts incurred prior to being declared insolvent and he and Catherine would be able to get on with their lives.

The Insolvency Court set down 5 March to deal with John's application. The meeting in the court on that day had been properly advertised and all the creditors were duly notified. A number of the creditors were legally represented in the court. A Hobart Town lawyer, Mr Lees, examined John in detail concerning business transactions he had undertaken.[292]

Lees asked detailed questions concerning John's relationship with George Rex. He asked John whether the money provided by Rex was merely a loan to establish the coach building business or whether Rex was actually his partner in the business. After John's insolvency application, it appears there may have been gossip in Hobart Town to the effect that George Rex would not have just lent £190 to John Copley, a man who only nine years earlier had been convicted of burglary and received a transportation sentence for life. The story appears to be that Rex was secretly John's business partner and that Rex had seen the writing on the wall in October 1855 and taken most of his equity out of the business. Such gossip would have attracted the attention of the creditors because, if Rex was John's business partner then he may have been liable for some or all of the money now owed to the creditors. John denied that Rex was his business partner. He told the court that Rex had lent him £90 eighteen months earlier to establish the business and that he had agreed to pay it all back to him by October 1855. He then went on to provide the court with a full explanation of his business dealings with George Rex.[293]

John almost certainly found the suggestion that George Rex was his secret business partner ironic, because Rex appears to have been the creditor who triggered the collapse of his business. By demanding his money back rather than taking the five chaise carts as agreed, Rex created financial difficulties for John and this in turn triggered the bank to demand he pay out his mortgage and a number of business creditors to press their claims and commence legal action.

Mr Lees went on to examine John's financial position when he incurred a debt of nearly £10 to John Austin, the ship chandler at New Wharf. These questions were clearly aimed at scrutinizing whether or not he contracted this debt without a reasonable expectation of paying it. In order to avoid gaol, John had to satisfy Fielding Browne in his answers to these questions. Lees based his line of questioning on John's admitted total debt of over £180 and he queried how John could have reasonably believed he was in a position to pay Austin the debts he continued to incur. John's answer was to provide the court with an insight into his business, where the price paid by purchasers for one of his chaise carts was a considerable amount more than the debt owed to Austin.[294] John was making the point to the court that, based on the financial turnover in his business and the price he received for chaise carts, it was reasonable for him to have believed he would be able to repay John Austin.

In his questioning, Mr Lees appears to have paid particular attention to the situation with John's finances at various times throughout the previous year. John's evidence to the court was that the actions of George Rex and the bank, together with the decline in the Tasmanian economy, had created his financial problems and that when all his debts were incurred there was a reasonable prospect that he would be able to repay them.

The other creditors and their legal representatives appear to have left the detailed questioning to Mr Lees. Lees had been trying to shake John to see if he could elicit more information than was contained in the Copley insolvency application. If George Rex was a secret partner or if John had money or assets that he had not declared, then perhaps vigorous questioning and the threat of gaol could cause him to reveal such information to the court. John provided no such information and he held his line that all creditors and assets had been declared and that when the debts had been incurred he had reasonable cause to believe he was able to repay them.

At the conclusion of the questioning, Mr Lees submitted that John should be required to provide the court with a detailed account of his financial transactions, both receipts and payments, over the twelve month period prior to his insolvency application.[295] Although the accounts of these court proceedings do not say so explicitly, it appears Lees was suggesting that John had a serious criminal record that involved convictions for theft and that the court needed to closely scrutinize what had actually happened to the money in his coach making business.

Commissioner Fielding Browne appears to have said very little during the proceedings on 5 March. With the sum of money involved and the insolvency petitioner's criminal record, it appears that he had no option but to make the orders requested by Mr Lees. The Commissioner concluded the proceedings by stating that he would order the petitioner to file 'a general account of his transactions during the last twelve months within fourteen days' and the meeting was adjourned to 26 March.[296] John still had a lot more work to do if he were to be discharged from insolvency.

John and Catherine's worries about the results of their insolvency proceedings would have deepened on 14 March, when a newspaper reported on proceedings that took place two days earlier in the Insolvency Court before Commissioner Fielding Browne. Although not able to read this report themselves, acquaintances and those who like to impart bad news no doubt regaled them with its contents. This report concerned the insolvency application of one Henry John Beamont. A number of Beamont's creditors had opposed the granting of an order discharging him from insolvency on the grounds that the insolvent had 'contracted debts without reasonable expectation of paying them'.[297] The Commissioner found that this submission was proven and stated that he knew of 'No part of the world where debtors were shown more moderation', but he had a duty to the 'mercantile & trading community' and therefore he sentenced Beamont to be imprisoned for three months.[298] The newspaper report stated that following this sentence, 'The Insolvent was taken into custody by the constable in attendance and conveyed to gaol.'[299]

Catherine and John were facing the possibility of their world collapsing around them. It is reasonable to assume that Catherine was very fearful. What would her future be if John were sent to gaol? She had no money or assets. She already had two young children and at this time she was more than four months pregnant with another. Unless she was supported by her brothers or friends, her young boys could end up in the New Town orphanage. If John were sent to gaol, she could find herself giving birth to her next child in a worse situation than in 1852, when she faced the prospect of having to give birth in the Cascades Factory. It would have been an extremely difficult time for the whole family.

The Henry Beamont court decision would have made it clear to John that it was vitally important every effort be made to be fully prepared for the Insolvency Court proceedings. He determined that when the matter went back to court he would have legal representation and he also obtained assistance in preparing the detailed accounts required under the orders made by Commissioner Browne.

In mid-March 1856, while John and Catherine were facing the trauma of the Insolvency Court, many people in Tasmania were greatly concerned about the general economic situation in the colony. On 19 March, the *Hobart Mercury* in its main article described the colony of Tasmania as 'living on droppings of richer neighbours'. The article went on to say that 'Our shop keepers now tell us that their trade is worse than it was before the diggings'. This poor economic situation was clearly reflected in the listings for the Insolvency Court on 26 March—John's was one of twelve cases to be dealt with by Fielding Browne on that day.[300]

Prior to his Insolvency Court meeting, John lodged with Commissioner Browne a detailed statement of his receipts and payments over the past twelve months and swore that 'to the best of my knowledge and belief their content are true'. These accounts showed his receipts for the twelve month period as amounting to £1395/1/1 and his payments for the same period as £1392/9/6.[301] They demonstrated that John had run a business with a reasonably strong cash flow and in fact the financial performance of the business had only marginally deteriorated over the twelve month period prior to his insolvency. The large amount of cash that had gone through John's business and his personal financial dealings supported his all-important argument that when he contracted the creditors' debts there had been a reasonable expectation that he would be able to repay them.

When John arrived in the courtroom for the insolvency meeting he received an unwelcome surprise. During the earlier proceedings, Mr Lees had represented John Austin's interests, but now Lees' place had been taken by Mr Brewer, another Hobart Town lawyer.[302] The last time John had seen Brewer in a courtroom was in April 1847 when he had represented James Fraser in the Supreme Court case involving the theft of property from the house of Christopher Harwood. Since both John and James Fraser were found guilty on that occasion, one suspects John would have found it a bad omen to see Brewer representing the creditor who was most determined to scrutinize his activities and if possible see him severely punished.

The proceedings commenced with John's legal representative Mr Washington McMinn applying for an order discharging the insolvent. McMinn argued that John had filed a full list of his accounts as required by Commissioner Fielding Browne's order. He submitted that the accounts showed nothing improper in John's business and other financial dealings. Mr Brewer made no detailed submission but merely asked that the Copley case be placed at the bottom of the list of cases set down for consideration that day so Mr Lees would be able to attend the court and deal with the matter. The Commissioner then asked McMinn whether he would agree to 'allow the case to stand over' to later in the day. McMinn indicated he did not support the request because standing the matter over would be hard on his client. However, he respectfully stated that he would leave the question of adjournment 'in the hands of the Court'.[303] Given McMinn's opposition to a delay and the fact that no substantial evidence was put to the court that precluded the granting of a discharge order, Fielding Browne went ahead and granted John's application to be discharged from insolvency.

When he returned to the court later in the day, Mr Lees appears to have been far from satisfied with Commissioner Browne's decision. He told the Commissioner that 'it was still his intention to oppose the issuing of the discharge and that he would communicate with the official assignee on the subject'.[304] Browne took little notice of Lees' comments and before the end of the day he issued an order that concluded 'I do hereby make this order for the discharge of the John Copley in writing'.[305]

John had gone through the insolvency process and had avoided a return to gaol. While this was a good result, it was far from the end of the problems he faced. However, Catherine could now concentrate on the forthcoming birth of her fourth child.

# 15  Opportunities and Risks

Following his discharge from insolvency, John was again able to earn a living in Hobart Town. Prior to being declared insolvent he had done his best to look after the financial interests of the tradesmen who had worked for him, and this no doubt assisted him to pick up small jobs around the city. He had also done his best to look after William Milner, who now owned the house he had built on Sandy Bay Road, and Milner continued to rent the property to John.[306] However, there were quite a few shopkeepers and businesspeople who were not happy that John had been discharged from insolvency and these people would have had no desire whatsoever to do anything to assist or support him.

On 22 April 1856 Catherine's older brother Denis was granted a conditional pardon.[307] He was the last of the three McMahon siblings convicted in 1849 to achieve conditional pardon status. Upon receiving his pardon, he decided to make another significant change in his status and marry a woman identified as Susan MacMahon. Denis was in the same position as John had been before his marriage to Catherine. Prior to their transportation sentences, both John and Denis had been married and, like John, Denis was a father. Denis's move to marry Susan was made at the first available opportunity open to him under the legal arrangements that applied at the time. He barely satisfied the legal criteria of a seven year separation from his previous marriage partner, because when he remarried it was only seven years and two months since he had been separated from his wife Julia following his arrest.

Denis's marriage to Susan was conducted on 28 May in the St George's Church of England at Battery Point.[308] This church was not too far away from the house John and Catherine rented on Sandy Bay Road. At the time of this marriage, there were apparently no hard feelings between Denis and John concerning the £27 John had owed to the McMahon brothers when he was declared insolvent, because John was the male witness to this marriage and he signed the marriage register.[309] Catherine, more than six months pregnant with her fourth child, no doubt also attended the wedding. She would not only have been celebrating her brother's marriage, but the day before this ceremony she had completed the full sentence of seven years and three months she received at the 1849 Clare Spring Assizes and her status was now 'free by servitude'.

In July, John finally achieved the same status in the convict system as his brothers-in-law when he was granted a conditional pardon. Notification of this to both John and the public was given with the following notice in the 15 July 1856 edition of the *Hobart Town Gazette*:

CONVICT DEPARTMENT
Comptroller-General's Office, 14th July 1856
It is hereby notified to the under-mentioned individuals, that His Excellency the Governor has been pleased to grant them Conditional Pardons, available every where save in the United Kingdom and the Island of Tasmania:-
1258 John Copley, per *Lady Raffles*.
942 Robert Rowden, per *Norfolk*.
W. NAIRN, Acting Comptroller-General

Under Tasmanian law, John was now able to leave the colony and travel anywhere with the exception of the United Kingdom. While John had been in the convict system for more than fifteen years, he had in fact achieved conditional pardon status far quicker than he could have hoped for when he was convicted of burglary in April 1847 and sentenced to be transported for the term of his natural life. The two year reduction in the time he was to serve due to his meritorious conduct on Norfolk Island had been a factor in this, but equally significant was the desire of the authorities in Tasmania to consign the convict era and the convicts themselves into the past. The best way to do this was to get them out of the system and hopefully get them to move out of the colony.

\*\*\*

It is unlikely that John had any serious thoughts of leaving Tasmania at this time. Instead, the family would have been waiting for Catherine to deliver her fourth child. This child, a son, was born on 15 August 1856 and given the name William. Catherine registered the birth of this new baby, gave her place of residence as Sandy Bay, and identified John Copley, the father, as working as a blacksmith.[310] A little over three weeks later, baby William was baptized at St Joseph's Catholic church and his male baptisimal sponsor was his uncle, William McMahon, after whom he had been named.[311]

Following William's birth, Catherine and John had to make a crucial decision about where their future lay. They now had the legal right under Tasmanian law to leave the colony and the logical place for them to move to was Victoria, which continued to have a booming economy fuelled by the gold rushes and goldmining industry. Alternatively, they could stay in Tasmania and John could try to build a future for himself and his family as a blacksmith. However, there had been no improvement in the Tasmanian economy and, after the insolvency and his creditors' loss of over £180, John would have faced significant difficulty in raising the credit to start and operate a new business in Hobart Town or anywhere else in the colony.

On the surface the idea of John, Catherine and their family moving to Victoria must have been very attractive, but there was one very significant problem. This problem was a law passed in 1852 by the Victorian parliament and given assent by the Governor that banned convicts from Tasmania with conditional pardon status from entering and residing in Victoria. Under this law, 'two justices of the peace were empowered to send' a male 'offender back to his place of departure, or to impose three years hard labour in irons on public works'. The punishments applicable under this law even extended to 'The master of a ship who bought to Victoria an offender' and a ship's master who committed this offence 'was liable to a fine of £100 or six months imprisonment, or both.'[312] This law was prompted by the widespread public perception in Victoria that the significant increase in crime that occurred with the gold rushes was caused by ex-convicts and conditional pardon men from Van Diemen's Land. In Victoria, these men were known as 'Vandemonians'.

The Vandemonian law was not just a politically attractive piece of legislation that was designed to look good to the general public. The provisions that applied in relation to its implementation were draconian in their terms and were contrary to the normal principles of natural justice. This law provided that a person, male or female, suspected of being a conditionally pardoned convict from Van Diemen's Land could be arrested without warrant. Then the arrested person had to prove that they were not a conditionally pardoned convict, otherwise a Justice of the Peace could order them to be held in custody. In effect, this law meant a suspected person had to prove they were innocent rather than the Crown having to prove that they were guilty. It also contained a strong incentive for people in the community to inform on individuals suspected of being conditionally pardoned convicts from Van Diemen's Land. A person convicted of this offence forfeited their property. Half of such forfeited property went to the colony of Victoria and the other half went to any informer.[313]

The potency of the Vandemonian law is seen in the fact that by January 1855, less than two and a half years after it was first introduced, 140 persons had been convicted under its provisions. Of this number, twenty-eight men and one woman were serving sentences in Victoria and eighty-three men and nine women had been returned to Van Diemen's Land.[314]

This law meant it would be both illegal and very difficult for John to get a ship to take him to Victoria. Further, if caught by the Victorian authorities, he was liable to serve a sentence of hard labour, forfeit all his property and be sent back to Tasmania. Such a conviction and sentence would clearly be disastrous for John, Catherine and their young family.

The rigorous approach taken by the authorities in policing the

Vandemonian law had been demonstrated to the Copleys in April 1855 when their friend John Goss was arrested by the police at Williamstown, near Melbourne, soon after he arrived in Victoria 'just fresh from Tasmania'. Goss was suspected by the Victorian police of being a runaway convict in breach of the Influx of Convicts Prevention Act and was held in custody for a number of days while his convict status was investigated.[315] However, by 1855 Goss had fully served the fifteen year transportation sentence he had received at the York Assizes in 1839 and after the police completed their investigation he would have been released. Goss's arrest had been written up in the *Hobart Courier* and the Copleys would have been aware of how their friend had been treated, even though he was not in breach of the Vandemonian law.

One final and not inconsequential matter was that if John had to serve a sentence of hard labour in Victoria it would be under the authority of John Price, the former Commandant of Norfolk Island. Since January 1854 Price had held the position of Inspector General of Penal Establishments in the colony of Victoria,[316] and in this position he was in charge of all prisoners serving sentences in Victoria and the facilities that held these prisoners. These facilities included the then newly established Pentridge Stockade just north of Melbourne and five prison hulks moored in Port Phillip Bay.

Catherine would have had a number of factors to consider before deciding whether she should press her husband into taking the option of moving to Victoria. In Tasmania, she appears to have enjoyed regular contact with her brothers Denis and William and this would be lost if she moved to Victoria. She no doubt also feared the consequences of John being caught under the Vandemonian law and she would have been well aware of the arbitrary and severe punishments that John Price had inflicted on her husband on Norfolk Island. Nevertheless, she also would have heard of many former convicts migrating to Victoria to follow the gold rushes in western Victoria. Above all she would have been conscious of the need to make a secure future for her three young boys—new-born William, two-year-old James and four-year-old John. Given the poor state of the Tasmanian economy, she may well have concluded that she could not see a future for her family in Tasmania.

As a young woman Catherine had shown a willingness to take risks to benefit her family. During the Irish potato famine she had participated in the theft and slaughter of Darby Rogers' sheep because it was necessary for the survival of family and friends. She did not just sit and starve, passively awaiting death. Now she and John could opt for no risk and stay in Tasmania or take a risk with the Vandemonian law and have a good prospect of achieving prosperity and security for themselves and their children.

\*\*\*

At the beginning of 1857, Catherine and John started to give serious consideration to making the move to Victoria. By March they would have heard about the latest report in the *Hobart Town Courier* concerning the gold diggings there. Under the headline 'OLD TIMES AGAIN ON BALLAARAT' the paper quoted an extract from the *Ballaarat Star* that it described as a 'cheering summary of the principal mining events of the bygone week'. This report stated that the aggregate weight of gold extracted from just seven claims on the Ballarat field over the previous week 'amounts to 10,080 ounces, or nearly half a ton weight; and the value estimated at seventy-nine shillings per ounce, reaches the imposing sum of nearly £40,000 sterling'.[317] This was just one more report that would have made it clear to Catherine and John that many normal working people from England and Ireland were making a fortune on the goldfields.

On 16 March, Catherine visited the Hobart Town post office and picked up her Free Certificate.[318] This certificate confirmed that she had fully completed her convict transportation sentence. It is likely that she applied for it at this time because she felt that they were close to finalizing their plans for the future. While possessing this certificate did nothing to address John's problem with the Vandemonian law, at least it made sure that she should encounter no such problems if they made the move to Victoria.

We can only speculate about what effect an event that occurred on 26 March at Williamstown near Melbourne had on John and Catherine's decision to risk the move to Victoria. On this day, a group of convicts from the prison hulk *Success* attacked and murdered John Price. The reports that first reached Hobart Town stated that the murder was 'deliberately concocted' by a group of thirty-five to forty convicts.[319] John would not have needed to hear the details to know that Price had finally paid for his authoritarian, arbitrary and unjust treatment of convicts. Whatever the outcome of a move to Victoria, John Price could now have no further impact on John's life. It was around this time that John and Catherine made the necessary arrangements to leave Tasmania.

We have found no written record of the voyage of the Copley family from Tasmania to Victoria and we would not have expected to. John and Catherine would have made certain that there was no record of their voyage. They may have secretly boarded a ship in Hobart Town and just disappeared one day. Alternatively, and perhaps more likely, they left Hobart Town and headed for the north of the island. This would have enabled them to say farewell to Catherine's brothers Denis and William, who were now living near Deloraine. If such a farewell did take place it was no doubt an emotional occasion for Catherine; after all, it was most likely to be her final contact with her Irish family. From Deloraine it was only a short coach trip north to Launceston, where John was not known. At Launceston, it would not have been difficult for them to take a passage to Victoria under assumed names on a steamer such as the *Royal Shepherd* or the *Black Swan*. A steerage passage for one adult on the *Royal Shepherd* cost £1/5/- with no provisions provided.[320] Catherine and John would not have been in a position to haggle about the cost of the passage across Bass Strait.

# 16   Seeking Gold

We do not know where the boat that carried Catherine and John and their three young boys berthed in Victoria. Infrequent crossings from Launceston to Port Fairy or Portland Bay were made at this time and, indeed, in early March 1857 it was advertised in the *Launceston Examiner* that berths were available on the *Adolphus Yates*, sailing from Launceston to Portland Bay.[321] The Copley family could have entered Victoria through one of these ports.

However, it is most likely that they entered Victoria via the Port of Geelong. There were frequent sailings between Launceston and Geelong and this route would have seemed a safer option for a conditional pardon convict than entering via Melbourne. It would have been reasonable for John and Catherine to assume that the Vandemonian law was more actively policed in Melbourne than in the far smaller port of Geelong, especially after the sensation caused by the killing of John Price. The family would have hoped to be out of the populated area of Geelong in no time, to become just one more group on the road heading west.

Like thousands of others, their destination was the goldfields, and in 1857 the major discoveries of alluvial gold were occurring in the west of the colony. This is another reason why Geelong would have been their preferred port of entry—it was closer than Melbourne to these goldfields.

A major rush occurred to Ararat in April, when Chinese miners discovered a major gold-bearing reef that was named the Canton Lead.

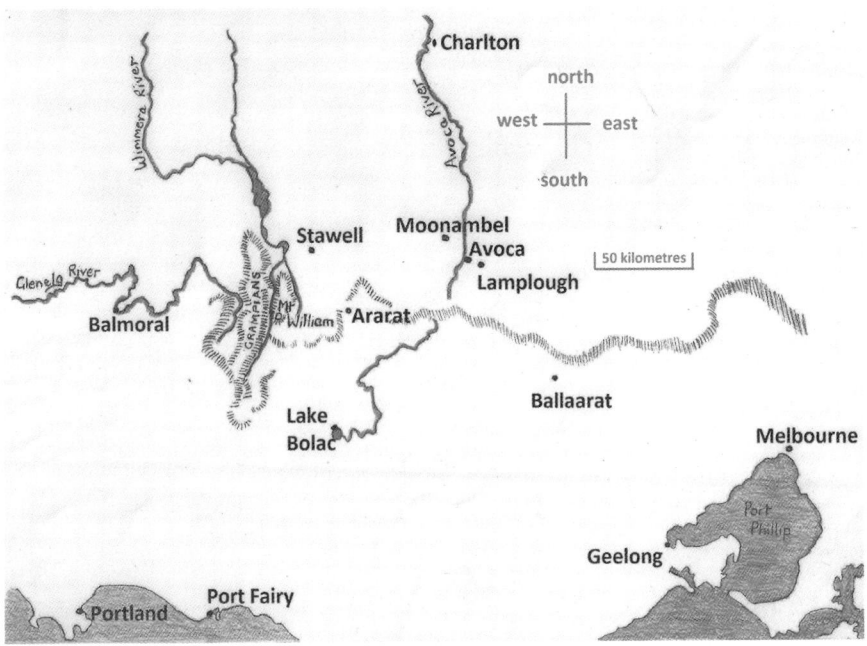

17. Map of western Victoria with significant locations identified. (Based on [Hughes, William 1817–1876, Victoria (cartographic material) 1865–1875, MAP NK 2456/140] contained in the National Library of Australia Maps Collection)

Within a couple of months, upwards of 30,000 miners and their families were living on the Ararat field. In June, soon after the Ararat field was established, a rush occurred to Pleasant Creek, subsequently renamed Stawell and located thirty kilometres to the north-west of Ararat. This rush to Pleasant Creek involved substantial gold finds in old river beds that had been buried long ago by volcanic lava. In September, the newly arrived Mining Warden, Vincent Murray, declared that he believed the Pleasant Creek field was of 'a permanent character'. He estimated the population on the field as 7050 males, 500 females, 400 children and 50 Chinese. Gold seekers continued to arrive and by the end of 1857, it was estimated that there were 30,000 people on the Pleasant Creek field.[322]

The Ararat and Pleasant Creek gold rushes in 1857 were the sort of rushes that would have attracted Catherine and John. They offered the opportunity to extract considerable wealth with a minimum of capital in a short period of time. Initially, much of the gold on these fields was surface gold, easily accessible to individuals and small groups of miners. It was easy for them to stake their claims and start to seek their fortunes. It was not unusual at this time for individual alluvial miners on the Pleasant Creek field to extract £1000 to £1500 of gold from their claim. Additionally, in 1857 the Ararat and Pleasant Creek fields were at the very edges of colonial settlement. There was not a strong police or law and order presence on these fields, and with a large number of people congregated there, a conditional pardon convict like John faced only a minimal risk of being detected as an illegal and taken into custody. Also, these new goldfields would have been a great place for a person with John's blacksmithing skills. A considerable amount of equipment on such alluvial fields needed the skills of a blacksmith to be properly maintained and he could have made good money.

In 1857 there was no rail connection that went anywhere near Ararat and Pleasant Creek and the Copleys and the other gold seekers had to travel on foot, by dray or buy seats on a coach to get to the new goldfields. From Geelong, they would have travelled a hundred kilometres to the major gold centre of Ballarat, where less than three years earlier the miners had rebelled against the government at the Eureka stockade. They would then travel on for another hundred or so kilometres to get to the Ararat and Pleasant Creek fields. This arduous journey would have convinced John that his coach building skills would also be in great demand on these goldfields. It was obvious that the carriages and drays that had to travel for so many kilometres over rough ground would need regular repair and maintenance work.

In the years immediately after their arrival in Victoria, Catherine and John and their three boys appear to have followed the gold rushes around western Victoria. The hardships that they had experienced in the Van Diemen's Land convict system would have toughened them up for life on the goldfields. While life was rough and there were minimal comforts in goldfield settlements, it would have been relatively easy to take compared to the Norfolk Island penal settlement or a harsh winter of hard labour at the Cascades Factory.

On the goldfields in 1859, John could not have avoided discussion and debate surrounding the election that year for the Victorian parliament. This was a very different election. It involved the implementation of a substantial part of the Chartist agenda that had prompted the failed Chartist rebellion in South Yorkshire two days before his arrest in 1840. In this 1859 election, for the first time, all adult males were eligible to vote for the lower house of parliament where the government was formed. Unlike in Tasmania, there was no property, wealth or income restriction that applied to the entitlement to vote or to the right to stand as a candidate. Additionally, in a world first, this election was carried out with the male electors voting by a secret ballot. While this was not the full agenda of the Chartists, it was a substantial part of it and it effectively meant that working men had the power to determine the government of the colony, free of intimidation or standover tactics.

In late 1859, Catherine and John participated in the gold rush to the town of Lamplough that was located sixty kilometres to the east of Ararat and five kilometres south of Avoca. This gold rush was typical of many rushes in western Victoria in the second half of the 1850s and the early 1860s. On 26 November two Welsh brothers, John and James Owen, claimed that they had struck payable gold and within a month of the initial discovery 10,000 or more people had arrived at the field seeking to make their fortune.[323] At Lamplough, most of the arrivals were diggers seeking to strike it rich. Others were seeking to make their fortune by providing support to the diggers in their pursuits on the field. Still others were providing the means for the diggers to spend the money they earned from the gold they extracted.

Once again, John's skills would have been in demand. The miners at Lamplough dug shafts to a depth of twenty-five metres,[324] and a considerable amount of equipment was needed to dig to this depth and then carry the gold-bearing ore to the surface. Maintaining and repairing this equipment provided plenty of work for a skilled blacksmith, as did the wide range of horse drawn vehicles the diggers used. The skills that John developed on Norfolk Island and used in his coach building business in Hobart could provide the Copley family with a good living on the Victorian goldfields.

In the early 1890s, John Chandler looked back on his years as a carrier from Melbourne to Lamplough and wrote that his three strongest impressions of the initial period of the Lamplough rush were dust, grog and wickedness. He recalled that the dust was halfway to the axle of his cart and that a glass of sour beer cost him a shilling. He went on to say that Lamplough at that time 'was a very hell for every wickedness and vice'.[325] It was in this environment that Catherine and John were now living and bringing up their young family.

In January and February 1860 mining operations at Lamplough were hampered by the absence of a plentiful supply of water and miners complained that there was not enough water for 'washing up' purposes. They did not simply complain. Instead, they asserted their rights in the newly democratic colony and 1500 of them crowded into a meeting at the Theatre Royal to petition the government to set aside money to improve the water supply for the town and the goldfield. Within six months, the government had responded to this petition by setting aside £1232 to construct a reservoir near the town.[326]

By April 1860 Catherine was more than eight months pregnant. When she arrived at Lamplough she was already four months into her term. She had spent a long, hot summer on a raw, rough, dusty and newly established goldfield, battling a shortage of fresh water and looking after seven-year-old John, five-year-old James and three-year-old William. To add to her problems, the health of young William was seriously deteriorating.

On 17 April, with the support and assistance of a Mrs Hogan, Catherine gave birth to a baby girl who was given the name Hannah.[327] Hannah was the name of John's mother who had died thirty-four years earlier in Thorpe Hesley. While there are no records that confirm it, young Hannah was almost certainly baptized soon after her birth by Father Fennelly, the Catholic priest born in County Tipperary, who at that time visited Lamplough every two or three weeks.[328]

Catherine and John did not rush to register the birth of their baby daughter. This could have been prompted by concerns for Hannah's health or just their own past experience. After all, in 1853 baby Catherine had died soon after birth. Catherine was eventually to have eight children with John and only four of these survived. The births of three of these children were not even registered in the colony records. The isolated locations of these births may partly explain the failure to register, but the main reason would most likely have been that the children died very soon after birth.

One other possible reason for the delay in registering the birth of baby Hannah was that Catherine and John were distracted by the continuing decline in the health of their third son, William. On 22 June, young William was examined by Dr Thomas H. Butler at Homebush, a small goldmining community four kilometres north of Lamplough. Dr Butler's diagnosis stated that the child was suffering from dropsy.[329] This involved the abnormal accumulation of fluid in one or more of the cavities in his body. Unfortunately, dropsy was a symptom of a more serious problem with William's kidneys and at that time Dr Butler would not have been able to recommend any treatment or medication that would stop the decline in his health.

On 6 July 1860, the birth of Hannah Copley was finally registered with a gentleman identified as W.H. Ratcliffe, the Registrar of Births, Deaths and Marriages on the Lamplough goldfield. Catherine, rather than John, took on the job of registering this birth and she marked the register with an X. Catherine gave the bare minimum of detail concerning the baby's father. He was identified as John Copley, a forty-three-year-old blacksmith born in Yorkshire, England. At this time, John Copley was in fact forty-eight years of age. In contrast, Catherine made no effort to hide her background details. She was now a free woman. The registrar recorded Catherine as identifying herself as thirty-year-old Catherine Copley, nee McMahon, who had been born in 'Skereith' in Ireland.[330] It was unusual for people at this time in Victoria to identify on the public record precisely where in England or Ireland they were born. Most people just gave the county of their birth. It was even more unusual for parents with a convict past, such as Catherine, to so clearly identify who they were. The inaccurate spelling of the name of Scarriff is explained by Catherine's lack of literacy skills and 'Skereith' was the spelling the Registrar, probably an Englishman, came up with based on Catherine's Irish pronunciation. Catherine also appears to have been just a little sensitive on the age front, giving her age as thirty years when she was actually thirty-three.

In mid-1860, Lamplough had the rudiments of an established goldfield settlement. There were three bank branches in the town. The Theatre Royal in Commercial Street put on a diverse range of performances with audiences of more than 1000 people. These performances included plays, singing acts and even a troupe of performing dogs and monkeys. This last act by the Klaer brothers was said to show 'the mastery of man over the canine and simian races'. Also a regular Court of Petty Sessions was held in the town. This court dealt with a wide range of cases, with the more serious cases referred to the General Court Sessions held at Carisbrook, thirty-five kilometres to the east. One of the cases dealt with at the Lamplough Petty Sessions was a sheep stealing offence where the person was convicted of the charge and received a sentence of six months gaol with hard labour.[331] This sentence contrasted greatly with Catherine and John's own transportation sentences of seven and ten years for the same offence.

On 6 August 1860, little William lost his battle against the kidney disease that had ravaged his body and he died just nine days short of his fourth birthday. In contrast to the delay in registering Hannah's birth, the formalities associated with William's death were dealt with promptly and were dealt with by his father. John notified W.H. Ratcliffe of this death on the day it happened and the funeral was also held on that day. William was buried in the Avoca cemetery, four kilometres from Lamplough, and despite being baptized a Catholic he was buried in the Church of England section of the cemetery. The death certificate states that at the time of his death, William had been in the colony for three years.[332]

\*\*\*

We do not know how long Catherine, John and their three remaining children stayed in Lamplough after the death of William. What we do know is that Lamplough was virtually abandoned by its population in December 1860, nearly as quickly as it had been established in November 1859. The reason of course was seemingly significant gold finds occurring elsewhere in western Victoria.[333] The miners and their families were continuing to chase that big gold strike.

Nor do we know where the Copley family went after they left Lamplough. Most of the thousands of people who left the town in December 1860 went to the new rush thirty kilometres away at Mountain Creek (subsequently renamed Moonambel). Not only did the people move to Mountain Creek but many of the buildings also made this move, including the Catholic chapel which doubled as a school and the Wesleyan chapel built of galvanized iron. This rush was even bigger than the late 1859 rush to Lamplough, with a population of 35,000 reported on the new field in December 1860.[334]

Alternatively, the Copleys could have left Lamplough before the start of the Mountain Creek rush and instead followed the October 1860 rush to the Londonderry diggings. These diggings were located in the Jallukar valley, fifteen kilometres west of Ararat. On 26 October 1860, it was reported that there were 5000 miners on this field and the usual support infrastructure for the miners including butchers, bakers and smithies was quickly established. Indeed the same report tells us that two dairy herds were heading to the Londonderry fields to ensure the diggers and their families had a readily available supply of milk.[335]

Between 1861 and 1867 the only mention we could find on the public record of Catherine, John and their family occurred in October 1865, when the following notice appeared in the Melbourne *Argus* in the section headed: 'Missing Friends, Messages': 'John Copley, blacksmith, left Hobart Town 1857—address Denis McMahon, Duke of Kent Hotel, Latrobe Street, Melbourne'.[336] At around this time Denis had moved from Tasmania to live in Melbourne.[337] He apparently knew nothing of Catherine and John's whereabouts in Victoria and was keen to make contact with them.

The continuing implementation of the Vandemonian laws explains why John was hard to locate in Victoria during this time. In the period from 1861 to 1866, the Victorian courts and the government continued to order the deportation back to Tasmania of convicts who had left the island colony with a conditional pardon. In 1864, James Shirley, a fifty-nine-year-old conditionally pardoned convict from Van Diemen's Land was deported back to Tasmania.[338] The city court in Melbourne made this order despite the fact that Shirley had been transported from England under a life sentence in 1828, had received his conditional pardon in 1840, and in the following twenty-four years had not been convicted of any offence in Tasmania.[339] In this same twenty-four-year period, John had received two transportation sentences and a far stronger case could have been presented to a Victorian court justifying his deportation.

Wherever they were living from 1861 to 1866, John and Catherine would have had to adapt to changes in the goldmining industry and to the Victorian economy. As the 1860s progressed, there were fewer gold rushes in western Victoria. Most of the major alluvial goldfields had been found and the relatively easy, near the surface gold had been extracted. Goldmining was now starting to become a business where substantial sums of capital were needed. Mine shafts had to be dug hundreds of feet below the surface and ore had to be carried to the surface and then put through various combinations of crushing and chemical processes in order to extract the gold. To participate in this new form of goldmining, you either had to have significant capital to invest in the new goldmining corporate entities or you worked for wages as a miner for these corporations.

During these years there are a number of directions that the Copley family could have taken, but there is nothing to suggest that they moved out of the western Victoria goldfields area. They could have followed the small isolated gold rushes but by this time, unless they were very lucky, these were not producing significant returns. It is unlikely that they moved into either Stawell or Ararat because the Copley name does not appear in the local government rate records as residing in either of those towns. Also the family would have known that there was a greater risk of John's status as a conditionally pardoned convict being discovered in larger established towns. The only readily apparent alternative to these options is that during some or all of this time, the Copley family lived on one or more of the large squatting runs in the Stawell and Ararat areas. A western Victorian squatting run would have been just the place for John to continue to keep a low profile. His blacksmithing skills were in demand on large squatting runs, and when combined with Catherine's experience of agricultural work in Ireland they would have been judged to be valuable additions to any squatter's workforce. The subsequent life experiences of both Catherine and John in the 1870s and 1880s show a strong interest in working the land, and working on a squatting run in the 1860s would have provided a perfect introduction to rural life in western Victoria.

In the mid-1860s, the squatters were starting to feel substantial pressure mounting against their hold over the tens of thousands of acres of land on which they grazed sheep. When the returns from alluvial goldmining began to decline in the late 1850s, political pressure from the diggers started to develop in the popularly elected lower house of parliament for them to have the right to purchase suitable land at moderate prices to set up family farms. This pressure was resisted by the squatter-dominated upper house of parliament that was elected on a restricted wealth based franchise. In August 1860, the first land selection bill was enacted by the parliament, but this only happened after a group of rioters stormed the parliament and apparently intimidated the squatting interests in the upper house. However, this 1860 bill and another land bill passed by the parliament in 1862 had little effect, with the squatters able to drive holes through the bills and use them as vehicles for the purchase freehold of significant tracts of land. A further land bill was passed through the parliament in 1865, but again this bill did not provide the means for a large number of families to take over good quality land from Victorian squatters. However, one aspect of the 1865 Amending Land Act that did open up substantial change in the control and ownership of land was a provision that enabled land within thirty kilometres of goldmining centres to be selected by genuine selectors for farming purposes. This provision opened up substantial land-holdings for selection in the heavily mined areas of Ararat and Stawell.

By 1867, John and his family obviously felt sufficiently secure in the colony to risk living at Quartz Reefs in Stawell. In this year, he appeared on the public record paying rates to the Stawell Council on a dwelling and land.[340]

It may be just a coincidence, but at the time John appeared on the public record in Stawell, the attitude of the Victorian Government and community started to soften in relation to former Tasmanian convicts who contravened the Vandemonian law. In November 1866 Samuel Knowles, a former Van Diemen's Land convict, was arrested at Amherst for contravening the Victorian Influx of Convicts Act. Amherst was eighty-five kilometres east of Stawell. The Amherst community did not applaud this arrest but instead rallied in support of Samuel and his family. They prepared a nearly 3000 signature petition extolling Samuel's virtues and begging that he be given a pardon. The petition stated that Samuel had 'conducted himself in every relation of life in a most upright and creditable manner, so much so that he obtained and still retains the respect and esteem of all classes of our community for his integrity, sobriety, and fair dealing.'[341] Samuel Knowles was eventually granted a pardon[342] and was permitted to live as a free man in Victoria. It appears that at this time John was starting to feel secure as a member of the community living in and around Stawell.

In 1868, the Stawell rate records describe John Copley as working as a miner and in 1869 they tell us that the Copley residence was located on Patrick Street near the Quartz Reefs.[343] In the late 1860s, deep quartz goldmining really took off in the Quartz Reefs. There the mines went down hundreds of feet underground and thousands of pounds of capital were required to extract and process the ore taken from the earth at these depths. Once again, John was ideally suited to pick up work associated with constructing and maintaining the infrastructure and equipment used in these goldmining operations.

Although John had work on the Quartz Reefs that provided a steady income, in late 1869 or early 1870 he decided to turn his back on goldmining work and use the capital he had saved to obtain and develop his own farm. John and Catherine had obviously done their research and understood that the 1865 Land Selection Act offered them a great opportunity, so John went ahead and took out a licence under the Act on eighty acres of land at Frying Pan Plains.[344] Frying Pan Plains was located in the Jallukar valley and the selection was fifteen kilometres south of Stawell and twenty kilometres north-west of Ararat. The Jallukar valley sits between the Mount William Range which is part of the Grampian Mountains and the Black Range of hills.

\*\*\*

The first white man to visit the Jallukar valley was Major Thomas Mitchell, a British army officer. In 1836, Major Mitchell undertook an exploratory trek from Sydney to the then small settlement of Portland located on Bass Strait. He then returned to Sydney. This trek covered around 3000 kilometres. Thirty-four years before John and Catherine took up their eighty acre Jallukar selection, Major Mitchell and five of his party passed through the Jallukar valley in their quest to climb Mount William and get the best possible view of the new sheep grazing lands they had discovered.

Before climbing Mount William, they camped overnight five kilometres to the north-west of the land that was to become John and Catherine's selection. On that evening, Major Mitchell wrote in his travel journal the most quoted words from his whole 1836 journey of exploration: 'We had at length discovered a country ready for immediate reception of civilised man and destined perhaps to become eventually a position of great empire'.[345] Major Mitchell also commented in his travel journal that this land had soil of excellent quality and an abundance of water and vegetation.

Although Mitchell and his party were the first Europeans to see the Grampian mountain ranges and the Jallukar valley, the Australian aborigines had lived in this area for at least 22,000 years.[346] The Jallukar valley was part of the land belonging to the Djab Wurrung people.[347] The Djab Wurrung knew the Grampian mountain ranges as Gariwerd, but Mitchell knew nothing of this and in fact his party only ever caught fleeting glimpses of the local inhabitants.

In the years immediately following 1836, squatters retraced the travels of Major Mitchell and claimed large squatting sheep runs in the Wimmera and Western District of what is now the state of Victoria. Because 1836 had been one of the wettest years that European man was to experience in south-west Victoria, the Jallukar area and western Victoria generally were not quite the incredibly fertile and rich paradise that Major Mitchell had reported. Nevertheless, within ten years of 1836, European man had taken over the Jallukar valley, the Aboriginal people had totally lost their lands and 70 percent of the Djab Wurrung people were dead.[348]

***

The eighty acre Jallukar valley selection taken up by John and Catherine was located on the Pentlands Creek that ran off the Black Range and was very near the Londonderry diggings where there had been a gold rush in October 1860. It was also only five kilometres south of Bellellen, where a small gold rush had occurred in 1868. The land they had selected was on the Lexington squatting run, which at this time was owned by William J.T. Clarke,[349] who was one of the largest squatters and land-holders in the Australian colonies. When he died in January 1874, Clarke left an estate valued at £2.5 million, plus he owned approximately 215,000 acres (87,008 hectares) of land that he held under freehold title.[350] This massive freehold title land-holding does not include the squatting run land that he controlled. The loss of eighty acres to John Copley would have made no impact on William J.T. Clarke.

The selection of this piece of land appears to have been well thought out by John and Catherine. Water usually flowed in the Pentlands Creek well into the summer. This would provide the Copleys with the means to grow vegetables and other crops in early summer and to support livestock all year round. There were only a handful of other selectors in the area and therefore they would be able to supply meat and vegetables to the prospectors and goldminers who were still active nearby. The location of this selection also put them in a position to be able to sell their produce at either Stawell or Ararat, the two major population centres in western Victoria. John no doubt counted on picking up some metal trades work from prospectors, miners and other selectors in the area to help supplement the family income.

The terms of the licence on this eighty acres involved John paying £4 in rent every six months for the three year duration of the licence.[351] This meant £24 in rent had to be paid over the licence period. During this period, £80 worth of improvements had to be made to the land. These improvements could be in fencing the land, building a permanent residence and/or constructing a dam. If these requirements were met within the first three years, John would have the option to take out a seven year lease covering this selection. The lease would also need to be paid off at the rate of £4 every six months, and if all these payments were made he would be the owner of these eighty acres. After achieving a lease, the lease and the land would become saleable property and John and Catherine could, if they wished, sell it off in the commercial marketplace.

Both Catherine and John almost certainly saw achieving ownership of this land as evidence of their success in Victoria and it would have compared very favourably to their family circumstances in Ireland and Yorkshire.

With Catherine now more than forty years of age and John in his late fifties, goldmining with its attendant hardships and difficulties would have held very little attraction. At this stage of their lives, holding, controlling and, even better, owning land appeared to offer a far more settled and reliable future for the family.

Among those who selected land in the Jallukar valley at the same time as Catherine and John was a forty-three-year-old Englishman, Thomas May. There is a possibility that Thomas was known to the Copleys before they met as selectors, but whether or not they knew one another in the past, Thomas was to become a significant player in the future of the Copley family.

## PART FOUR
## THOMAS MAY

# 17 Growing up in a Royal Seaside Resort

The precise date of the birth of Thomas May is not known. We do know that he was christened on Sunday, 22 April 1827, at St Nicholas Church in Brighton on the south coast of England.[352] In the early nineteenth century, normal practice was for English parents to wait several months after a baby's birth to christen the child, and therefore it is reasonable to assume that Thomas was born in the first few months of the year.

Thomas Henry May was the first child for his father Thomas, a sailor, and his mother Mary Anne May (nee Martin) who had married in April 1826. Baby Thomas was born in Nottingham Street in Brighton.[353] At this

18. Map of south-east England showing places of significance in the story of Thomas May. (This map taken from: d-map.com/carte.php?lib=south_east_england_map&num_car=16357&lang=en)

time Nottingham Street had the reputation as one of the worst streets in Brighton and was well known as the haunt of tramps and beggars. There were three beer shops in the street and it was common for up to seventeen people to crowd into rooms to sleep in the many lodging houses. This area of Brighton had imperfect and insufficient drainage and numerous cesspools lay around the streets.[354]

While in early 1827 baby Thomas was living in one of the worst of environments in England, only a few hundred metres to the west, King George IV was residing at his Brighton palace, the Royal Pavilion.[355] The king had progressively constructed the Royal Pavilion over the preceding forty years. He wanted the Pavilion, with its grand Oriental Indian exterior design and its opulent interiors, to project an image to the world of prestige, power and the very latest in fashion. Perhaps, the most extreme example of the opulence of the Royal Pavilion is the music room, which is richly decorated in an oriental

19. A small part of King George IV's Royal Pavilion which so strongly influenced life in early nineteenth-century Brighton.

theme and has nine lotus-shaped chandeliers hanging from a domed ceiling that is made up of 23,000 golden gilded cockle shells.[356]

Unfortunately for Brighton, by March of that year George IV spent little time appreciating his golden cockle shells and instead spent most of his time ensconced in his bedroom and private apartments. He was sixty-six years old and his health was in serious decline. Brighton was starting to lose its appeal for the monarch. For four decades, he had brought other members of the royal family to the seaside resort and the royal presence had made Brighton the place to visit. The fashionable flocked to take the sea air. Now, however, the King had lost interest in entertaining the fashionable. He simply wanted to do whatever he could to alleviate the pain associated with his numerous ailments. At the very time of Thomas May's birth, the king had apparently decided that this would be his last visit to the seaside resort.

When Mary and Thomas May first arrived in Brighton, the town was still flourishing. Jobs and economic activity had been created by the need to service the infrastructure that grew up around the royals, their entourage and other fashionable visitors. However, when George IV ceased visiting his Royal Pavilion the town declined and by the end of 1827 there was a surplus of labour in Brighton to meet the requirements of the town. For people like Mary and Thomas, Brighton was a very expensive place to live; in fact, the cost of living was higher than in London.[357] Brighton took great pride in the appearance of the Royal Pavilion and the fashionable beach front, but little regard was shown for the people who lived in the back streets like Nottingham Street and who provided the energy and labour to maintain this appearance.

Tragedy struck the May family in the early 1830s. By this time Mary had given birth to a second son, Richard, and shortly after that her husband Thomas died. The details of his death are not known. In the 1830s, there was no income support or workers' compensation for the widow and children of a dead sailor. With no husband, two very young sons and no income support to compensate for her husband's death, Mary must have been in a desperate economic situation. Later in her life, British census records identified Mary May as working as a charwoman,[358] so most likely in the early 1830s she worked as a cleaner in the hotels and grand houses of Brighton in order to support herself and her two sons. In this environment, with his mother away at work and little money in the family, young Thomas would have been free to roam the rough and seedy back streets of the town.

By June 1839, life had changed again for Mary May and her two sons. Mary now lived as the wife of Henry Phillips, a journeyman plumber, and she went by the name of Mary Phillips.[359] While in the 1830s a journeyman plumber was still a reasonable job, it was not the job it had been some years earlier. During the construction boom in Brighton that had lasted from the late eighteenth century until well into the 1820s, there had been a great demand for all sorts of tradesmen. The sea baths for which Brighton had become famous had been a great source of work for plumbers. However, in the decade following the death of George IV, the town not only lost its fashionable lustre but very little new construction work was undertaken. Henry Phillips would have had plenty of competition for the limited employment opportunities now available to plumbers. Henry Phillips was a widower with seven children when he met Mary and he lived at 52 Egremont Street.[360]

This change of address did not signal any serious improvement in living conditions for Mary and her boys. Two adults and nine children were crowded into the Phillip's lodgings,[361] and Egremont Street itself was then one of the worst possible addresses to reside at in Brighton. This street and the area around it were considered an intolerable nuisance by the local authorities. It was known as the resort of tramps, begging imposters, thieves and prostitutes of the lowest description.[362] Egremont Street did however provide its unfortunate residents with a good view of the fashionable and pleasure-seeking resort town because it runs up a hill that overlooks the coast and the English Channel. From outside the house in which he lived, Thomas May could see the Chain Pier that ran more than 320 metres from the beach front out into the sea. The pier provided a stark contrast to the squalid conditions of Thomas's Brighton. It had been constructed in 1823 at a cost of £30,000 and in the 1830s it was considered by many people to be one of the wonders of the world. It was made up of four suspension bridges in a row, with iron columns secured in the sea bed, and each of the bridge spans had a length of over sixty metres.[363] On June summer days, thousands of people paid twopence per occasion for entrance to the pier, where they promenaded up and down and took in the sea air.[364]

There is no evidence to suggest that prior to June 1839 Thomas had ever gone to school. Roaming freely around the back streets, he would have been exposed to criminal activity and considerable depravity, whereas along the seafront and in the fashionable areas of town he would have seen the luxuries that were available to anyone if only they had money. It was an environment full of temptation for a young boy.

Twelve-year-old Thomas succumbed. On 13 June 1839 he was arrested and charged with stealing a plate from William Hall,[365] who ran a bakery in George Street.[366] Another boy, Jesse Summerford, was also arrested and charged with the same offence.[367] George Street was situated approximately 700 metres down the hill from Egremont Street and only a couple of blocks back from the grand houses and hotels on the beach front road. However, while it was near the fashionable area, George Street housed shops and businesses that serviced the needs of the working people.

Stealing a metal plate from a bakery was one of the classic crimes that boy street thieves committed in early nineteenth-century England. In a bakery, these boys could find large pieces of metal, such as cooking plates, which attracted a good price if sold to a scrap metal dealer. Many such dealers knew not to ask any questions when boys approached them to sell large metal objects. The beauty of this trade for both the boy thieves and the scrap metal dealer was that soon after the sale was made, the object would be placed in a foundry melting pot and often, long before the baker even knew of the theft, the stolen object had become a blob of molten metal and could never be traced.

However, on this occasion Thomas and Jesse did not succeed with their theft and they were caught either in the act of stealing or soon after, in possession of the plate. Thomas was about to have his first experience with the British justice system.

On 1 July 1839, Thomas and Jesse stood in the dock at the Lewes Courthouse. They both faced a charge of simple larceny.[368] Lewes is an old market town located twelve kilometres to the north-east of Brighton and the criminal Quarter Sessions for the Eastern Division of Sussex were held there.

This was the first court appearance for both boys but it is quite likely that around the criminal back streets of Brighton they had picked up some ideas about how they should handle themselves. Both gave their age as eleven years[369] when in fact they were both twelve. It appears they understood that the younger the age they gave, the harder it would be for them to be convicted, and a younger age would probably reduce the seriousness of any punishment meted out. English law at this time held that for a child of between seven and thirteen years of age to be found guilty of larceny, the child had to understand that they were stealing. The onus of proof in relation to this issue rested on the prosecution.[370]

Thomas and Jesse both pleaded not guilty. They had no legal representation in the court. While we do not know the evidence that was presented against them, the jury had to be convinced that the boys had been found with or seen in possession of the bakery plate to have a realistic prospect of sustaining the charge. The boys did not impress the jury and both were found guilty.

The magistrate then moved to determine and announce their punishment. He sentenced them both to one week in prison with hard labour and both were to be privately whipped.[371] Soon after their conviction, the boys were taken off to Lewes prison that was located on the edge of town, less than a mile to the west of the courthouse.

The punishment for Thomas and Jesse could have been worse. Up until 1847, children found guilty of offences were legally liable to the same forms of punishment that applied to convicted adults, such as execution, transportation, imprisonment and fines. The short sentence of imprisonment for one week with hard labour and a private whipping had the benefit of being a lot cheaper than transportation or imprisonment for an extended period of time. The Sussex treasury had already incurred the sum of £2/13/- in expenses in bringing successful criminal prosecutions against the boys.[372]

Thomas and Jesse were already familiar with Lewes prison. After their arrest on 13 June they had been held in custody there awaiting their trial. However, during that time they would not have been subjected to the discipline of a convicted criminal. After their trial, this changed, with the boys' diet reduced to the bare basics of bread and water. The hard labour part of their sentences would have been served with time on the prison treadmill and, at some point during this period of one week, the boys would have received their whipping.

This private whipping of the two boys involved their bare buttocks being whipped with a birch rod. Prior to his whipping, Thomas would have been stretched across a wooden frame known as the whipping horse. Canvas straps were used to tie his body to the horse and to make sure he could not move during the punishment. The prison officer responsible for giving the whipping was known as the punishment corporal and he would have given Thomas a good birching with all the vigour he could muster.[373]

After his release, Thomas returned to the back streets of Brighton, where he once again rubbed shoulders with thieves and prostitutes. His dismal social circumstances remained unchanged. At this time, English law worked on the basis that the time in prison, the treadmill and a good whipping should have had the effect of belting some sense into juvenile offenders. Unfortunately Thomas's punishment did not deter him from future thievery.

# 18    Rabbit Pie

During September 1841, a transformation occurred in Brighton. On 21 September, the opening of the Brighton to London railway took place. At around noon on that day, the first London train entered the newly built railway station.[374] Prior to this, it took five hours to travel by horse-drawn coach from London to Brighton and it cost thirteen shillings for a ticket to sit on the outside of the coach. By rail, this journey only took two hours, and a second class rail ticket sitting under cover cost nine shillings and six pence.[375] The railway opened Brighton up to the masses from Britain's capital and in the next couple of years the town would be transformed. The fourteen-year-old Thomas would have been very much aware of the coming of the railway. On that September day, virtually everyone who lived in Brighton stood in awe at the arrival of the locomotive with a train of carriages. Many people did not understand the great change the railway would bring to their town, but it apparently didn't take young Thomas long to appreciate that some new opportunities to make a few shillings had been created by the mass of middle-class tourists who now arrived on the train.

On the night of 26 October 1841 an event occurred that changed the direction of Thomas May's life. He was once again involved in a property theft. He was arrested next morning along with three other boys on suspicion of stealing three rabbits from John Parsons,[376] a twenty-year-old cooper who lived at 6 Dorset Gardens.[377] The three other boys who were arrested also had the Christian name Thomas; Thomas Head, Thomas Dix and Thomas

Sargent. All four boys told the police that they were thirteen years of age,[378] although Thomas May and Thomas Dix were in fact fourteen.[379] Dorset Gardens was a small street that ran off James Street and it was quite near to the bakery of William Hall, from which Thomas and Jesse Summerford had stolen the iron plate in 1839. Jesse was not involved in this theft. He no longer wandered the back streets of Brighton with Thomas because he was in the Work House, subject to rigid discipline and hard work.[380]

John Parsons, the cooper, lived with his wife Harriet who was also twenty years of age and they had a one-year-old son.[381] Their house in Dorset Gardens faced out on to the only parkland in the area where many of the working people of the town lived. No doubt the Parsons collected grass from this parkland to feed their three rabbits. John Parsons may have kept these rabbits for domestic consumption or he may have planned to make a few shillings by selling them. With the coming of the railway, a good rabbit pie was just the sort of food that the middle-class citizens of London liked to eat during their stay at the seaside resort. This new middle-class market explains why the Brighton police gave the three stolen rabbits the surprisingly high value of nine shillings.[382]

Thomas Sargent, like Thomas May, already had a criminal record. Sargent had three convictions for vagrancy, having been found on each occasion in dwellings for the purpose of committing a felony.[383] He worked as a chimney sweep,[384] and at only 1.37 metres in height he was well suited to climb down chimneys and remove soot. It appears likely that on the three occasions Sargent had been caught inside dwellings for the purpose of committing a felony, he had used his chimney sweeping skills to enter the premises.

Thomas Dix lived in Bread Street, Brighton, just a couple of blocks to the north-west of the Royal Pavilion. He worked as a shoemaker and was fourteen years of age. He did not live with his parents but with his seventeen-year-old sister Anne and two younger brothers.[385]

Thomas Head, like Thomas May, lived in Egremont Street. Thomas was twelve or thirteen years of age. He lived with his father William, who worked as an agricultural labourer, and his mother Ellener and he was the only child in this household.[386]

On 1 December 1841, the four Thomases stood in the dock at the Lewes Courthouse. Since their arrest on 27 October, May, Sargent and Head had been held in custody at Lewes gaol. Dix obviously had some support behind him because, after being charged by the Brighton police, he was given bail.[387] The four juveniles faced charges of larceny and all four pleaded not guilty.[388] The proceedings were conducted before two local magistrates.[389] The Chairman Magistrate was Robert Willis Blencowe, a thirty-nine-year-old barrister,[390] who also acted as a magistrate at Lewes.

John Parsons told the court that at 10 pm on 26 October he fed the three tame rabbits at his home at Dorset Gardens, but they were gone by 6 the next morning.[391]

The most damaging evidence against Thomas May was presented to the court by James Coppard, a forty-seven-year-old baker who lived at Kensington Garden in Brighton.[392] Kensington Garden was just a couple of blocks to the north-west of the Royal Pavilion and was near where Thomas Dix lived in Bread Street. Coppard told the court that on the night of 26 October, May and Dix offered to sell him two of the rabbits that were the property of John Parsons. Coppard went on to confirm to the court that he accepted this offer and purchased the rabbits.[393]

This evidence indicates that after stealing the rabbits from John Parsons on the night of 26 October, May and Dix and perhaps also the other two boys headed across the centre of town to sell the rabbits. It would have seemed a clever strategy to approach Coppard. His bakery was not in the immediate vicinity of John Parsons' home and it was unlikely to be the first place that the police would approach after the theft was reported. Also by selling the rabbits to the baker, the boys would have believed that they would soon be converted to rabbit pie. This would have made it impossible for the police to trace the thieves.

We do not know why this strategy failed or why James Coppard did not

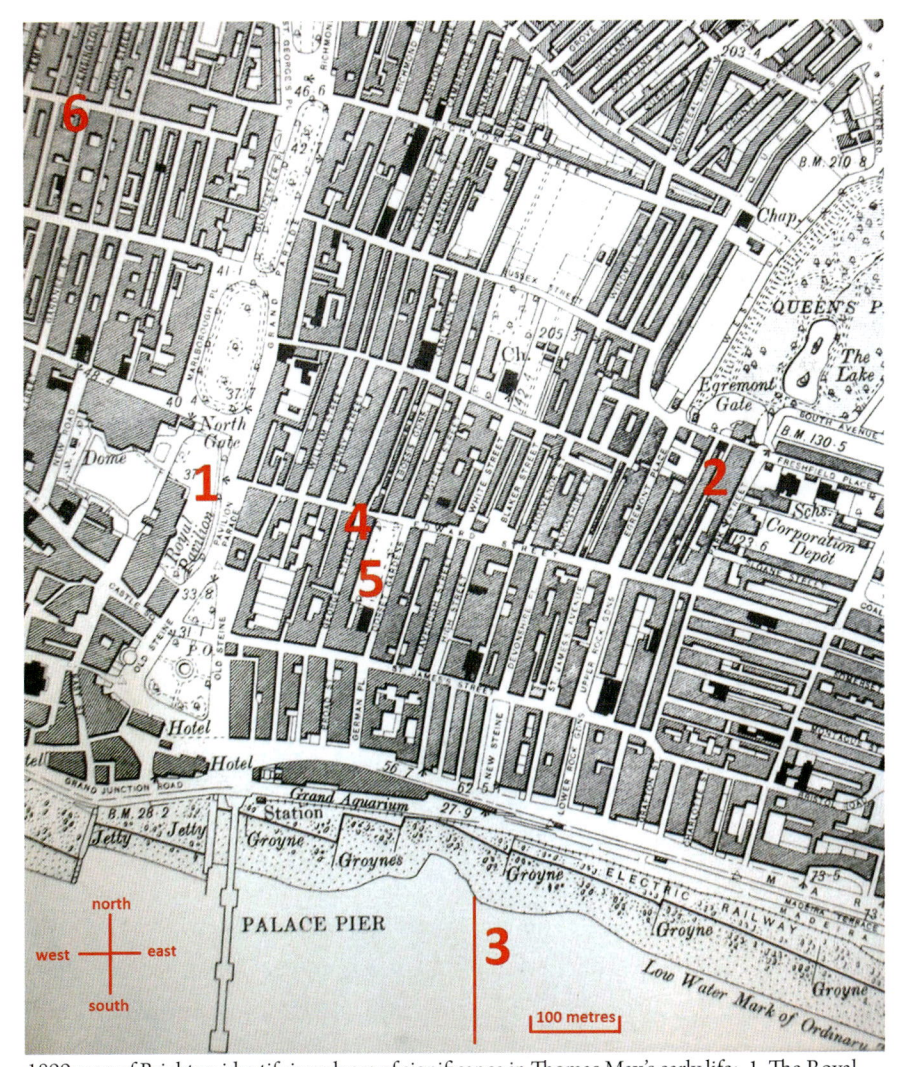

1899 map of Brighton identifying places of significance in Thomas May's early life: 1. The Royal Pavilion; 2. Egremont Street (now Tillstone Street) where Thomas May lived; 3. The location of the Chain Pier which no longer existed in 1899 when this map was published; 4. George Street where William Hall's bakery was located; 5. Dorset Gardens where James Parsons' home was located; and 6. Kensington Garden where James Coppard's bakery was located.

end up before the court on a charge of receiving stolen goods. However, fail it did and Coppard's evidence, along with that of William Halliday, sealed Thomas May's fate.

Forty-year-old William Halliday who lived in Warwick Street provided evidence to the court that was devastating for Thomas May.[394] He told the court that May and Dix had admitted to him that they had stolen two live rabbits and one dead rabbit from John Parsons. Halliday went on to say that May had told him that he sold one rabbit for five shillings but that he only gave sixpence to Thomas Head.[395] It was not only by the theft of the three rabbits that Thomas May displayed his dishonesty. By admitting to only giving 10 percent of the value of the rabbit to Thomas Head, he showed a willingness to cheat and deceive not only the rabbits' owner but one of his own peer group and a partner in crime. This would not have reflected well upon his character.

Additional evidence was presented to the court by George White, an inspector of police in Brighton, John Sanders, a mariner who lived in High Street, and Ambrose Gates who lived in Bread Street.[396]

When all the evidence had been presented, the jury adjourned to consider its verdict. A short time later it returned and announced that both Thomas Head and Thomas Dix were not guilty of the larceny charges but that Thomas May and Thomas Sargent were guilty as charged.[397] The jury effectively decided that May and Sargent were the key players in stealing the rabbits. Perhaps the jury members did not believe that Head and Dix fully understood the concept of theft and hence, given their ages, they were unable to convict them.

Magistrate Blencowe and his colleague on the bench then brought down their decisions on the punishment for May and Sargent. Their decision was that both of the convicted juveniles should be sentenced to transportation for seven years.[398] Blencowe concluded this sentencing by stating: 'These boys are only thirteen years old each; May in 1839 had been convicted of felony, and Sargant had been thrice summarily convicted of a vagrancy, having been found in each instance in a dwelling house for the purpose of committing a felony. Their only chance of being reclaimed is by their being sent to the Parkhurst Reformatory, and I earnestly recommend and hope that they be sent there.'[399]

At this time, a transportation sentence for convicted juveniles meant they would be sent to Van Diemen's Land. The concluding statement by Magistrate Blencowe that he recommended and hoped they be sent to Parkhurst Reformatory meant he wanted them to spend time in the Parkhurst Juvenile Reformatory on the Isle of Wight before they were sent out to Van Diemen's Land. At that time, the reformatory had only been established for three years. It was a prison specifically designed for juvenile male offenders and it was meant to impose discipline on them before they were transported. It also aimed to develop skills in the boys that employers in the colonies would find to be of value. Magistrate Blencowe apparently believed that discipline and training were needed if there was any hope that May and Sargent could be reclaimed from their criminal ways.

# 19   A Boy Convict

Soon after their conviction, Thomas May and Thomas Sargent were sent to the prison hulk *Euryalus* that was moored at Chatham on the Medway River in Kent.[400] Here they were approximately eighty kilometres away from Brighton. At this time, *Euryalus* was used exclusively for juvenile boys.[401]

It is not clear why the two boys were not sent to Parkhurst Reformatory as recommended by Magistrate Blencowe. However, there were always more criminal children sentenced to transportation than available places at the reformatory, and therefore a selection process was applied. The governor of Parkhurst had the right to decide whether or not he would accept hardened offenders who could undermine his regime of discipline.[402] Magistrate Blencowe, with his statement about the problems of 'reclaiming' May and Sargent, may well have unintentionally ensured that the authorities at Parkhurst were not prepared to accept the two Brighton rabbit stealers.

If the Parkhurst Reformatory was considered the best possible prospect of reclaiming May and Sargent, then by 1841 everyone who had an interest in the treatment of juvenile offenders knew that the place with the least prospect of reclaiming them was the *Euryalus*.[403] As a naval ship, the *Euryalus* had an impeccable pedigree in English history. It was constructed and launched in 1803 and it saw service in 1805 at the Battle of Trafalgar. After the famous battle, Admiral Collingwood, who took charge of the British fleet following Lord Nelson's death, used *Euryalus* as his flagship.[404]

However, the glory days for the *Euryalus* were over and it was now simply a repository for England's troublesome youth. In 1835, Thomas Dexter, who as a youth had been a prisoner on hulks, told the Parliamentary Select Committee on Gaols and Houses of Correction that 'It is said that frequently judges sentence a boy out of mercy to the hulks—but if it were a child of mine I would rather see him dead at my feet than see him sent to that place.'[405] In the early 1830s, J.J. Capper, the Inspector of Hulk Establishments, told the Parliamentary Select Committee on the Police that the results from placing juveniles on hulks were not encouraging. He specifically mentioned the conduct after their release of convict boys who had been on hulks: 'I am sorry to have to say it has been very indifferent, for eight out of ten that had been liberated returned to their old careers.'[406] On hearing such reports, the committee recommended that the hulks should be abandoned for juvenile offenders, but in the 1830s and 1840s these recommendations were ignored.

On their arrival at the *Euryalus*, the conviction and punishment of May and Sargent for stealing three rabbits worth nine shillings was starting to look very expensive. The cost of the criminal proceedings in the Lewes Court was £6/15/8. The cost of moving them from Lewes to the *Euryalus* was £4/17/-.[407] This total of more than £11 took no account of the costs that were going to be incurred at the hulk, in transporting the two boys to Van Diemen's Land, or in overseeing them when they arrived in the colony.

On his arrival at the *Euryalus*, Thomas May was given the hulk convict number of 4440.[408] Most of the juvenile prisoners were between eleven and nineteen years of age, although there were about half a dozen older men. The boys on the *Euryalus* did not work outside the ship. In fact, with the exception of visits to the hospital ship, they never left the hulk. The daily regime involved nine and a half hours of work making clothing for convict establishments and one hour of schooling. It also provided one hour of exercise in the open air, which in reality meant walking around on the deck of the ship. Games were not permitted during this one hour exercise period.[409] The silent system where prisoners were not allowed to talk to anyone applied, even during exercise periods. Thomas had his problems on the hulk and for a period he was denied any bread due to 'idleness'.[410]

One fortunate aspect of Thomas's time on the hulk was that it was comparatively short. Some juvenile convicts spent years on the hulks before they were finally transported or the term of their original sentence elapsed. On 29 March 1842, a little more than three months after he first boarded the *Euryalus*, Thomas boarded the transport vessel *Elphinstone* at Sheerness.[411] On leaving the *Euryalus*, Thomas's hulk report described his conduct as 'indifferent'.[412]

On 1 April the *Elphinstone* left Sheerness and commenced the voyage to Van Diemen's Land. During this voyage the ship was known as the *Elphinstone (4)* as it was the fourth convict transport voyage it had made to the Australian colonies. On board there were 230 male convicts and of these, 222 were described as convict boys and eight were adults.[413]

As the journey commenced, William H.B. Jones, the Surgeon Superintendent on *Elphinstone (4)*, issued his 'Rules and Regulations to be observed on board'. The Surgeon Superintendent was responsible for the preservation of discipline on board and he had powers similar to a Justice of the Peace. His orders were hung up in a conspicuous place within the prison ship and those orders listed here give us some idea of what was expected of Thomas and the other boy convicts during the voyage.

* The greatest possible respect is to be paid to the Surgeon, Captain and Officers …

* It is expected that strict attention will be paid to the Chief Wardsman's orders and those of the Overseers.

* Swearing, fighting, stealing, wrangling and all improper behaviour will be punished with the utmost severity.

* No buying, selling or trafficking with provisions or other articles will be allowed.

* It is to be understood that when the bell is rung strict silence must be observed and the Wardsmen are to observe this as not a whisper will be allowed.

* Any boy accusing another falsely will be severely punished.

* It is expected that every boy will be clean in his person and clothing.
* Strict attention is to be paid during Divine Service ...
* Any boy pretending to be ill will be punished.
* It is to be recollected that the future welfare of Prisoners in general depends entirely on their conduct here. A book is kept for noting down any misconduct.[414]

We learn from the records that on 16 April 1842 the convicts on the *Elphinstone (4)* went on to salt rations; that in May one of the convict boys John Winford went into the ship's hospital where he died; and that in June J. Robinson was 'placed in irons for attempting an unnatural act'. The passage from Sheerness was considered a healthy voyage, and on 28 July 1842, after 108 days at sea, they reached Hobart Town.[415] At the end of the voyage, the Surgeon Superintendent described Thomas May's 'general conduct' during the voyage as 'good'.[416]

On arriving in Hobart Town, the adult convicts were disembarked and Thomas and the other boy convicts stayed on board. The Registrar of the Probation Department came on board the ship and he recorded the particulars of the young convicts. The following information was recorded on Thomas's convict record.

Thomas was four feet, seven and a quarter inches high. He was listed as thirteen years of age although according to his birth record he was actually fifteen. He was described as having a large head with dark brown hair and a broad face with a high forehead, a freckled complexion and no whiskers. His eyebrows were black, his eyes hazel and his nose, mouth and chin were described as medium. He had a scar on his right knee, a scar over his left eye and three small scars on his forehead. His religion was Protestant, he could not read or write and his occupation was given as labourer.[417]

While Thomas had arrived in Hobart Town, he had actually not finished his journey. The *Elphinstone(4)*'s convict transportation contract involved delivering the bulk of the boys to the boy convict settlement at Point Puer. Point Puer was sited near the Port Arthur convict settlement which had been established on the Tasman Peninsula in south-east Van Diemen's

Land. On 6 August, the *Elphinstone (4)* weighed anchor with only 205 boy convicts still on board.[418] The convict authorities had apparently decided that sixteen of the convicts were no longer boys and they would go through the normal adult convict system. Three days later, the *Elphinstone (4)* arrived at Port Arthur,[419] where the boys were handed over to Captain Charles O'Hara Booth. The Captain had responsibility for both the Point Puer boy convict settlement and the main settlement at Port Arthur.

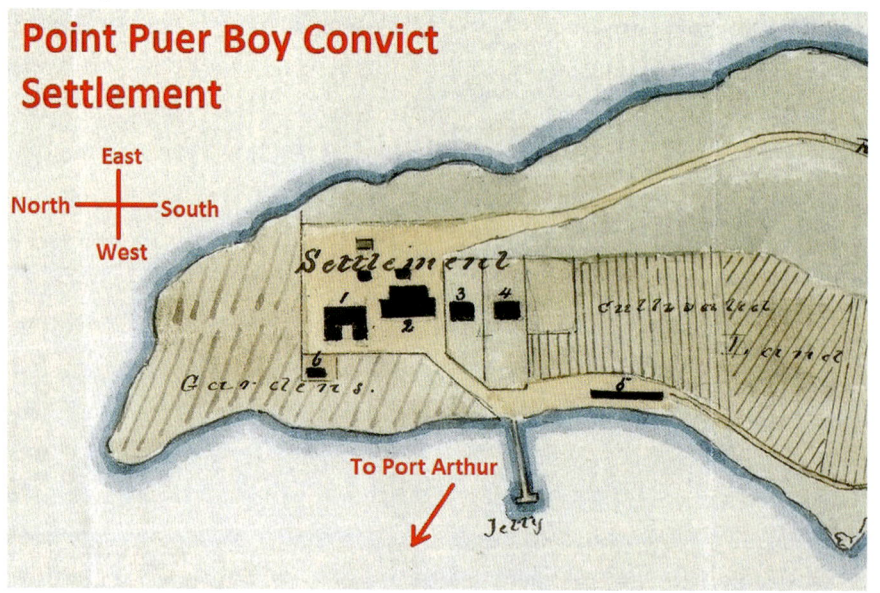

21. Part of 1840s map of the Point Puer Boy Convict Settlement showing: 1. Workshops; 2. Boys Barracks; 3. Chaplain's Quarters; 4. Superintendent Quarters; and 5. Saw pits.

The Point Puer boy convict settlement had been established in 1834. It had been set up near the large Port Arthur settlement as a means of reducing its establishment and running costs. A separate settlement for juveniles was deemed appropriate because the convict authorities had been concerned about exposing boy convicts to the corrupting influences of adult male convicts. They also wished to impose an appropriate regime of discipline on the boys at the start of their time in Van Diemen's Land and to give them appropriate skills that would make them employable in the colony. Like Thomas, many of the boy convicts had no education and no experience on the land or in any trade or occupation.

While the location at Point Puer saved on administration costs, it was not an appropriate site for a settlement. The soil on the point was very sandy and not well suited for agricultural pursuits. Also there was no water supply available, so all water required for the settlement to operate had to be carted in from outside. This shortage of water meant that for general cleanliness and hygiene, the boys had to bathe in the protected bay that faced the Port Arthur convict settlement. While this was no doubt quite enjoyable in summer, it would not have been a pleasant experience in midwinter.

On 9 August, Thomas commenced a two year probationary period of service at Point Puer. At the start of their probation, new boys like Thomas were either employed on labouring jobs such as making roads, cutting and carting timber and cultivating ground for agricultural purposes, or on domestic tasks such as washing and cooking. Thomas almost certainly had his first experience of growing vegetables and crops while working on the thirty-five acres of land that was under cultivation at the settlement.

He would have experienced a tough, disciplined regime at Point Puer. The boys rose at 5 am, then said prayers and listened to scripture readings before breakfast at 7 am. Working hours were from 8 am to noon and from 1.30 to 5 pm. Lunch was at 12.30 pm. They ate their evening meal at 5.30 pm and this was followed by one hour of formal tuition from 6.15 to 7.15. The day ended with prayers, hymns and scripture reading before bed. On Sundays, religion was the main feature of the day with prayers at 9 am, Divine Service at 10.30 am and a second service at 6 pm. After the services, the boys were questioned on their understanding of the sermon.[420] Adapting to this tightly structured regime would have been very difficult for a young boy like Thomas.

Great emphasis at Point Puer was placed on the boys learning trades.

After the initial period of employment on labouring jobs, there were many trades that the boys could learn such as blacksmithing, baking, shoe making, book binding, tailoring, boat building, coopering and gardening.[421] The main trades in which Thomas worked were shoe making and baking.[422] Thomas had been forced to travel to the other side of the world but finally he was getting some schooling and he was doing some honest work in a bakery.

The bakery at Point Puer was located near the top of the promontory that made up the settlement. Just below the bakery were barracks where the boys slept. Both the bakery and the barracks faced out across the water to the west and towards the main Port Arthur convict settlement. Just off the northern end of Point Puer there is a small island known as the Isle of the Dead. It was the Port Arthur and Point Puer burial ground. Whenever Thomas and the other boys saw a whale boat row out from Port Arthur to the Isle of the Dead they would know that another poor convict was to be laid to rest.

During the time that Thomas spent at Point Puer, the settlement held its largest number of boys. At the end of 1842, 712 boys were housed there.[423] In January 1844, Thomas's conduct at Point Puer was described as 'fair'. On 6 August, at the end of his two year probationary period, the Superintendent described Thomas as a shoemaker, but qualified it by stating that he 'cannot earn his livelihood'. At this time Thomas's conduct was reported as 'good'.[424]

After his time at Point Puer, Thomas was transferred to the convict hiring depot at New Town where he worked on the farm at the Queen's Orphan School, waiting to be hired out. In late 1844 he was hired to a Mr Jepson at New Norfolk, and to a Mr Clarke at Bushy Plains. During 1845, with the economic recession in Van Diemen's Land and the great surplus of convict labour, he spent a considerable amount of time in convict hiring depots. In January 1846 he again worked for Mr Jepson but this time at Fingal, sixty kilometres east of Perth in the centre of Van Diemen's Land. On 17 March 1846, around the time of his nineteenth birthday, he was granted his ticket-of-leave which allowed him to make his own way in the colony, subject to reporting to the police once a week.[425]

Thomas's only serious conflict with the government authorities in Van Diemen's Land occurred in 1848, when on 25 February he was charged with 'misconduct in hired service' while working for a Mr Burke at New Norfolk. Thomas was found guilty of the charge and the Police Magistrate sentenced him to one month of hard labour in a house of correction and he had to forfeit the wages due to him.[426] We do not know the details of the 'misconduct' but Thomas would have served this sentence in chains undertaking heavy labouring work and he may have spent time on a punishment tread mill.

By the end of 1848, Thomas had served out his seven year sentence. He was now a free man but he chose to continue to live and work in Van Diemen's Land.

# 20   A Second Chance

After gaining his freedom, Thomas settled in Hobart Town, where in the early 1850s he worked as a baker.[427] By 1852 he had made the decision to marry and start a family and in September that year he married sixteen-year-old Anne Bottrell in St George's Protestant church.[428] This was a good marriage for the baker who had arrived in the colony as a boy convict. Anne Bottrell was the step-daughter of Sergeant John Watson, a member of the local police. On his marriage certificate Thomas once again understated his age, saying that he was twenty-one years of age when in fact he was well past his twenty-fifth birthday. Soon after their marriage, Thomas and Anne moved into a house in Brisbane Street.[429] At this time, they may well have met John and Catherine Copley, who also lived in Hobart Town. However, we cannot say for certain that any contact was made between the two couples.

In early 1853, Anne found that she was pregnant and on 4 August she gave birth to a son who was given the name Thomas Fredrick May. On 10 August, John Watson, the Sergeant of Police, attended the births and deaths registry office and registered the birth of his stepdaughter's child.[430] Unfortunately, by late that month it was evident that all was not well with baby Thomas Fredrick. His had been a premature birth and he struggled rather than thrived. On 11 September he died and his death was registered by his baker father, Thomas May.[431]

In the mid-1850s it is very likely that Thomas fell victim to the poor state of the Tasmanian economy and that he, like many other ex-convicts, started to struggle to find regular employment. No doubt the idea of finding his fortune on the goldfields had an irresistible attraction and he decided to make the move to Victoria. We do not know precisely when he left Tasmania but records show he was living in Victoria by September 1857. What happened to Anne remains a mystery. The only clue we have is that Thomas is on record in 1891 as stating that his wife had been dead for twenty years.[432] However, we have not been able to locate any record of her death in Victoria and there is no record of her death in Tasmania or of a divorce.

By September 1857 Thomas was living in western Victoria but he first appears on the historical record working on a large sheep station and not on the goldfields. At that time he was working as a shepherd on the Ledcourt squatting run that was located twenty kilometres to the west of the gold rush settlement of Pleasant Creek on the edge of the Grampian mountain range.[433] This squatting run was first established in 1840 by Robert Briggs, a former army officer, who was the first squatter to follow the 1836 tracks of the explorer Major Mitchell.[434] By 1857, Ledcourt was owned by a Scotsman, Thomas Swinton Carfrae, and it covered 74,500 acres and had the capacity to carry tens of thousands of sheep.[435]

Records show that Thomas worked as a shepherd on Ledcourt until December 1857 and was paid £10/6/- for this work or around £1 a week. He was also paid a further £3/5/6 for work expenses he incurred.[436] There is no evidence to suggest that Anne was with him on the station. On Ledcourt, Thomas would have used some of the skills associated with working and living on the land that he first learnt as a boy convict at Point Puer in the early 1840s. At this time, many of the shepherds on the large squatting runs in western Victoria were former convicts. It was said that the hardships of the convict system provided a good grounding for the isolated and tough life of a shepherd. It is quite possible that Thomas spent more time on Ledcourt than is indicated here. There are significant gaps in the station records throughout the 1850s and 1860s.

Ledcourt station was to go on to find a place in Australian history because, in the mid-1860s, the author and journalist Marcus Clarke was its manager. After leaving the Stawell area, Marcus Clarke went on to write the acclaimed novel on the Van Diemen's Land and Norfolk Island convict experience, *For the Term of His Natural Life*.

Like the Copleys, Thomas was among the thousands who flocked to Lamplough when gold was discovered there in late 1859.[437] Again we cannot be certain whether he met up with John and Catherine on this goldfield but it is certainly a possibility. However, Thomas only stayed in Lamplough for a short time before returning to Stawell where, on 23 March 1860, he was admitted to the hospital suffering from dysentery.[438] Dysentery is typically caused by unsanitary water containing micro-organisms which damage the intestinal lining and it results in severe diarrhoea. We cannot be sure where Thomas contracted dysentery but it is quite possible that this occurred at Lamplough. Gold rush mining communities often had problems with access to supplies of clean water and the water that was available was sometimes polluted by the poor disposal of faeces and other waste. In a very short space of time, Lamplough had gone from being an isolated spot in the bush to a bustling goldfield with a population of more than 10,000 and we know that at the end of summer in early 1860 it had major water supply problems.

On his admission to the Stawell hospital, Thomas was recorded as being thirty-three years old.[439] This is the first recorded occasion where he gave an accurate account of his age. This hospital had only opened twelve months earlier and it was constructed half of bark and half of calico. It had three rooms that could take between twelve and sixteen beds.[440] Despite the primitive building, the hospital provided the care that Thomas needed and thirteen days after he was admitted he was discharged. The hospital records tell us that he had been 'cured'.[441]

# PART FIVE
# JALLUKAR SELECTORS

# 21 Obtaining Land

We know nothing about Thomas May's life from the time that he left hospital in April 1860 until March 1871, when he took up occupancy of sixty-seven acres of land that he had nominated for selection near the Mount William Range.[442] This land was around four kilometres west of the eighty acre selection that had been taken up by Catherine and John Copley. A surveyor from the Lands Department surveyed the land in January 1871 and on 8 March a selection licence for this land was issued to Thomas. This three-year selection licence required him to pay £3/8/- every six months to the Lands Department and to make at least £68 worth of improvements to the land. If he met these obligations he could then take out a lease on the land. Under a lease, his six-monthly payments of £3/8/- would have to continue for a further seven years before he could receive the full land title and gain ownership of the sixty-seven acres.

This was a good selection. It had access to water that was provided by run-off from the Mount William Range and with this water Thomas could grow vegetables and raise livestock to sell in the booming deep quartz goldmining town of Stawell, twenty kilometres away.

\*\*\*

From September 1870 through to April 1873 things appear to have gone well for Catherine and John on their selection. John regularly paid his licence payments to the Lands Department,[443] and he also paid the annual rate bill that was due on the land to the Ararat Shire Council. By 1871, John and Catherine had built and moved into their own home on their own selection.[444]

A worrying event occurred in 1871 when their son James was admitted to the Stawell hospital suffering from concussion.[445] He must have had a serious fall to warrant the fifteen kilometre trip to Stawell. This hospital was not the bark and calico building where Thomas May had been treated for dysentery in 1860. In 1861, a new hospital located near the Quartz Reefs had been constructed at a cost of just over £2500.[446] On admission, James gave his occupation as farmer, his place of residence the Black Range and his age as nineteen when in fact he was only seventeen.[447] At that time, he was working with his parents on their selection at Frying Pan Plain near the Black Range. Fortunately, he made a full recovery.

By May 1872, ten acres of land on the Copley selection were described as cultivated land where grain crops like wheat, barley and oats were grown and vegetables such as carrots, potatoes and turnips were cultivated. The remaining seventy acres were pasture where livestock could be grazed.[448] This land today is sheep country and we can be almost certain that Catherine and John ran a few sheep on their block. No doubt they kept a close eye on them. They would certainly have been aware of the risk to their flock from sheep stealers.

In the early 1870s, a mining boom was taking place in Stawell at the Quartz Reefs. Money from Ballarat and further afield was leading to the opening of new mines. These miners had money and they were doing hard and heavy work that created quite an appetite. The vegetables and livestock produced by Catherine and John and by their neighbour Thomas May were attracting good prices from the local shopkeepers.

***

At around this time Thomas probably had his first contact in more than thirty years with rabbits. In 1859, twenty-four rabbits had been released in the countryside near Geelong by an Englishmen who was homesick for the animals and for the sport that had been available in the English countryside. In 1867, a group of four rabbits, descendants of the Geelong rabbits, arrived in Ararat on the Ballarat coach. These rabbits were greeted with great joy by the locals who called them 'four little strangers'.[449] They were released near Ararat and within a few years, the descendants of these rabbits were starting to spread throughout the wider Ararat and Stawell areas. We do not know how Thomas reacted to his first contact with rabbits since 1841 in Brighton, but surely he got a certain satisfaction from being able to enjoy a good pot of rabbit stew.

In the first twelve months on his selection Thomas cleared five acres of land for cultivation. This involved removing all trees and scrub from the heavily timbered land and then ploughing the ground ready for sowing a crop of wheat and barley. He recorded a few years later that he experienced great success with this first crop of wheat and barley as it produced a yield of ten bushels an acre.[450] It appears he was deriving some dividends from his experience with agricultural work thirty years earlier at Point Puer. During this time he also constructed a home on his land and started to construct a fence around his boundaries.[451]

In 1872, the area alongside the eastern edge of the Grampian mountains where the Copleys and Thomas May had their selections was formally named. It was given the name Jallukar. This was the same name that the local Aboriginal tribe had given this land long before the advent of white settlers. At this time, it was very unusual for places to be given Aboriginal names.

\*\*\*

At the start of 1873, John came up with a plan to further expand his landholdings in the Jallukar area. The Copley eighty acre selection on Pentlands Creek was located about ten kilometres from Redman Bluff and twelve kilometres from Mount William. The view of these mountains from the Copley selection was very similar to the view that had so impressed Major Mitchell at his nearby camp site in July 1836. The mountain range ran for virtually as far as the eye could see to the north, and to the south-west was Redman Bluff with its imposing red rock cliff face and Mount William, the highest peak in the range. In winter, their peaks were sometimes covered in snow and they always had a powerful presence.

Obviously John saw more than this. He must have noticed that these mountains were often covered in cloud when there was no cloud anywhere near his block and realized that they were magnets for rain.[452] He then determined that a selection of land on a water course at the base of Mount William and Redman Bluff would be the best place in the Ararat and Stawell districts to grow vegetables, crops and raise livestock for the expanded market created by the Stawell miners. However, there was one major drawback—land at the base of these mountains was extremely isolated, with no selectors much less any settlement for miles around.

This drawback did not stop John and on 26 February 1873 he signed and submitted an application for a licence to select a hundred acres of land near the base of Redman Bluff.[453] At the same time he paid a £6 application fee to the Lands Department. In early April, his application to select this land was approved.[454] However, despite expending £6 and gaining this approval, for some unknown reason John did not proceed with this selection application.

22. View of the Grampian Mountains from the Copleys' eighty acre selection block. Mount William dominates the centre skyline with Redman Bluff on the right.

April 1873 was a good month for the Copley family. Four days after the Lands Board at Ararat approved their selection application, Catherine and John's first-born son, John, married Jane Stonehouse at the Catholic priest's house in Ararat.[455]

Young John Copley was twenty years of age and Jane Stonehouse was twenty-two. Jane's father Robert Stonehouse was a blacksmith. The Stonehouses also had a family background in Van Diemen's Land, with Robert Stonehouse's grandfather John Marsden being transported to the island in 1812 after being convicted of sheep stealing at the Nottingham Assizes. Initially, Marsden had been sentenced to death for this offence but the sentence was subsequently commuted to a life transportation sentence. While he escaped death at the hands of the English authorities, he was not so lucky when he encountered a group of Aborigines near Launceston in September 1827. The Aborigines attacked and killed the then sixty-six-year-old.[456]

In August 1873, there was further good news for Catherine and John. They had successfully completed the initial three year licence period on their selection. They had progressively made the total of £24 in payments to the Lands Department and they had also been assessed as making at least £80 worth of improvements to this land. On 29 August, the Lands Department granted John a lease covering this selection.[457] He could now if he wished, sell this land in the commercial marketplace. Alternatively, he could hold onto the land and make the necessary lease payments and he would be granted full ownership. The Copley family move onto the land at Jallukar had been fully vindicated.

On 2 April 1874, Catherine and John became grandparents for the first time when their daughter-in-law Jane gave birth to a daughter. The proud parents named her Catherine; the name shared by both the baby's grandmothers.[458] It was Catherine Copley who supported Jane during her labour and, along with a Doctor Galbraith, she was in attendance at the birth. On the birth certificate the baby's father, John, was identified as having been born at Launceston. It appears that someone in the family had decided that Launceston had less of a convict association than Hobart Town, where John had in fact been born to his then pass holder convict parents.

\*\*\*

In the first half of 1874, while things were going well for the Copley family, Thomas May was experiencing major problems in holding on to his Jallukar selection. Thomas had made only one of the six licence rental payments of £3/8/- that he was supposed to have made to the Lands Department and the three years of his licence period had concluded in early March.[459] We do not know why Thomas failed to make these licence payments.

In late May, Mr W. Matthews, a selector at nearby Moyston, wrote to the Lands Department on behalf of Thomas. The letter stated that for the previous two months Thomas had been attempting to pay the licence rental arrears he owed, but due to some identity confusion with a James May he had been unable to pay these arrears to the Lands Department office in Ararat.[460] James May was a selector in the Jallukar area who was no relation to Thomas.

At around the same time as this letter was sent the Lands Department received five rent payments, each of £3/8/-, from Thomas. This covered the money he owed for the full three year licence period.[461] Thomas was apparently hoping that by making this large payment, the department would overlook his failure to make the payments at the due time and grant him a selection lease with little further scrutiny. However, the Lands Department had concerns about the bona fides of this large payment and determined that they would not at that stage formally accept and process it.

The response of the Lands Department office in Melbourne to the receipt of this payment was to write to Thomas and ask him to forward to them a declaration of the improvements he had made to the selection.[462] It was a prerequisite for the granting of a lease that the department be satisfied that at least £1 per acre worth of improvements had been made during the licence period.

In his declaration, Thomas stated that he had lived as required on the selection since January 1871, when he first took out the licence. He explained that during that time, twenty-five acres of land had been cultivated and ploughed. From this cultivation, carrots, turnips, wheat and oats had been harvested with a value of £25. He claimed that one weatherboard and slate roofed dwelling house measuring twenty feet by sixteen feet had been constructed as had two outbuildings. These were given an improvement value of £20. He added that grubbing work had been undertaken on six acres of land. Grubbing was backbreaking work as it not only involved clearing the land of trees, but of the stumps and roots as well. He gave this work the value of £60.[463]

There was, however, one problem. Thomas could only claim that forty-eight chains (965 metres) of fencing had been constructed around his boundaries. Under the terms of his selection licence he had committed 'within two years from the issue of this licence [to] enclose the land described therein with a good and substantial fence',[464] and to fully enclose the selection he should have erected 170 chains (3410 metres) of fencing. The Lands Department was not impressed and Thomas started to strike serious problems. The Melbourne office believed that he might not be a genuine selector and that he could be acting as a cover for a squatter, who on a prearranged basis would assume ownership of the land after the department granted a lease.

At this time, it was relatively common practice for squatters to plant people known as selection dummies on prime pieces of land on their squatting run. These dummies then appeared to do the bare minimum to gain a lease on the selection, and after the lease was granted the dummy handed the land back to the squatter. This practice was totally contrary to the purpose of the Land Selection Acts. These Acts were meant to open up the land to family farming, whereas what the dummies did was to give the squatters the means to convert their tenuous squatting hold on land into secure freehold title.

In mid-June, the Melbourne office of the Lands Department directed that the Crown Lands Bailiff investigate and report on Thomas's bona fides as a selector.[465] This was a serious situation for Thomas because if the Crown Lands Bailiff was not satisfied with his performance, then almost certainly he would not be granted a lease and he would be thrown off the land.

On 29 June Mounted Police Constable James Hornibrook of the Stawell police, acting for the Crown Land Bailiff, inspected Thomas's Jallukar selection. This visit proved to be the most positive contact that Thomas was to have with any member of a police force. Constable Hornibrook submitted a glowing report to the Chief Commissioner of Police and all importantly he stated in his report, 'I believe him [Thomas May] to be a bona fide selector'.[466]

It is apparent from Constable Hornibrook's report that Thomas must have had considerable assistance in the period between 11 and 29 June because much work was done during that time to improve his selection. We do not know who assisted Thomas. Was it friends, fellow selectors like the Copleys or the local squatter? They are all possibilities. What we do know from Constable Hornibrook's report is that by then the selection was enclosed by 125 chains (2510 metres) of fencing that was in good repair. He stated that fencing enclosed the north, south and east sides of the selection and there was a water course on the western side. He also reported that twenty acres of the selection had been grubbed and cleared; considerably more than the six acres declared by Thomas earlier in the month.[467]

The Lands Department accepted Constable Hornibrook's report and accepted Thomas's licence rental payments that he had forwarded earlier in the year.[468]

\*\*\*

Around the time Constable Hornibrook inspected Thomas May's selection, Catherine and John's son, John, submitted an application for a licence for a forty acre selection that bordered on the southern side of Thomas's sixty-seven acres.[469] This selection backed onto the Mount William Range and two creeks ran off the range into these forty acres. It appears that on this small selection John was planning to use the water from the mountains to grow vegetables and grain crops to sell in Stawell. John's selection application was the first made anywhere near the May selection and certainly by now there would have been at least a working relationship between the Copley family and Thomas May.

In October, the Mines Department indicated it had no objection to young John Copley's selection licence application,[470] and on 1 December 1874 the Lands Department approved this forty acre selection. By the end of 1874 John had already paid £4 in licence rental payments to the Lands Department.[471]

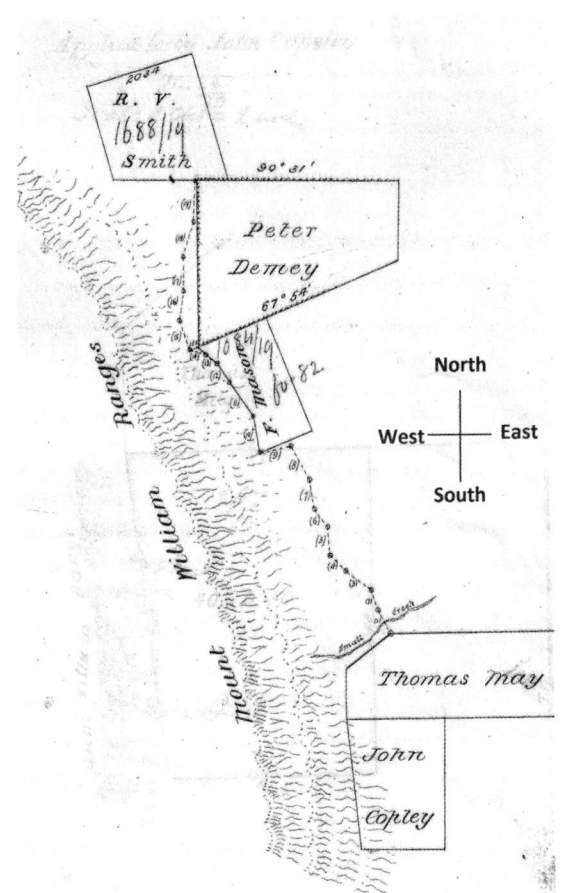

23. March 1875 Lands Department drawing of the sixty-seven acre Thomas May Jallukar selection and the bordering forty acre selection held by the younger John Copley, son of Catherine and John.

Also in October 1874, John Copley senior applied for a selection licence for 125 acres of land at the base of Redman Bluff.[472] This licence application covered the hundred acres of land that he had been given approval to farm under a selection licence back in April 1873.

It is not clear why John did not take up this selection licence in 1873. It could be that he decided to first secure a lease on the eighty acre selection on Pentland Creek. However, this does not explain the extended delay. Perhaps Catherine and John had decided to strengthen their financial position before they took on new land. After all, John had already experienced insolvency in Van Diemen's Land and they would not have wanted a repeat of that situation.

Furthermore, John may have started to appreciate the major challenge that the selection of land under Redman Bluff represented. This land was so isolated that it was not even covered by a land area parish recognized by the Lands Department for selection purposes. It was a considerable distance from both Stawell and Ararat and access to markets would therefore be time consuming and difficult. Additionally, this selection and all the land in the vicinity was squatter's land, part of the Lexington squatting run with the Barton squatting run located nearby. A selection at the foot of the mountains raised the prospect of interference with a major source of water for these squatters. By this time, John must have been aware that the squatters would be far from pleased if this area was opened up for land selection.

The other factor that may have been playing on John's mind and holding him back from pressing ahead with the Redman Bluff selection was concern about his health. By mid-1874, John was starting to experience symptoms associated with valvular heart disease.[473] These symptoms can include weakness, dizziness, palpitations, chest pains and swelling in the ankles, feet or abdomen. Any one of these symptoms would have been good reason for John and Catherine to pause and consider whether they really wanted to go ahead with this new selection.

Nevertheless, John and Catherine decided to proceed with their selection application.[474] The size of the proposed selection was increased from a hundred acres to 125 acres and at around this time John sold the eighty acres he held under lease on Pentlands Creek. The sale of this land would have provided important capital to help make the move to the land underneath Redman Bluff successful. John had identified what he believed to be the best land in the area and both he and Catherine appeared to believe that land, and particularly good land, was what would provide them and their family with long term security. No longer young, they were about to take on a whole new selection in an area where no one else before them had selected any land. It was virgin bushland.

*\*\*\**

By November, Thomas May had submitted his application for a lease covering his sixty-seven acre Jallukar selection. This application contained much of the same information contained in the Constable Hornibrook report and Thomas informed the Lands Department that £105 worth of improvements had been made on the selection over the three year licence period.[475]

After a two and a half month wait, Thomas got the news he'd been hoping for; in February 1875, the Board of the Lands Department approved his application and granted his selection lease.[476]

# 22  The Farmer From Redman Bluff

In January 1875 John Copley senior's selection licence application was approved by the Lands Department. Not surprisingly, there were no objections raised to this application because there had been no mining activities anywhere near this land. On 1 February, the then Acting Governor of Victoria, William F. Stawell, completed the formalities when he signed the selection licence document which gave John 'full licence and authority to enter upon and occupy' the 125 acres of land just below Redman Bluff.[477] At this time, William F. Stawell was the long serving Chief Justice of Victoria and the town of Stawell had been named after him.

Following the granting of this selection licence, the Copley family—John sixty-two; Catherine, forty-seven; second son James, twenty; and daughter Hannah, fourteen—moved onto their new land. At this time John and Catherine's eldest son, John, and his wife Jane lived about five kilometres away from them to the north on their forty acre selection that bordered Thomas May's. John and the Shalders family who had taken up a selection five kilometres to the north-east were their nearest neighbours. To the east, in the adjacent Moyston selection parish, their nearest neighbour was a farmer identified as D. Kane whose land was more than six kilometres away.[478]

These 125 acres of land were in an incredibly beautiful and isolated spot. Redman Bluff was a kilometre to the west and each day, at least an hour before sunset, their selection was covered in the shade of the mountains. Mount William was only four kilometres to the south-west. Mount William, like Redman Bluff, featured rocky escarpments and steep cliff faces and both mountains towered over this new Copley family home. The family shared their new land with native birds and animals and no doubt once their crops were planted, they were in a state of constant warfare.

Between the new Copley selection and their nearest neighbours were many hundreds of acres of bushland that few white men had entered. In fact, bushland is pretty much all that the selection was at this time. There were a few large red gum trees that had grown on the land for hundreds of years but much of the acreage was densely timbered with honeysuckle and tea tree and, due to its close proximity to the mountains, the ground was covered in ferns.[479] One of the downsides of selecting land in such a wet, fertile area was that the native vegetation was thick and profuse and very difficult to clear.

Having lived in gold rush settlements and at Pentlands Creek, the family would have been accustomed to the sounds of the Australian bush, but they were now surrounded by a veritable symphony orchestra of birdsong. Even today, at daybreak and evening in the bushland of the Grampians, the sound of galahs, cockatoos and kookaburras fills the air.

However, in early 1875 it is unlikely that the Copleys had time to appreciate the flora and fauna on their new selection. A house made of sawn slabs and measuring twenty feet by twelve feet was soon constructed.[480] The family gave this house the appropriately modest and geographically accurate name of Mountain Hut.[481] After providing themselves with shelter, a priority job was to start clearing, grubbing and cultivating an area of land in preparation for planting a crop. Within four or five months, about six acres of land had been cleared and grubbed, and here the Copleys planted an oat crop.[482]

Under the terms of the licence, a boundary fence for the selection boundary covering more than 4500 metres had to be constructed within two years. After the oat crop was sown, work started in earnest on constructing this fence. Some of this fencing was of a post and rail construction and some was constructed of logs and brush.

In June 1875, John paid the Lands Department their second rental payment of £6/5/-.[483] Under their selection licence, six payments of £6/5/- had to be paid to the department six months apart over the three year period of the licence. John and Catherine knew that these payments had to be made and the other terms of the licence met if John were to be entitled to a selection lease covering this land. Such a lease would then run for a further seven year period and they would be required to make another fourteen payments of £6/5/- to obtain full ownership. They knew it would be 1885 before John fully owned this selection, and by then he would be over seventy years of age.

Eventually the Lands Department established a new selection parish of West Moyston that included the Copley holding. However, the Copleys had very little contact with Moyston and they always saw their land as being part of Jallukar. The nearest selectors to them lived in Jallukar. They saw Stawell, rather than Ararat, as their main market and regional town and they travelled through the Jallukar area to get to Stawell.

At the end of 1875 the Copley family harvested the oat crop planted on the six acres of cultivated ground. The yield was a modest one and a half bushels per acre.[484]

In March 1876 John applied to the Lands Department to expand his Jallukar land-holding.[485] He submitted a licence selection application for a further 115 acres of land adjoining the eastern and northern boundaries of his 125 acre selection. If granted, this would take John's total holding to 240 acres. With the eighty acres at Pentland Creek that he had already selected and sold and 240 acres near Redman Bluff, he would have selected a total of 320 acres. This was the maximum amount of land that one individual was entitled to select under the colony's land selection laws.

The rationale for this further selection application appears to have been that they had to obtain the maximum amount of land that was possible to help create a viable and secure farm. At this time John's health was almost certainly continuing to deteriorate from the heart disease he had first experienced in mid-1874, but nevertheless he and Catherine pressed on with their plan to obtain more land. They knew that people such as John Cutt and Darby Rogers, substantial land-holders at Thorpe Hesley and Cappabane, had been the ones with real economic security. John and Catherine were relying on the land to provide them with that same security.

By early May, the local lands board at Ararat had approved John's application for a licence covering the further 115 acres of land and had sent the application on to the department's office in Melbourne for final consideration.[486]

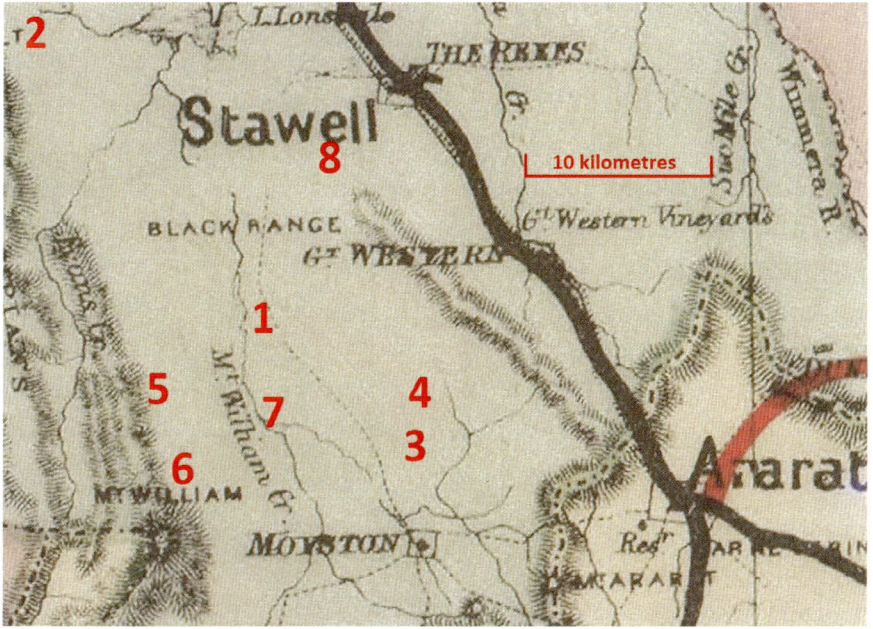

24. 1884 map of Stawell, Ararat and Grampians mountain area with significant locations marked: 1. Major Mitchell's July 1836 camp site; 2. Ledcourt squatting run where Thomas May worked in 1857 and 1858; 3. The 1860 Londonderry gold diggings; 4. John Copley's eighty acre selection; 5. Thomas May's selections and the younger John Copley's forty acre selection; 6. John and Catherine Copley's 240 acres of land under Redman Bluff; 7. Jallukar township; and 8. Illawarra. (Part of the [Sands & McDougall Limited Victoria (cartographic material) 1884 MAP RM 3865] contained in the national Library of Australia Maps Collection)

While they were awaiting final approval from Melbourne, Catherine and John received news from John and Jane of the birth of their first male grandchild. Like his father and his grandfather before him, the baby was named John. On his birth certificate his full name was given as John Robert Copley.[487] John and Jane were to eventually have six children. When registering the births of these children, John was to repeatedly change the name of the town in Van Diemen's Land where he was born. This time he correctly stated that he had been born in Hobart Town.[488] He obviously knew of the convict background of his parents but it seems he was never quite sure whether or not he should acknowledge that he had been born in the centre of convict administration.

At around this time, Catherine and John planted a crop of oats for the 1876 season covering a further six acres of new ground.[489]

In early July, final approval was given by the Lands Department for John to have a selection licence for the additional 115 acres.[490] John, at sixty-four years of age, had now become what anyone in his Yorkshire birthplace of Thorpe Hesley would consider to be a significant land-holder. This would have made him a man of some importance in the community. It must have

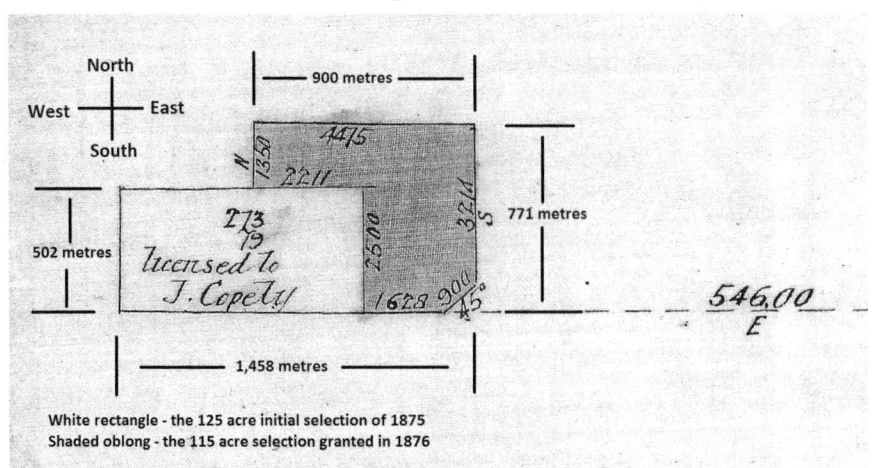

25. May 1876 land selection drawing showing the two Copley selections located near Redman Bluff. The measurements in chains on this drawing and on other Lands Department drawings have been converted to metres to help show the size of the selections.

given him considerable satisfaction to know that despite his convict past he had transformed his life and now farmed a sizeable acreage.

There was an immediate downside to obtaining the approval for the further 115 acres and this was the amount of selection licence rental payments that had to be paid. Under the licence for this land, every six months for three years Catherine and John had to make payments of £5/15/- to the Lands Department.[491] Combined with the licence payments already due on their other Redman Bluff selection, this meant they had to make rent payments of £24 a year. To put the value of this financial obligation into context, at this time a miner working for wages at the Quartz Reefs at Stawell was paid around £2/8/- a week or £125 a year.[492] At this time, £24 a year was a substantial sum of money, particularly when it was considered that the Copleys also faced considerable expense in establishing their farm.

Life was made much more difficult for the family when soon after they gained the licence on the 115 acre selection, there was a marked deterioration in John's health. The symptoms of heart disease became worse. Weakness and severe chest pains would have meant he was able to do little or no work. Valvular heart disease involves abnormalities or dysfunction occurring in one of more of the four valves that operate the heart and it was a very serious problem indeed. The body of John Copley had gone through a great deal and it was not going to permit him to go any further.

By early August 1876, John had been admitted to the Stawell hospital where he was treated by Doctor Robert Colquhoun, who had been the resident surgeon since 1859. Doctor Colquhoun would have made it clear to Catherine and John that he had little hope of recovery.

On 7 August 1876, John prepared his last will and testament. Apparently he was too sick to actually sign this document, so he marked it with an X. This document read as follows:

> I John Copley being very ill but of sound mind and understanding hereby make and declare this to be my last Will and Testament whereby I give and bequeath unto my wife Catherine all the property either real or personal of

which I may die possessed of or be entitled to, and hereby appoint my said wife sole executrix of this my will—In witness whereof I hereunto set my hand and seal this seventh day of August 1876.

Signed, seal and delivered by the said John Copley as and for his last Will and Testament in our presence and which we hereby attach our names as witnesses at his request this seventh day of August 1876 in the Pleasant Creek Hospital at Stawell.

(Sgd)     X

    John Copley

Mountain Hut

Moyston

(Sgd) Robert Colquhoun—witness

(Sgd) Alexander Black—witness[493]

Despite his serious heart problems, John was a strong man and he continued to linger for a further eleven days. On 15 August, the weather in Stawell turned very cold, with hail storms and snow covering the hills,[494] but despite this John's weakened heart continued to beat until on 18 August he died in his hospital bed.[495]

On 20 August, John formally reported his father's death to Edward James Bennett, the Deputy Registrar of Births, Deaths and Marriages in Stawell.[496] In examining the death certificate arising from this report, it is apparent that John produced a sanitized version of his father's life for the public record.

The certificate stated that John senior had lived in Tasmania for six years. This was far from accurate. John had been in Tasmania for twelve years and on Norfolk Island for four. There was no mention of Norfolk Island on the certificate. This reference to a six year period which is one year less than the minimum transportation sentence of seven years appears to be suggesting he migrated to Van Diemen's Land in the mid-1840s as a skilled migrant.

The certificate also stated that John had lived in Victoria for twenty-four years, which meant he arrived in Victoria in 1852. This suggests that like many free men, he left Van Diemen's Land to find his fortune as soon as gold had been discovered in Victoria. John in fact arrived in Victoria in 1857. Son John must have known that the suggestion his father arrived in 1852 was nonsense. After all he had been five years old when they left Tasmania and on the death certificate he recorded his own age as twenty-three. John knew that his father had a convict past and he was doing his best to camouflage this in the formal record of death.

Some things are difficult to hide. During his hospitalization and after his death, the hospital staff and the Stawell undertaker, Thomas Lymer, would have gained an insight into his convict past. The floggings he almost certainly received on Norfolk Island with the cat-o'-nine-tails would have left permanent scars on his back that would surely have been recognized by those treating him and preparing the body for burial.

John was buried on 20 August 1876 in the Church of England section of the Stawell cemetery. The funeral was conducted by the Reverend Stone, the Church of England minister. On death people are usually identified by their name and then a simple statement concerning their occupation or status in life. On the death certificate, son John identified his father as a blacksmith.[497] There are many other ways in which John could have been identified—nailor, labourer, sheep stealer, convict, burglar, coach builder, illegal migrant, miner or selector, but almost certainly he would have best appreciated the Stawell cemetery records entry that reads 'John Copley, farmer'.[498]

# 23 Catherine's Battle Begins

After John's funeral, Catherine would have headed home with a great deal on her mind. She had lost her husband of more than twenty-four years and was no doubt mourning this loss deeply, but to add to her woes she had an immense amount to consider about her own future and the future of the Jallukar selections.

John had left all his property to Catherine. The terms of John's will appear to have been quite straightforward but the situation was nowhere near so simple. With the making of his will, all the livestock, material and equipment on the two land selections, as well as any capital that he possessed, became the property of Catherine. The problem arose in relation to who now held the two selection licences covering the 240 acres near Redman Bluff. With this will, John attempted to transfer his position as the holder of the licences to Catherine. However, Victorian law, as provided in the Land Selection Act that went through the colony's parliament in 1869, stipulated 'No will or codicil or the granting of any probate or letters of administration shall be deemed to be an assignment or transfer [of a licence] within the meaning of this Act'.[499] This provision meant that John's will had no power to transfer the two land selection licences to Catherine. If the Copleys had not been so ambitious in relation to owning land, then this legal problem would not have existed. If John had not taken out the two Redman Bluff selection licences and had instead retained the eighty acres on Pentlands

Creek, the eighty acres of land that was under a selection lease would have smoothly transferred to Catherine on John's death. In the coming years, Catherine was to find out that Victorian law and powerful institutions in the community were strongly hostile to John's deathbed wish that she should have the opportunity to become a successful selector and farmer at Jallukar.

Following John's death, Catherine and her two children continued to live in Mountain Hut, but the question that still had to be faced was the legal status of the two selection licences. In a strictly legal sense, it appears that the licences died when John died. We do not know whether Catherine received any legal advice but she seems to have taken the wisest possible approach to secure her hold on the selections. She did absolutely nothing.

If Catherine had notified the Lands Department of John's death shortly after it happened, the department may have taken the view that the Copley family had only held the 125 acre selection licence for eighteen months and the 115 acre selection licence for a couple of months and therefore little would be lost if they were forced to leave the land. Catherine was not going to risk this and instead she, twenty-two-year-old James and sixteen-year-old Hannah just continued to develop and work the two selections.

John and Jane may also have given some support and assistance because at this time they were no longer living on their forty acres of land at Jallukar. In August 1876, on reporting the death of his father to the Deputy Registrar of Births, Deaths and Marriages, John had stated that his usual place of residence was Stawell rather than Jallukar. Although he had made the six payments of £2 each that he was due to make under the selection licence for the Jallukar land,[500] there is no record of him converting this selection licence to a lease.

Towards the end of the year, the six acre oats crop that had been sown before John died was harvested, and again it produced a yield of one and a half bushels per acre.[501]

Catherine, James and Hannah continued to make improvements to the selections in accordance with the two licences. This included the hard physical job of clearing and grubbing the land and continuing to construct fences around the boundaries of both selections. With the addition of the second 115 acre selection, they now faced the formidable task of constructing more than 6000 metres of fencing by mid-1878.

During April and May 1877, they planted out a crop of wheat on five acres of new ground that had not been cultivated in their previous two years on the selection. Towards the end of the year, this wheat crop was harvested with the now very familiar yield of one and a half bushels per acre.[502]

In 1877, Catherine was able to make all required selection licence payments to the Lands Department. This amounted to a total payment of £24.[503] She had successfully met all the financial obligations that were due under the two selection licences John had taken out.

By the start of February 1878, Catherine must have felt confident that she and her family had overcome the major obstacles that in August 1876 had stood in her way to becoming a successful land-holder. Two dwelling houses had been constructed and more than 4000 metres of boundary fencing had been erected around the 125 acre selection as well as most of the fencing around the second selection. More than thirty acres of land had been cleared of dead timber and crops had been planted and harvested on seventeen acres.[504] This meant that Catherine had met the necessary requirements for the licence on the first selection to be converted to a lease. With a selection lease Catherine would no longer be subject to any Lands Department review beyond making the necessary lease payments. Additionally, with a selection lease she knew she would be free if she wished to sell the land on the open property market. She now awaited the expiry date of the licence on the 125 acre selection.

This was an incredible achievement. In the 1870s, many selectors in Victoria failed to last the difficult and challenging first three years under licence on their selection. The life was just too tough. They had to clear, fence and cultivate the land and grow food for themselves and their family. Additionally, they had to grow enough food to sell in the marketplace to provide the money to pay rent to the Lands Department and also to purchase whatever else was needed for the farm and the family. Catherine, with the support of her children, had done this, despite John's death eighteen months earlier. To clear their heavily timbered and fern covered land, backbreaking work would have been the daily lot of all three family members and the isolated location of the two selections meant that there were no near neighbours to call on for assistance. Together, Catherine and John had selected land in this remote area but it was the widowed Catherine who had ensured that it had been a success.

26. Mountain Hut beneath Redman Bluff where Catherine Copley lived in the late 1870s and the 1880s. This photo was taken around 1911, more than twenty years after Catherine sold her land and this house.

In early February Catherine received a letter from the Melbourne office of the Department of Lands and Agriculture that was addressed to John. This letter stated the following:

> I have the honor to inform you that the term of the licence issued to you under Section 19, 'Land Act 1869', for the land described in the margin will expire on the 1st February 1878, and that if you have complied with the

conditions specified therein you are entitled at any time within thirty days after that date to apply for a Crown Grant or for a Lease of the said land.

I enclose a form on which you can make such application and beg to inform you that any reasonable assistance in filling up and completing the same will be afforded without charge, by any of the officers of this Department stationed in your district.

The declaration on oath embodied in the form of application can be made by you before any Justice of the Peace.

The application, when completed, should be handed or posted to the nearest District Surveyor, who will forward it to this office.

To ensure the issue of your lease or grant within a reasonable time after the expiry of your licence, you are requested to make your application without delay.

When your application shall have been approved, of which due notice will be given, the fees payable, viz., £1 for the Certificate of the Board of Lands and Works, under Section 20, 'Land Act 1869', and £1 for each Crown Grant or Lease, which will have to be paid.[505]

This was the letter that Catherine had been waiting for. She knew that she had met all the requirements to be granted a lease covering this selection and that there was no practical reason why it should not be approved. She had every reason to believe that it would be a formality to obtain her lease. There was only one possible issue; she had met the requirements after John had died.

On 27 February 1878, within the thirty days period stipulated in the Lands Department letter, Catherine submitted her application for a lease covering the 125 acre selection.[506] Catherine did not have the literacy skills necessary to fill out this application so she sought the assistance of William O'Callaghan, the publican of the Railway Hotel in Stawell.

***

William O'Callaghan was much more than a hotel publican. In the 1860s he had been the Chairman of the Land Reform Association in Ararat. This Association campaigned for working people to have the right to readily select land for farming. In the ten year period between 1868 and 1878, William unsuccessfully stood for election to the lower house of the Victorian parliament on three occasions,[507] and when he first stood for election for the seat of Ararat he strongly supported the establishment of land selection laws that gave working people the opportunity to select land that was held by the squatters. He considered land selection as the 'paramount question' facing the electors because it involved 'the prosperity, the stability and the greatness of this country'. He believed that the selection of land afforded 'the working class, the means of living in comparative comfort'.[508] He not only spoke in support of selectors during election campaigns, but in the 1860s and 1870s he gave considerable unpaid assistance to selectors and working people interested in taking up land. He gave this assistance by making representations on their behalf to the Victorian Lands Department. Catherine was about to gain considerable benefit from William's commitment to assist working people with land selection matters.

27. William O'Callaghan, MP for Wimmera from 1880 to 1883.

Catherine had far more in common with William O'Callaghan than an interest in land selection and ownership for working people. William was born in Skibbereen in County Cork and he left the town in 1853 or 1854 when he migrated to Victoria.[509] Skibbereen, like the Scarriff area where Catherine came from in County Clare, was one of the worst places to live during the Irish potato famine. A government report in December 1846 records that in the six week period from 5 November to 17 December a hundred dead bodies had been found in the lanes and cabins of Skibbereen town—many of them half eaten by rats. The official writing the report gave an account of how he was approached by a woman begging in the street who had a dead child in her arms. The report concluded that 'nothing can exceed the deplorable state of this place'.[510] While Skibbereen in the famine years was a place of starvation, disease and death, there was actually plenty of food in the town for most of this time. At the same time that the November/December 1846 government report was filed, there were plentiful supplies of fish, meat and bread at the Skibbereen market. During the famine, there was more than enough food in Ireland—working people just had no means to obtain it. William's strong stand in the 1860s and 1870s for working people to own land and therefore to be able to grow sufficient food for their families and communities appears to have been based on his experiences in Ireland during the potato famine. William would have had no problem understanding why Catherine and her brothers stole Darby Rogers' sheep in February 1849.

***

With William's help, Catherine completed her lease application form. She described herself as a farmer and she signed the form with an X mark. In filling in the form, Catherine did not address the issue of John's death; she simply declared 'That I have complied with all the … conditions of the said Licence'.[511] She confirmed that all fees due on the licence had been paid and stated that she lived on the selection with her family. She declared that one weatherboard house and one slab house had been constructed on the selection. She stated that improvements to the value of £246/2/8 had been made to the selection and this included the erection of 243 chains (4886 metres) of fencing. Not only had Catherine more than fulfilled the requirements of the Lands Department to gain her lease, she had in fact exceeded the value of improvements that were required for the application to be approved by £121.

In their March 1878 assessment of Catherine's application for a lease on her 'selection in the Parish of Moyston', the Lands Department agreed that she had complied with all conditions of the licence for the granting of a selection lease. However, while this was all positive, the department then determined to write to Catherine informing her that: 'If she applies for a lease of John Copley's selection and this licensee [John Copley] is deceased, it will be necessary to forward letters of Administration or Probate of Will to this Office for information.'[512]

At this point Catherine would have begun to realize that obtaining a lease was not going to be easy. It was obviously going to be far more complex than just proving she had met all the requirements. On 2 April 1878, on Catherine's behalf, William wrote the following letter to the Minister for Lands in Melbourne:

> I have the honour by request of Mrs Catherine Copley (widow of the late John Copley) to reply to your communication of 15th March 'that (Catherine) forward to the department letters of administration before a Lease is Granted to her for 125 acres in the Parish of Moyston held by her late husband'. In reply, I beg to say that she is too poor to incur the expense incident to such process but with your permission she will forward her marriage certificate with the certificate of her husband's death which you will please accept instead.[513]

The Lands Department in Melbourne took more than a month to reply to this letter. On 7 May, the Surveyor General, stated in a file note that the department should enquire if Catherine's 'husband left a will and what family she has. Also if she held any other property besides' the 125 acres selection.[514]

In replying to a departmental letter apparently based on this file note, William decided to take a different approach. This time, he wrote the introduction to the letter but then quoted Catherine. This letter dated 11 June 1878 reads:

> In reply to your queries … 'if my husband (John Copley[515]) left a will and what family he had, also if he held any other property besides this'. I beg to say, he made a will bequeathing this property to me, and making me sole executrix. I have got three in family. My husband also left me in the same manner 115 acres under licence similarly to the allotment in question.[516]

In August 1878, the Minister for Lands wrote back to William and told

Catherine that 'Probate of will must be obtained'. The Minister went on to ask that Catherine immediately act on this request.[517] This request for prompt action appears unreasonable because most of the delays in dealing with this matter over the previous six months were caused by the tardiness of the Minister or his department in responding to correspondence from Catherine.

On receipt of this letter, William decided an immediate response should be sent to the Minister for Lands, and two days later he sent the following letter to the Minister:

> I have the honour by request of Mrs Catherine Copley of the Parish of Moyston to acknowledge your communication --- asking for probate of Will of her late husband previous to the issue of her lease, and in reply to state that she is too poor to afford the cost of such instrument. (I know this of my own knowledge.) I here however enclose certificates of marriage and death of her late husband and sincerely trust the poor creature will shortly obtain her lease as she is making a hard struggle to keep her family together.[518]

The Lands Department took more than two months to consider this letter, but when they eventually responded they had not moved one inch from their previous position. In October, the department wrote to William and enquired 'if steps are being taken to obtain letter of administration'. The department asked for 'an immediate reply' to this request.[519]

The department was showing no understanding of Catherine's financial position and in fact was stepping up the pressure on her to go through the full probate process in relation to her entitlement to John's estate. The implication was clear that should she fail to do so, her only course of action was to abandon the selection. Although Catherine and her children had developed and worked the land for more than three and a half years, it appears that some senior people in the department were trying to make it as difficult as they possibly could for Catherine to obtain a lease covering the 125 acres.

The department's approach to Catherine was a strange one. The authorities knew that the 1869 Land Act clearly stated: 'No will or codicil or the granting of any probate or letters of administration' had any legal status in determining what should happen to land under a selection licence. This makes it clear that going to probate would make absolutely no difference to the status of Catherine's entitlement—it would simply be a considerable financial imposition on her. Undoubtedly the Lands Department was hoping that obstacles like this would weaken Catherine's determination. However, John's intentions were clear. His will clearly indicated that he wanted Catherine to remain on the selection and she had shown that she could fulfil all requirements necessary to obtain a lease. Catherine determined to proceed.

At same time as she was fighting the department to secure a selection lease on the 125 acres, Catherine was continuing to work to put herself in the strongest possible position to also secure a lease on the second selection of 115 acres. In September 1878, she paid the Lands Department the final two selection licence rental payments of £5/15/- each on this land.[520] She was telling the department that she was determined to secure selection leases covering the full 240 acres that she farmed at Jallukar.

William O'Callaghan responded quickly to the Lands Department's October 1878 letter that pressed Catherine to obtain letters of administration covering John Copley's estate. On 29 October 1878 he sent the following letter to the Minister for Lands:

> I have the honor to draw your attention to the application for lease, of Mrs Catherine Copley whose late husband was the licensee of a small piece of land in the ranges near Stawell and who died some time back in the Stawell Hospital and to state that the widow (Catherine Copley) has with her children continued to reside on the allotment referred to and effected the required improvements under difficulty being too poor to obtain letters of administration. She forwarded to the Department Certificate of her marriage and Registrars Certificate of Death of John Copley in August last ----- In doing this she has done all possible ------ for her to do ---- she is heroically maintaining her family from the small profits of a few head of cattle. If she obtains her lease she will battle on otherwise she will have to succumb. Trusting you will

direct the issue of her lease, the instrument of her future prospects.[521]

(At this time the word 'cattle' referred to all livestock on a farm; cows, sheep or pigs were all recorded as cattle.)

Following receipt of this letter, the Lands Department in Melbourne appeared to have finally moved significantly in its dealing with Catherine's lease and they determined to deal with it as a 'poor widow' case.[522]

In early November, the department wrote to Catherine enclosing a form that they requested she fill out and sign 'in the presence of a competent witness' and then return to them at her earliest convenience.[523]

It was 21 December 1878, before William returned this form to the Lands Department.[524] The main reason for the delay was that Catherine's two sons, John and James, had to sign one of the attached documents and at this time they were working with John's father-in-law, Robert Stonehouse, who was a blacksmith in Charlton 150 kilometres to the north of Jallukar. It took time for the documentation to be forwarded to John and James and then returned to William in Stawell. Four other documents that were cited as being required by the department were also attached to the form.[525]

The first attached document was the Lands Department pro forma 'poor widow' application form on which Catherine declared:

> I the undersigned being the widow of John Copley who selected the land specified in the margin hereof apply for a Lease to issue to me, being too poor to take out letters of administration to the estate or probate of the Will of my late husband and herewith forward the certificate of his death and the certificate of my marriage and supply the information hereunder which is true and correct.'

John's death certificate was attached to this document.

The second attached document was a statutory declaration where Catherine again confirmed that she was the widow of John Copley and that letters of administration of the estate 'have not been applied for or granted to any person'. Catherine also declared 'That I have paid and satisfied all debts due owing and payable by the said John Copley'.

The third attached document was the certificate of the marriage of John Copley and Catherine McMahon in Hobart Town on 15 March 1852. This certificate identifies both John and Catherine as pass holder convicts and so by December 1878 the department definitely knew about their convict past.

The fourth attached document was a declaration by Catherine's three surviving children. This letter was signed by John, James and Annie (Hannah) Copley. This declaration reads as follows:

> We the undersigned being the children of the late John Copley and Catherine Copley do hereby Consent to the issue of a lease of 125 acres land in the parish of Moyston formerly licensed to the late John Copley, to the above named Catherine Copley.

This document graphically shows the discriminatory and demeaning treatment of women that existed in relation to property. At this time, Catherine was fifty-two years of age. She had given birth to John, James and Hannah and coped with the loss of five other children. She had raised these three children and, along with John, provided for them through very tough times. Before he died, John had signed a will where he clearly indicated that he wanted Catherine to assume his position in relation to the Jallukar selections. Yet despite all this, Catherine's three children had to give their 'Consent' before she could be issued with the selection lease. The Lands Department appeared to believe that Catherine was not capable of making legitimate and reasonable decisions concerning what she wanted to do with her life without the approval of her children.

This discriminatory treatment of women in relation to property was far from unusual. In fact up until 1886 in the colony of Victoria, married women had no rights whatsoever to hold or own property and if a woman held or owned property, ownership automatically transferred to her husband upon marriage.

When by Christmas 1878 Catherine had still not received her selection lease for the land under Redman Bluff, she would have felt extremely frustrated. Nevertheless, the correspondence William had just sent off to the Lands Department would have led her to hope that her long wait would soon be over.

\*\*\*

Something much worse than mere frustration was about to ruin Christmas for the Copleys. Catherine was forced to watch as a bushfire raced across her land, destroying years of hard work.[526] It would have rivalled her most frightening experiences in the Van Diemen's Land convict system. We learn from Catherine's later application for a lease covering the 115 acre selection that the fire destroyed all the fences on this selection. These fences had measured 102 chains (more than 2000 metres) in length and had been of log and brush construction. We do not know what effect this bushfire had on the 125 acres where Catherine had two houses but it was unlikely that it survived completely unscathed.

The frightening and devastating effect of fire on the Australian bush is well known today. Residents in the Jallukar area are very well aware of the devastation that can be caused by bushfires. In January 2005, fires pushed by a strong, hot, north-westerly wind roared over the Grampian range into the Jallukar area. Lives were lost, and in one afternoon healthy bush and farm land was incinerated into grey powdered ash. We do not know the intensity of the fire that burnt Catherine's land in 1878 but we can be certain that it must have been truly frightening. At that time her nearest neighbour was five kilometres away and she was totally surrounded for kilometres by highly combustible bush land. Her two houses were constructed of wood and it would only have taken one piece of flying ash to set a bark roof alight in a flash. To make things worse, we know that earlier in December both John and James were living more than 150 kilometres away and we do not know whether they had returned to Jallukar for Christmas. It is quite likely that Catherine faced this bushfire with only her eighteen-year-old daughter Hannah for support.

While experiencing the bushfire must have been truly terrifying for Catherine, the financial consequences would have been devastating. We know from her 125 acre selection lease application that her log and brush fencing had been valued at five shillings and four pence a chain,[527] and this value was not contested by the Lands Department. In the Christmas 1878 bushfire she lost 102 chains of log and brush fencing which meant a loss of £27/10/8 just for fencing alone.[528] Of course, under the terms of this selection licence, Catherine was obliged to replace all this destroyed fencing. Most if not all of the grass was burnt and therefore this land had no or little value as grazing land for livestock until, at the earliest, the spring of 1879. On top of this, Catherine had to cope with the financial consequences of any fire damage to the land, fencing, crops, and houses on the 125 acre selection.

***

Meanwhile at the Lands Department office in Melbourne, the officials were experiencing further problems with the paperwork associated with Catherine's application for her first selection lease. In January 1879, the department wrote to William O'Callaghan at the Railway Hotel in Stawell seeking a copy of the death certificate for John Copley.[529]

In February 1879, William replied to this letter, enclosed yet another copy of John Copley's death certificate and stated that he trusted they would 'expedite the issue of her lease'.[530]

On 10 March the Lands Department completed the review of Catherine's 'poor widow' application for a lease. It noted that all the required documentation had been provided by Catherine and it recognized that £246/2/8 worth of improvements had been made to the 125 acre selection.[531] Here they acknowledged that Catherine had easily met the legislative requirement for selection improvements to entitle her to receive a lease.

In their review, the department made the following very legalistically worded recommendation: 'That the succession to the interest in the license pass to the widow.'[532] This recommendation was approved by the government and on 24 March 1879 the Lands Department wrote to Catherine informing her of this decision to issue her with a selection licence,[533] not the lease that she had been expecting.

Catherine would have been devastated. All her hard work had been in vain. She had applied for a lease, not a licence. The issuing of a licence put her back in exactly the same position John had been in more than four years earlier. It gave her no security of tenure on her land. Effectively what the department and the government were saying was that she had to work and develop this land for another three years before she could again apply for a lease. It was a decision that could have destroyed Catherine but she remained strong.

Never, in her original application and subsequent paperwork, had Catherine given any indication that she was seeking anything other than a lease. More importantly, in proposing the 'poor widow' approach to deal with Catherine's request, the department had never suggested that anything other than the granting of a lease was under consideration. Catherine decided that she would not accept this decision and determined to continue to press for a lease. Consequently, on 30 April 1879 William O'Callaghan sent the following letter to the Lands Department in Melbourne on her behalf:

> Referring to your letter dated 24/3/79 stating 'that the Governor in Council has sanctioned the issue of a <u>Licence</u> to Catherine Copley of the land held by her late husband -----.' As the land in question has been held under licence during the past five years, Mrs Copley requests me to apply on her behalf for the issue of her <u>lease</u>. She is very poor and the possession of that instrument would afford her temporary accommodation.[534]

At last a breakthrough occurred. After receiving this letter, the Lands Department finally backed off in its endeavours to deny Catherine a lease and on 8 May 1879 it determined that her request for a lease on the 125 acre selection would be approved.[535] Soon afterwards, this decision appeared in the government gazette. Catherine had won a significant battle but it was not to be her last battle with the authorities in relation to her Jallukar selections.

# 24 Catherine and the Squatters

At around the same time that Catherine finally received approval for her lease, she received notice from the Ararat Shire Council taking her to court for failure to pay rates to the shire. Since Catherine and John had first moved on to the 125 acres in 1875, no rates had been paid to the council. In contrast, when they lived on the Pentlands Creek selection they had paid the rates in full whenever they fell due.

It is not clear why the Copleys failed to pay their rates after their move to Redman Bluff. They appear to have gained no benefits or services from the council. They had provided their own access to their selection; making their way through isolated bush land where there were no established roads or tracks. They saw Stawell as their regional centre and market town and their contact with Ararat seems to have been limited to dealings with the regional office of the Lands Department.

Whatever the reason, on 27 June 1879 Catherine was called upon to appear in the Ararat Court of Petty Sessions to respond to an application from 'The President & Councillors & Ratepayers of the Shire of Ararat' for a judgment for her to pay £6 in rates to the Shire of Ararat.[536] Interestingly, while the shire council application in the court was for £6, the council rate book shows that she owed £3/15/-.[537]

Three days before she was due to appear in court, Catherine paid the council £1/1/-. The Shire rate book stated that this payment was for rates owed on 125 acres in Moyston parish, North Riding.[538] This rate payment was apparently part of an agreement she had negotiated with the Ararat Shire because the court minute book recorded that the Catherine Copley matter was 'settled'.[539] Catherine was no doubt pleased to avoid her first court appearance since 1851 in Hobart Town when she was found guilty of falsely representing that she had no shoes.

On 2 July Catherine requested that the Ararat Shire Council give her an exemption from paying any further rates that were owing because at this time she was unable to afford them.[540] She no doubt cited her losses caused by the bushfire in this letter.

It is not surprising that Catherine would make this request for an exemption and she was not the only person to do so. At its April meeting, the council received correspondence from Robert Spears, a farmer requesting an exemption from rates. The *Ararat Advertiser* on 8 April 1879 reported that Spears advised the council 'that a large portion of his land & fences had been burnt by the recent bush fires and consequently rendered useless and he was asking therefore that a proportionate reduction be made on his rates'. Spears held 1099 acres of land at Watgania,[541] where he had been established on the land since 1865.[542] In 1879, his annual rate bill from the council was £4/1/-.[543] After considering Spears' letter, the council determined that 'Collection of rates be not enforced against Robert Spears for the present owing to his grass and fences being burnt'.[544] Catherine was nowhere near as well established on the land as Spears and a large amount of her land and fences had also been burnt by the bushfires.

Unfortunately, the Ararat Shire Council did not view Catherine's request as sympathetically as they did that of Robert Spears and the minutes of the 4 July council meeting recorded that 'The request of Mrs Copley for exemption from rates was not entertained'.[545]

In accordance with this decision, on 8 July 1879 James McLean, the shire council secretary, wrote to Catherine stating: 'I have the honour to acknowledge the receipt of your letter of the 2nd instant asking remission of the rates due by you to the Shire Council, and in reply I am to inform you that the Council declines to comply with your request'.[546] Mclean then went on to state that Catherine must make arrangements to pay the £4/15/- she owed without delay. This time the rate books show Catherine owing only £2/14/-.[547]

The background of the members of the Ararat Shire Council may explain why they had so little sympathy for Catherine's request for a rates exemption. Eight of the nine shire council members attended the 4 July meeting, seven of whom were large land-holders. Three were squatters including the President of the Council, Cr William Hood, and between them they held over 66,000 acres in the shire. Four were graziers with substantial properties averaging around 2000 acres. The odd man out was Cr. George Harriott, a publican from Wickcliffe in the south of the shire with land-holdings of forty-two acres.[548] Secretly, Harriott probably welcomed the business he got from the selectors and their families.

The seven squatters or graziers on the shire council were among those who paid the bulk of the rates in the shire and they had multiple votes in council elections. Consequently they controlled the council. These people saw selectors such as Catherine as posing a threat to their idea of the proper utilization of the land in the shire. Catherine's selections were in prime squatting land at the very top of the watersheds that ran off Redman Bluff and Mount William. Squatting and grazing interests would have been concerned that if Catherine were successful on her land then other selectors would move into the area and into similar areas in the shire. Not only would this reduce the amount of land available for large scale grazing but, even more importantly, selectors would take a large proportion of the limited supply of available water for their cultivation and horticultural purposes. This would significantly reduce the water available for graziers and their livestock.

Catherine's response to the letter from the shire requesting prompt payment of the £4/15/- in rates was to do nothing. By the time she received this letter, her attention would have been dominated by a very important forthcoming family event—her daughter Hannah's wedding.

On 16 July, Hannah was married at the then recently constructed St

Patrick's Roman Catholic church in Stawell. St Patrick's was close to the Quartz Reefs where she had lived for a number of years as a child. The ceremony was conducted by the Stawell Catholic priest Father Fitzgerald. Hannah married Thomas Green a twenty-five-year-old bachelor who on their wedding certificate described himself as a 'farmer' and gave his usual place of residence as Jallukar. On the marriage certificate, nineteen-year-old Hannah gave her usual place of residence as Jallukar and in the section concerning 'rank/profession' she simply stated that she was 'living with mother'.[549] As Hannah was under twenty-one years of age, Catherine had to give her consent to the marriage. Like most mothers, Catherine would have experienced a mix of emotions as she watched her daughter's marriage and the one she must have felt most acutely was a great sense of loss. She would no longer have the full-time company, support and assistance of Hannah on her isolated Jallukar selections. The Copley family witness to Hannah's marriage was her brother James, who should have been very familiar with the new St Patrick's Church because descendants of James recall being told that he worked there as a stonemason during its construction. It appears that some time before his sister's wedding, James had returned from Charlton to live and work with his mother on their farm near Redman Bluff.

# 25  A Struggling Widow

By August 1879, the full three years on the second selection licence covering 115 acres had reached its expiry date and battle resumed with the Lands Department to secure Catherine's hold on all of the 240 acres of her land. When this licence expired, Catherine wasted no time waiting for the department to invite either her or John to put in an application for a selection lease and straight away submitted an application.

In her application Catherine declared that she had paid £34/10/-, which covered all the fees due on the August 1876 selection licence, and that she had 'complied with all the other conditions'.[550] She went on to state, 'within two years from the issue of the said Licence I enclosed the said allotment with a good and substantial fence'. She also informed the department that although 'The block was all fenced with log and brush but got entirely destroyed with bush fires last Christmas', the 115 acres were now 'all enclosed' with new fencing of 'Brush & spar' construction.[551]

She confirmed that she resided with her family on her leased land which adjoined this block and she declared that she had 'no other occupation'. She also stated that the 115 acres of land covered by this application was only suited for 'grazing purposes' and it was 'quite unfit for cultivation'.[552]

In her February 1878 lease application for the first 125 acre selection she had declared that 'No person' occupied 'the adjoining lands',[553] but now she acknowledged that she had squatters as neighbours and declared in her application that 'the occupiers of the adjoining lands' were 'Wilson & Co Squatters'.[554]

The squatting run on which John and Catherine had selected the 240 acres was the same Lexington squatting run that had covered the eighty acres of land near Pentlands Creek. In 1874, on the death of William J.T. Clarke, his land-holdings in Victoria, including the Lexington squatting run, were taken over by his son Sir William Clarke, who built the Rupertswood mansion near Sunbury. In the late 1870s, ownership of the Lexington squatting run passed to 'Wilson & Co.'[555] The 'Wilson' in Wilson & Co. was Alexander Wilson, who had operated large squatting runs in western Victoria since the 1840s.[556] In 1879, Wilson & Co. paid rates to the Ararat Shire on 7000 acres of squatting run land in the Jallukar Parish.[557]

In late August and early September, the Lands Department in Melbourne undertook an evaluation of Catherine's lease application.[558] The department determined that this application was in 'Substantial compliance' with the requirements for granting a lease. They determined that Catherine had made all the required licence payments and that the selection was fully fenced. They expressed some concern that only £25/10/- worth of improvements that been made to this selection, when under the 1869 Lands Act £1 worth of improvements were supposed to be made for each acre of land, but they overcame this concern by taking account of the £246 worth of improvements that had been made to the first 125 acre selection.[559] This meant that with a total of 240 acres of land, Catherine had made more than £270 worth of improvements and therefore the criteria of £1 worth of improvements for each acre had been met.

The department's response to this application from Catherine was to write to her in September and invite her to make a 'poor widow' application for a lease covering the 115 acres.[560]

Later that month, Catherine made contact with forty-three-year-old[561] Daniel J. Sullivan who was the head teacher at the Moyston State School.[562] Daniel Sullivan was born in Mitchelstown in County Cork and had migrated to Victoria in 1861.[563] Catherine needed to see him because she had to make a statutory declaration in front of an authorized person in support of her 'poor widow' application. It is quite possible that Catherine knew Sullivan before he signed her statutory declaration. As well as being a schoolteacher he was a botanist who, in the 1870s and 1880s, walked throughout the Grampians and identified over 700 different plant varieties in the mountains.[564] He is now recognized as having played a key role in bringing to public attention the breadth and beauty of the flora in the Grampian ranges and he was known to have a particular interest in the mosses and ferns located in the gullies in the Mount William Range. In exploring these gullies, it is quite likely that he occasionally called in at Catherine's home, isolated as it was at the base of Redman Bluff and Mount William.

Catherine duly placed her X on this statutory declaration and Sullivan certified that it had been signed in his presence. Catherine provided much the same information in this declaration as she had in the one that accompanied her earlier 'poor widow' lease application. The only real point of difference occurred in her response to the question: 'How many children have you? Give their names and ages. If any are of legal age their consent in writing, duly attested, must be forwarded herewith.' In reply, Catherine stated she had three children but she only gave the required details for 'John Copley twenty-six years' and 'James Copley twenty-four years'.[565] She failed to give the required details concerning the name and age of her daughter Hannah and she did not include their written consent.

Catherine was obviously worried. Since December 1878, when she filled in this same form, Hannah had married and was now Hannah Green. Apparently Catherine feared that if the Lands Department knew her youngest child was no longer dependant upon her, it would harm her chances of gaining approval for this selection lease application.

In early October, the Lands Department reviewed Catherine's 'poor widow' application. The department file noted that the required documentation had been 'duly filed' but predictably it was determined to ask for the consent of her children of legal age.[566] In late October, Catherine was again requested to provide written consent from her children if she were to be granted a lease.[567]

While Catherine normally responded promptly to Lands Department requests, it took her three months to do so on this occasion. There must have been considerable family discussion about how Hannah should sign this document. When the document was finalized, it was headed 'Moyston Jan 7th 1880' and it read: 'We the undersigned being the Children of the late John Copley and of the applicant for Lease 115 acres parish of Moyston do hereby Consent to the offer of the Lease to our Mother Catherine Copley'. Below this statement were the signatures: 'John Copley, James Copley and Annie Copley'. In the end, Hannah did not sign the document under her married name but under her maiden name as Catherine's dependant daughter. A carefully worded letter from William O'Callaghan dated 24 January 1880 accompanied this document. It read: 'Herewith are the names of Mrs Copley's children as requested by you in your letter of 20th October which I beg to enclose here'.[568]

In late January and early February 1880, the necessary approvals were given by the Lands Department,[569] and after a long drawn out struggle Catherine and John's dream of land ownership was finally realized.

*\*\**

While this was certainly very good news, by this time Catherine was in significant financial trouble. By February 1880 she owed the Lands Department £42/15/- in lease payment arrears and £4 for the issuing of the lease documentation covering the two selections. This was a grand total of £46/15/-. As well as this she owed the Ararat Shire Council £4/10/- for rates and she was still suffering from the devastating financial consequences of the Christmas 1878 bushfire and no doubt from the costs associated with Hannah's wedding.

Catherine could have been excused for thinking it was all too difficult, but she obviously got the best advice she could and determined on a course of action. She wanted to stay on her land and she hoped that the 1880 Land Act that had just gone through the Victorian parliament was going to help her to do so. Her first move was to ask that the department bring her two selection leases under the terms of new provisions in the 1880 Act.[570] Under the 1869 Land Selection Act, Catherine had to pay two shillings rent per acre per year. This meant that on her 240 acres of selected land she would have had to pay £24 a year to the Lands Department in lease payments. However, section 3 of the new Act provided that these lease payments could be set at one shilling per acre per year and this would halve Catherine's annual lease payments. The total amount that Catherine would eventually be liable to pay the Lands Department was not reduced by the 1880 changes to the land selection laws; it simply meant that she would be required to make these lease payments for fourteen years rather than for seven.

Catherine was not just seeking to bring her leases under the 1880 Land Act for future lease payments, but she also wanted the department to retrospectively apply these provisions to the back payments she owed on both selections. This would make the amount she owed far more manageable. Both she and John had lost everything when he was declared insolvent in 1856, and she had no desire to repeat this experience. She was doing everything possible to avoid it.

In seeking support to get her two selections under the 1880 Land Act, Catherine sent a letter to Mr David Gaunson, MLA, member of parliament for the lower house seat of Ararat.[571] The geographic area of the seat of Ararat included Jallukar and Catherine's selections. Although Catherine did not get a vote, Gaunson was her local member of parliament.

28. David Gaunson, the MP for Ararat from 1875 to 1881.

We cannot be absolutely sure who wrote the

May 1880 letter to Gaunson for Catherine but the handwriting style of this letter is very similar to that of Daniel Sullivan, the botanist and head teacher at the Moyston school.[572]

Catherine was very fortunate to have Gaunson as her local member. At that time, he was considered a leading Australian-born liberal MP and a prominent member of the colony's parliament. He was admitted as an attorney to the Melbourne bar in 1869 and while in parliament continued to practise as a lawyer. Two months after Catherine sent her letter, Gaunson was engaged as legal counsel in defence of the bushranger Ned Kelly, after Kelly's arrest in July 1880 at the Glenrowan siege. From August to November 1880, he was prominent in conducting Kelly's legal defence, arranging a mass meeting in support of Kelly and, after he was sentenced to death, presenting a petition in support of clemency for him.

Catherine wrote as follows in her late May 1880 letter to Gaunson:

> Being a struggling widow I believe I am right in thinking that you would kindly assist me under present difficulties. I am behind in my rent through family misfortunes and want, if it can be done, my land (240 acres) brought under the new regulations viz the payment of 1 shilling per acre per annum. Also please let me know if the back rent could be brought under that head. By assisting me on this matter you would confer a great boon on me just now. The land is situated near Mount William in the Parish of Moyston.
>
> I am, Dear Sir,
>
> Yours truly
>
> Mrs Catherine Copley[573]

On reading this letter, Gaunson forwarded it to George Arthur Walstab, the senior clerk in the Department of Lands with an accompanying note that stated 'Please see what can be done & kindly inform me'.[574]

This letter, in Catherine's own name, is the first letter concerning her land selection problems that did not come under the name of William

O'Callaghan. The reason for this was that in March 1880 William had, at his fourth attempt, been elected as a member of the Victorian parliament.[575] He was elected by a comparatively small margin, as one of the two members for the lower house seat of Wimmera that covered tens of thousands of square kilometres of countryside to the west and north of Stawell. William now had his own responsibilities for an electorate that did not cover Catherine's selection at Jallukar. Nevertheless, it cannot have done any harm to Catherine's cause that William O'Callaghan, who had strongly supported her, was now a member of the Victorian parliament.

The letter to David Gaunson does seem to have assisted Catherine. Soon after Gaunson's note was received by Walstab, Catherine was provided with the necessary application forms and, on 15 July 1880, she submitted two Lands Department applications for both her Jallukar selections to come under the 1880 Land Act provisions.[576] In both applications Catherine stated: 'In explanation of my rent not being fully paid up to date I have to state that I cannot take up my lease unless it is transferred to section 3 Land Act 1880'.

While the Lands Department was considering what to do with Catherine's application, the Ararat Shire Council was considering what to do about overdue rate payments. On 8 August 1880 the *Ararat Advertiser* reported that at the monthly council meeting the 'President drew attention to the fact that there was a very considerable falling off in the money coming in from rates'. After discussion, the shire council decided to adopt what is known in the twenty-first century as a name and shame policy and endorsed the following resolution: 'That an advertisement be inserted in the newspaper calling on all rate payers to pay their rates during the current month after which legal proceedings to be taken and the names of all defaulters advertised in the local paper'.[577]

On 10 September, the Ararat Shire Council followed through with the threat contained in the resolution and a very large advertisement appeared in that day's edition of the *Ararat Advertiser* headed:

SHIRE OF ARARAT

Rate payers in Arrear Up to 31st March 1880

There were then 198 names listed under the various parishes that made up the shire but the two relevant to our story were: 'Copley, John = £1/5/-, Copley, Catherine = £6/10/-.'

Just in case the very public naming of these tardy ratepayers had not been enough to remind them of their responsibilities to the shire, the advertisement concluded with the threat that: 'Orders have been issued by the Shire Council that the above names be handed to the Shire Solicitor who will take immediate legal proceedings for the recovery of the several sums'.

According to this advertisement, only two of the 198 rate payers listed owed more than Catherine and she was by far the worst of the defaulters in the Parish of Jallukar. However, once again the actual shire council rate book for this year showed a somewhat different story, with Catherine listed as owing £4/10/-.[578]

The 'Copley, John' listed as owing '£1/5/-' was Catherine's son John. There was no justification for the shire council citing John as having overdue rates. Council claimed that the rates were owed on the forty acre selection at Jallukar that bordered Thomas May's land, but, as we know, at the conclusion of the three year licence period John did not proceed to take out a lease and he abandoned the selection. At the end of the three year licence period, John was fully up to date with shire council rate payments. The alleged rate arrears accrued from the period after mid-1876 when he had already left the selection.

After this advertisement appeared in the local newspaper, it seems the Ararat Shire Council received a fair amount of criticism. Between October and December 1880, the shire council acknowledged that two people named in the 10/9/1880 advertisement in fact owed no rates at all and the council apologized to these rate payers.[579]

Also, as the weeks went by, the Ararat Shire Council was shown to be a paper tiger. It did not follow through with its threat to take to court rate payers who were overdue in making payments and in fact, in the period between September 1880 and May 1881, it did not initiate any court proceedings for overdue rates. Possibly the council had second thoughts about the wisdom of this course of action. The pursuit of rate arrears through the courts would have caused a problem for them. In 1879, Justice Sir Redmond Barry in a court decision in Melbourne determined that courts could not give orders for court costs against rate payers in cases where councils were claiming payment of overdue rates.[580] This decision was subsequently upheld in April 1881 in a case in the Ararat Court of Petty Sessions.[581] This meant the Ararat Shire Council would have faced a very hefty legal bill if it had followed through with its threat of legal action.

After this advertisement appeared in the *Ararat Advertiser*, Catherine made no move to make any rate payments to the Ararat Shire Council. It is possible that this advertisement made Catherine even more determined to avoid paying her rates.

# 26   The Upright Thing

Catherine spent more than two months waiting to hear the Lands Department's decision on her application for her selection leases to be brought under the provisions of the 1880 Land Act. It was not the issue of the two selections coming under the new lease provisions that was causing this delay. It was her request that the lease payment provisions apply retrospectively to when the selection licences concluded in February 1878 and August 1879. The Lands Department had to decide when the two new leases would take effect and what payments Catherine owed the department.

There appeared to be differing views within the department on this issue. Depending on which side carried the day, Catherine could have been required to pay either a maximum of £60/15/- or a minimum of £4. The £4 would cover the cost of the establishment of the leases, and once that was paid she would only be required to make lease payments from the time of issue of the two new leases. Catherine would not have dreamed of asking for such a favourable deal as this.

By 7 October it appeared the Lands Department had reached a final position when its Secretary wrote to Catherine confirming that her two selections would be covered under the lease provisions in the new 1880 Land Act. While we do not have a copy of this letter, subsequent correspondence from Catherine asserted that in this letter, the department agreed to issue the new leases on the payment of the £4 in establishment fees. The department's position in this letter apparently was that the issue of rent arrears will 'stand over' and the letter apparently contained nothing concerning the commencement date of the two new leases under the new Act.[582]

Soon after receiving this letter, Catherine attended the Ararat office of the Lands Department and paid the department the £4 fee.[583] George F. Clarke, the senior department officer at the Ararat office, was not happy with the departmental decision. He felt that Catherine should not be granted her new leases without paying approximately £28 as well as her £4. This £28 would cover lease payments back to the dates when the licences expired and it was in fact what Catherine had initially applied for.

The key decision makers in the Lands Department ignored Clarke. Once the Melbourne office of the Lands Department received the £4 in lease establishment fees it followed through with implementing the terms of the 7 October letter to Catherine and on 15 November 1880 the Governor in Council approved Catherine's new lease covering the 125 acre selection.[584] In early December, approval was granted for the new lease covering the second selection of 115 acres.[585]

However, some people in the Lands Department supported Clarke's view, and even after the Governor had signed both documents approving Catherine's new leases they still tried to force her to pay the £28 in arrears covering her 240 acres at Jallukar. Throughout December 1880, the department sent letters to Catherine demanding the payment of lease arrears before she could receive the new selection leases even though they had already been approved by the Governor.[586]

After she received these letters Catherine realized that she still had a serious problem, so once again she visited the Railway Hotel in Stawell. On this occasion, she was assisted by Daniel O'Callaghan, the twenty-one-year-old son of William. In reply to the December 1880 Lands Department letters, Catherine sent the following letter, drafted by Daniel, to the Secretary of the Lands Department:

I have to acknowledge receipt of your communication dated 7$^{th}$ and 24$^{th}$ December wherein you demand payment of arrears of rent prior to the issue of a new lease. I desire respectfully to draw your attention to the contents of your letter bearing date 7$^{th}$ October 1880 in which the Department agrees to issue the new lease upon payment ----- fees for preparation. I cannot now understand how after your correspondence on the subject I am having paid the necessary fees you should make this request for payment of the arrears.[587]

Catherine further stated that she was led to believe that everything was settled and that the department was satisfied. The letter went on to conclude:

I may say that to comply with this the last and most extraordinary (under the circumstances) request would mean ruination to me and further that after the R&P [Receiver and Paymaster—Lands Department] at Ararat having accepted my money that it is not the upright thing now for the Lands Department to go back on their agreement with me which I shall not now go back from myself.

I will esteem it a favour if you say it is not the determination of the Department to enforce this claim prior to the issue of the new Lease.

I am Sir, your obedient servant,
Catherine Copley[588]

In sending this letter, Catherine was no doubt focusing on obtaining the new selection leases without having to pay rent arrears but, as a former transported convict, she may well have gained some pleasure from telling a senior government official that his department was not doing 'the upright thing'.

The Lands Department continued to push for payment[589] and Catherine received two more letters demanding that she pay the rent arrears on both selections before the new selection leases would be issued.[590]

Then the department appeared to retreat a little from its hardline position and forwarded Catherine the formal lease documentation covering the new selection lease for the 115 acres.[591] However, she still was not given the agreement document covering the 125 acre selection where the better land was and where her house was sited. A further visit to the Railway Hotel was required and in March 1881, Daniel O'Callaghan sent a letter to the Secretary of the Lands Department stating:

> What appears to be strange to Mrs Copley is the receipt by her of two letters from the Department --- demanding again the arrears that you so long since agreed to have stand over. She cannot understand too why the other Lease (that for 125 acres in the same parish) has not been sent up.
>
> It would be much more satisfactory if she could understand from the Department thoroughly the intentions of the Secretary in her case as today she is told by letter the arrears will stand over and tomorrow from another branch of the office that they must be paid now.[592]

On receipt of this correspondence, an officer at the Lands Department in Melbourne noted in the file that the lease documentation covering the 125 acre selection had been sent off to the Ararat office for execution on 14 January.[593] It appears that George Clarke had decided to hold on to this documentation and continue to press Catherine to pay rent arrears to the department.

While Clarke wanted to continue the battle with Catherine,[594] on 11 March 1881, more than three years after she first applied for a selection lease, the board of the Lands Department in Melbourne decided that it would finally settle the disputes in relation to her selections. On this day, the board determined that 'Both leases endorsed for 14 years from 1/1/81'.[595] This meant the department would not pursue her for any rent arrears and that payments under the new selection leases would only be payable from the stated date.

This final settlement was in fact far better than Catherine had asked for in her letter to David Gaunson, MLA. In this letter, Catherine had simply requested that the reduced one shilling per acre lease payment provisions in the new 1880 Land Act be applied from when the three year licences on both selections had expired. If her request had been granted she would have had to pay the Lands Department £24/10/-, then not an insignificant sum. However, as a result of the settlement no arrears at all had to be paid, only the £4 in lease establishment fees. Catherine could not have wished for a more favourable outcome.

By March 1881, four and a half years after the death of her husband, Catherine had, against all the odds, developed a 240 acre working farm at Jallukar. Additionally, she had gained secure tenure over this land. In doing so, she had achieved a major victory over the bureaucrats in the Lands Department and the squatting and large grazing interests in the Shire of Ararat. It had been a long drawn out and no doubt very exhausting struggle for a largely illiterate woman, but luck had been with her when she met William O'Callaghan, his son Daniel and Daniel Sullivan—three men who had significantly assisted her.

## 27   Working the Land

In 1881, after she obtained the new leases covering both her Jallukar selections, Catherine paid £12 to the Lands Department.[596] This payment fully met her obligation in terms of lease payments from the commencement of the new selection leases. Now that her struggles with the department were finally over, she could concentrate on working and improving her land.

In the same year, an incident occurred that showed how very different the system of justice in the colony of Victoria was to that which had applied in the 1840s in Ireland. In the second half of 1881 a local selector, Joseph Marshall, was charged with stealing two sheep from the Mokepilly squatting run. At this time Mokepilly carried over 10,000 sheep. The police presented evidence to the court that Marshall sold two sheep skins bearing the Mokepilly brand to a police officer, Constable Hadfield, who was disguised as a sheep hide and skin dealer. The Stawell jury that considered this case determined that there was not enough evidence to convict Marshall and that selling the skins with a value of £6 could not be considered a serious crime.[597] This jury was made up of a cross section of the local male population. This contrasted with the juries that convicted John and Catherine of sheep stealing in the 1840s. They were solely made up of men of financial substance most of whom owned a significant amount of property. If Catherine had heard of this case she would have been amazed at the changes that had occurred in the years since her own conviction in 1849.

1881 was also a significant year in the life of Catherine's neighbour

Thomas May. He now had no selection lease payments to make to the Lands Department. On 22 October 1880, Thomas had paid his last £3/8/- lease payment on his sixty-seven acre selection at Jallukar.[598] Since 1874, when he had come close to being thrown off his selection, Thomas had kept up to date with his lease payments and in November 1880 he was given full title to his land. This was a considerable achievement for Thomas, growing up as he did in the worst of the back streets of Brighton and then being transported to Van Diemen's Land as a juvenile convict.

On 18 January 1882, life changed again for Catherine when her second son, James, celebrated his marriage to Mary McGee, a twenty-five-year-old spinster who had been born in County Londonderry in the north of Ireland. Her family had migrated to Victoria when she was one year old and before her wedding she lived at Jallukar on her father's selection. The celebration took place in Stawell and the marriage was conducted by Father Fitzgerald at St Patrick's Catholic church.[599] James had been living on the selection with Catherine since Hannah's marriage, but now Catherine must have been aware that sooner rather than later she would be left alone at Mountain Hut.

In August 1882, the Ararat Shire Council again considered the situation with arrears in the payment of shire rates and at their monthly council meeting they ordered that 'the usual steps be taken for the recovery of all outstanding rates'.[600] Catherine had made no further rate payments to the council since 24 June 1879 and the shire rate book showed that she now owed £7/13/-.[601] Although she continued her non-payment of rates, no legal action was taken against her.

This habitual non-payment only applied to shire council rates and Catherine made regular lease payments to the Lands Department. There appears to have been no problems with the financial performance of her Jallukar farm because in this year she paid three rather than the required two selection lease payments.[602] This meant she forwarded £18 to the Lands Department and this extra payment put her six months ahead in paying off the selection leases. Obviously the monies used for this extra payment could have been used to pay the council but Catherine appears to have been hostile to the Ararat Shire Council. She cannot have been impressed with the September 1880 name and shame council advertisement in the *Ararat Advertiser* which named her son John as being in arrears in rate payments when in fact he was not. Also since her contact with Ararat was still very limited, it is possible that she felt under no obligation to give the shire any of her hard earned cash.

By 1883, none of Catherine's children were living with her on an ongoing basis on the Jallukar selection. Hannah lived in Stawell with her husband Thomas and James and Mary had moved from Jallukar to Whittlesea sixty kilometres north of Melbourne, where he was working as a quarryman.[603] In the 1880s, a building boom was taking place in Melbourne and there was great demand for skilled labour in the building industry and in the industries that serviced and supplied it. At this time John, Jane and their children were Catherine's nearest family because John had again taken up a Jallukar selection.

While in 1883 Catherine was having less contact with her children, Thomas May was starting to have a considerable amount of contact with those same small creatures that had led to his downfall in the past—rabbits. At Jallukar at this time, rabbits were no longer the cute novelty that they had been in the late 1860s. On 20 October 1883 the *Pleasant Creek News and Stawell Chronicle* reported, 'We learn that rabbits are beginning to make their appearance at Mokepilly station in considerable number' and Mokepilly station was within five kilometres of Thomas's selection. The newspaper story went on: 'A gentleman who was in that district a few days ago, states that he met with scores in every direction in which he travelled, and that there is every appearance of the plague assuming formidable proportions if active steps be not taken to destroy the vermin'.

Thomas would not have escaped their assault on his land and crops. Undoubtedly they would have been damaging the grain and vegetables he was growing on his sixty-seven acres. Still the situation was not all bad—this rapid growth in the rabbit population provided a cheap source of meat. Thomas was probably not cooking rabbit pies like the bakers did in Brighton in 1841, but almost certainly he was cooking rabbit stew and adding his own home-grown vegetables.

In 1884, despite his rabbit problems, Thomas made a bold decision to take on a new land selection at Jallukar. Since he first selected land there in 1871, the number of selectors in the area had steadily increased. The development of Jallukar can be seen by the opening of a post office in 1884.[604] Much of the land around Thomas's selection had by now been taken up by members of the Morcom family, the Hold family and a Frenchman, Peter DeMay.[605] It would have been clear to Thomas at this time that it was now or never if he was going to take up additional land near his existing holding.

On 15 October 1884 he took the plunge and submitted an application to the Lands Department Surveyor at Ararat for a selection licence covering more than 200 acres of land half a kilometre to the north of his existing selection. In this application, Thomas gave his address as Jallukar, C/o the Golden Age Hotel, Stawell.[606]

In January 1885, the Lands Department completed a survey of the land covered by this licence application and it was found to cover 224 acres and 25 perches. The surveyor reported that the land was undulating and that the soil was sandy. He further reported that the vegetation on the land was made up of wattle, honeysuckle, gum, ferns and grass-tree.[607] The Lands Department received no objections to the proposed selection from the Mines Department or from anyone else and the application for a selection licence was approved by the Governor in Council on 16 June.[608] Thomas, at fifty-seven years of age, had his new selection.

The terms of this selection licence were very similar to the licence he had been granted in 1871. The major difference was that under the 1880 Land Act, the selection licence lasted for six years rather than three. With this increased time frame he was required to pay annual licence payments of one shilling rather than two shillings per acre. This meant that for the six year period of the licence, twelve payments of £5/12/6 had to be made to the Lands Department at six monthly intervals.[609] He was also to cultivate at least twenty-three acres and make a minimum of £225 worth of improvements to the selection.

If all twelve payments were made to the Lands Department and the required improvements were made to the selection, Thomas would be entitled to obtain a selection lease covering this land in June 1891. In 1885, Thomas would have known that land values were increasing substantially beyond the £1 per acre value that applied under the land selection laws and he would have been well aware that if he could achieve a selection lease then he would almost certainly be able to make a large capital gain on selling the land.

While Thomas was applying for and obtaining his new selection licence, Catherine continued to make the required lease payments on her land. In each of the years 1883, 1884 and 1885, she made two payments of £6 to the Lands Department.[610] With the other payments she had made since the 1881 start of the new selection leases, she now only had to pay a further £102 in lease payments over the next ten years to have full title to the 240 acres at Jallukar. With rising land values, she was now in a strong financial position. Catherine must have seen this as vindication of the belief that she and John had shared—that possessing and owning land was the means to provide economic security for themselves and their family.

*\*\**

Although Catherine was making her required payments to the Lands Department, she had paid no monies to the shire council since 1879. At the start of 1885, the Ararat Shire rate records show that Catherine owed £9/15/- in rates,[611] and at this time the shire council decided that it would adopt a more aggressive approach with her. On 27 January James Maclean, Shire Secretary and Collector, wrote as follows to 'Mrs Catherine Copley, Jallukar': 'I beg to remind you that you are now due rates to the council of this shire amounting to £11/10/- and that you are hereby notified to pay the same within one week from this date otherwise my instructions are to take legal steps for the recovery of same.'[612]

Catherine's response to this letter was to do nothing within the one week deadline. However, on 13 February she paid £1/15/- to the shire council in rates. The council rate book states that this was for rates that fell due in 1876.[613] After she made this payment, there is no record of the shire council taking any legal action against her. Later in 1885, Catherine went further, and on 29 August she paid £9 to the Ararat Shire Council.[614] With new rates that had fallen due during the year, this meant that she was now only 15 shillings in arrears in rate payments.

We do not know why Catherine finally paid the vast bulk of her rate arrears. She may have believed that the shire council really was just about to take her to court and she may not have relished the idea of facing yet another struggle with, this time, a local government authority.

\*\*\*

By 1886, it must have been apparent to Catherine that there was little prospect that any of her children and their families would be interested in living with her full time on her Jallukar selections.

On 1 March of that year her eldest son, John, sent a letter to the Minister for Lands that showed what he considered to be a priority in relation to where his family resided. He wished to obtain a selection of one hundred acres in Jallukar which he understood was open for leasing or selection. He gave his reason for wanting this selection closer to town: 'As I am situated far back in the bush and 8 miles from the nearest school the land would be most convenient for me for educating my children as it is impossible to send young children such a distance through scrubby country'.[615]

John may have been slightly exaggerating in suggesting that his existing selection was eight miles from the nearest school but the crucial point is clearly made—it was a threshold issue to John that wherever he and his family lived they needed good access to education. When he wrote this letter to the Minister for Lands, John and Jane had five children. They saw it as essential that these children learn to read and write. His mother's dependence on William O'Callaghan to help her secure tenure on her selections would have reinforced John's belief in the vital importance of literacy. Obviously neither John nor Jane would have been interested in moving their children further into the 'bush' and 'scrubby country' to where his mother lived in the isolation of Mountain Hut.

By 1886, Hannah had three children and she and her husband Thomas Green showed no desire to move full time to Catherine's Jallukar selection. At around this time, Hannah and Thomas did show interest in taking up a selection but it was located at Bellellen[616] where there was a school and where they would have been in close proximity to Stawell.

Catherine's second son, James, also showed no interest in moving back to Jallukar and in fact his life was heading in the opposite direction. In 1886 or 1887, he moved from Whittlesea to live in the Melbourne suburb of Footscray where he worked as a quarryman.[617] In Footscray, James and his wife Mary had access to education for their two young daughters and at this time there was plenty of well paying work in Melbourne associated with the building and construction industry.

Once Catherine realized that her children had no desire to return to Mountain Hut and work with her on her selection, she must have begun to question whether she herself should continue to stay on this land. She was now nearly sixty years old and no doubt was still working hard to maintain and further develop her property. Due to these demands and the isolated location of the selection, she would not have been able to see anywhere near as much as she would have liked of her three children and their growing families. It would have been a lonely and isolated existence. While Catherine's childhood and upbringing at Cappabane had been firmly based on working on the land, it was working the land as a total family activity involving her parents, brothers and to a lesser extent the neighbouring families. This was not the situation on her 240 acre selection. Catherine had a decision to make.

\*\*\*

In March 1887, Catherine took out a mortgage covering the 115 acre selection lease. This mortgage was with a gentleman identified as Archibald Gray.[618] We do not know why she took out this mortgage, the value of the mortgage or its terms, but we do know that at this time Catherine was six months ahead in her lease payments on both selections. She was also up to date in her rate payments to the Ararat Shire Council. We can only speculate that she may have needed the money for some improvement to the selection or to her house or she may have been using her now substantial equity in the 240 acres of land to provide funds to assist a family member or friend.

\*\*\*

By July 1888, Catherine had finally made a decision concerning her future. On 25 July the ownership of the two selection leases covering the 240 acres of land near Redman Bluff was sold to Ronald MacMaster, a farmer who lived at Lake Bolac,[619] fifty kilometres south of Ararat. The MacMasters were a Catholic family who originally migrated to Victoria from Scotland. We do not know how much Catherine received from Ronald MacMaster for these two leases, but when she sold them there was only a further £78 that had to be paid to the department for full ownership of the land to be granted.[620]

The first 125 acre selection contained a substantial amount of good agricultural land. Even into the 1950s, when hardly any vegetables were grown in the Jallukar area, crops of potatoes were still being regularly planted and harvested on land within this selection lease.[621] Additionally, two creeks ran through the 125 acres carrying rain that fell on Redman Bluff and Mount William. Today a number of dams are located on these creeks and this was an improvement that could have been made at any time to ensure a secure year round water supply for the selections. There were few selection blocks anywhere in the Ararat and Stawell areas that could provide such a secure water supply. This 125 acres was good land.

The second 115 acre selection was only fit for grazing and therefore it would not have had the same value. Indeed, we do not know whether this block had been fully cleared of the heavy timber cover that was on it in 1876 when John first received the selection licence. Nevertheless, by 1888 this land would have been worth substantially more than the £1 per acre value that applied under the Land Selection Acts.

No doubt the isolated location of this land had a slightly negative impact on the amount Catherine received from Ronald MacMaster. However, by the late 1880s land values had increased substantially and she would have made at least £500 on selling these two selections. This was a considerable sum of money at that time. At sixty-one years of age, this money should have been enough to provide her with financial security into old age.

In selling and leaving these two selections, Catherine did so at a time of her choosing and on her terms. This compared very favourably with the situation she found herself in nearly twelve years earlier when John died. If she had not then developed the land and fought to gain selection leases she would have been forced to leave with nothing.

Fifty-two years earlier, the explorer Major Mitchell had declared that the Jallukar area was 'destined perhaps to become eventually a position of great empire'.[622] In 1888 there was no 'great empire' in the Jallukar area, but surely it was a far greater achievement that a society had been established where a woman who had been transported to Australia as a convict had been able to achieve secure tenure over 240 acres of land, farm that land successfully and then receive a substantial sum of money when she decided to leave the land. Catherine had not given in to hunger and despair in famine-ridden County Clare and she did not give up on the land that she and John had selected. It was a remarkable achievement.

## PART SIX
## CATHERINE AND THOMAS

# 28 Thomas Secures his Selection

It appears highly likely that for most of the time between August 1888 and May 1891 Catherine lived in Stawell near the Quartz Reefs. In 1889, a woman identified as Elizabeth Copley, widow, first appeared in the Borough of Stawell rate book as living at Fisher Street, near the Quartz Reefs.[623] This woman continued to be listed in the Stawell rate book as living at Fisher Street until 1892,[624] but we could find no trace of her on the public record after this date. This was the area of Stawell where Catherine had resided during the late 1860s. On 9 October 1890, Hannah Green gave birth to her fifth child, a boy, at the home of 'Mrs Copley' in Fisher Street.[625] Although the rate book shows the Mrs Copley at this address to be named Elizabeth, it was almost certainly Catherine, as it is reasonable to believe that Hannah gave birth to this child at her mother's house and not that of a stranger. No explanation, however can be offered for the use of the Christian name Elizabeth.

In the 1880s and early 1890s Stawell was a considerably different place to live than on the 240 acres of land under Redman Bluff. There was not the natural beauty of the Grampian mountains or the morning chorus of the cockatoos and kookaburras. Instead, the mining operations at the Quartz Reefs went twenty-four hours a day, six days a week, and miners and carters bringing supplies such as timber to the mines were on the move from early morning until late in the evening. The sound of quartz crushing operations

29. Stawell in 1880 from the top of the Quartz Reefs. St Patrick's Catholic church (left) is located on Patrick Street.

was an ever-present background noise in the Quartz Reefs area. Perhaps the regular social events and entertainments in the town provided some compensation for this noisy, dusty, industrial environment.

One such entertainment that caused a sensation in Stawell occurred on 13 August 1890. It involved 'Professor Price' inflating a canvas hot air balloon measuring seventy-five feet in height and 150 feet in circumference and rising to 3000 feet above the town. As if this was not exciting enough for the residents, when the balloon reached this height, the Professor's 'aeronaut' assistant 'Mdlle Millie Viola', her 'petite figure' arrayed in 'a tight fitting costume', successfully parachuted from the balloon to the ground.[626] Such entertainment was certainly not available on the farming selections near Redman Bluff!

\*\*\*

In the second half of the 1880s, Thomas May had his hands full with his new 224 acre Jallukar selection. The main reason for this was its size; it was three times larger than the sixty-seven acre selection he took up in 1871 and which he still continued to farm. Nevertheless, this new selection had some positive features. Under the 1880 Land Act provisions, he had six years to fully fence the boundaries, rather than the two years allowed in the 1869 Land Act. Also, some of the boundaries bordered directly on existing selections that were already fully fenced.[627] By 1891 he had cultivated forty acres of the land covered by the new selection licence. On this cultivated land, he grew wheat, oats, peas, carrots and other root crops. He also grew wattle trees as a harvested crop.[628] The wattle tree was not grown to provide food for human consumption. Its value was in the bark of the tree that was used as a dye.

By this time, Thomas would have been facing a seemingly endless battle with rabbits that were by now in plague numbers throughout the Ararat Shire. His grain and vegetable crops and his pasture land would have been under constant rabbit attack and to limit his losses to these pests he would have had to spend a large amount of time trapping and killing them. At this time, the rabbit plague was so bad that the Ararat Shire Council spent several hundred pounds a year on rabbit extermination programmes and employed a full-time rabbit inspector, paid £225, to oversee these programmes. In 1887, the Ararat Shire paid a bounty of one shilling for each 24 rabbit 'scalps' that were brought in to the council.[629]

Surely, while engaged in this seemingly never-ending quest to exterminate the rabbits on his selection, Thomas occasionally thought about the changing value of rabbits. In 1841 in Brighton, he sold one of John Parsons' rabbits for five shillings. In 1887, he would have needed to capture and kill 120 rabbits to be paid five shillings by the Ararat Shire. What a fortune he could have made if, as a juvenile in Brighton, he had had access to all these rampaging Jallukar rabbits!

The ingenuity of farmers in the Stawell district as they attempted to control the rabbit plague is seen in an article in the *Pleasant Creek News and Stawell Chronicle* in April 1891 where a farmer stated that his poison jam method 'surpasses everything else that he has used' to eradicate rabbits. The farmer's formula for poison jam involved combining 'fruit 18lb, common sugar 12lbs and 1 once of strychnine …boiled together for several hours until thoroughly mixed'. This produced a concoction that contained twelve grains of strychnine in each ounce of jam. The potency of this brew is seen when you consider that three grains of strychnine are enough to kill a man.[630]

After producing this poison jam, the farmer then ladled it onto pieces of bark 'in the vicinity of the burrows'. In ladling out the jam, the farmer had to be careful not to touch the bark because 'the rabbits are exceedingly keen in detecting' human contact. The farmer then recounted that 'the bunnies eat the jam greedily'. On one occasion, 'a very small quantity' of jam 'laid around one burrow over night produced 118 dead rabbits in the morning'. The jam was so potent that the rabbits died before they could return to their burrows.[631] We do not know whether Thomas had his own potent formula for poison jam but we can be sure that farmers like Thomas would be desperate for a solution to this problem.

In either late 1890 or early 1891, Thomas sold the sixty-seven acres of land he had first selected in 1871 to Dr William Symes, a surgeon in Stawell.[632] We do not know his reason for selling this land but no doubt his priority at the time would have been getting a selection lease covering his 224 acres. Since taking out the selection licence on this land in 1885, Thomas had been six months behind in making the six monthly licence payments on two occasions,[633] so the money from the sale of the sixty-seven acres would have been very useful.

Thomas experienced a major setback in early 1891 when his 224 acre Jallukar selection was hit by a fire. We know from land selection records that his two-room thirty feet by ten feet slab and bark house was destroyed by bushfire at around this time.[634] It is highly likely that this would have been the Black Saturday bushfires that occurred on the weekend of 14 and 15 February, because one of the blazes that made up the Black Saturday fires started on the Lexington squatting run near Thomas's selection.[635] By the end of the day on 15 February thousands of acres of land had been burnt out in the Ararat, Moyston and Jallukar areas.[636]

Obviously Thomas would have experienced other losses in this bushfire apart from his house. In a detailed account in the *Ararat Chronicle* on 18 February it was reported that, 'Many heart-rending scenes the poor farmer had to witness, themselves objects of great compassion, seeing favourite horses, cows and dogs roasting in the flames, while machinery, houses, furniture and all utensils and improvements representing years of toil were consumed before them as if by magic'. Since Thomas was already six months behind in his selection licence payments such losses would have been a major setback, making it much harder for him to secure a lease covering his 224 acre selection.

After the destruction of his slab and bark house, Thomas stopped living on his Jallukar selection and moved into Stawell, where Catherine was now living.[637] Catherine and Thomas almost certainly knew each other quite well before the 1891 bushfire but after Thomas moved into town a closer relationship developed between them. Both had experienced the devastation caused by fire. Catherine, who had watched as the 1878 blaze tore through her Redman Bluff selections, would have been able to sympathize with Thomas in his troubles and he needed any support and assistance he could obtain from a financially secure friend such as Catherine.

On 28 May 1891, Catherine and Thomas were married in Stawell by the local Roman Catholic priest, Father Thomas Guilfoyle. On their marriage certificate they both gave Stawell as their 'Present' and 'Usual' address and they both understated their age. Although both were sixty-four, Thomas gave his age as sixty-one and Catherine stated that she was sixty. Thomas described himself as a 'farmer' and Catherine stated that her occupation was 'domestic duties'. Thomas signed the register but Catherine marked it with an X. Catherine identified her father as James McMahon, a farmer, and her mother as Margaret Blake and she stated that she was born at 'Skarriff, Co Clare, Ireland'. Thomas identified his father as Thomas May, a sailor, and his mother as Mary Martin and his birthplace was listed as 'Brighton, England'. Thomas acknowledged that he had been married previously and stated that he was widowed in 1870. Surprisingly, he claimed that he had no children either living or dead, apparently forgetting his son Thomas Fredrick May who died when he was one month old in Hobart Town in 1853. Catherine stated that she had been married previously and was widowed in 1878 (actually 1876) and that she had three children living and five children who had died.[638]

The witnesses to this marriage were M. Fitzmaurice and Annie Doyle. Annie was the then forty-nine-year-old widow of Martin Doyle,[639] who from 1869 to 1880 was the Town Clerk of the Borough of Stawell.[640] Annie had been born in County Wexford, Ireland, and it appears that she and Catherine were friends.

Even though it was certainly not acknowledged at the time, this marriage had some broader historical significance. Initially the settlement of Australia from 1788 had been built on convict marriage or at least convict relationships, and this marriage between two former convicts well into their sixties must have been one of the last of many thousands of such marriages.

When this marriage took place, all three of Catherine's children were busily occupied with their own lives. Only Hannah lived in Stawell with her husband Thomas and their five children. Caring for her husband and young family would have absorbed all Hannah's time and energy and Catherine's involvement with her daughter would have been limited to helping care for the children. By marrying Thomas, Catherine was starting a new life and she no doubt believed that she would be able to provide him with support and assistance on his selection or in any other ventures that they might undertake together.

In marrying Catherine, Thomas was gaining a partner who had considerable experience of successfully working the land. He was also gaining a wife who, due to the sale of her Jallukar selections, was financially very comfortable.

Thomas married Catherine at a crucial time in relation to the future of his 224 acre selection at Jallukar because the six year selection licence covering this land was due to expire on 1 June 1891,[641] four days after the marriage. Obtaining a selection lease on this land was vital if he was to achieve long-term financial security. On 11 June, a bare fortnight after the wedding, the last of the twelve required licence payments of £5/17/6 was paid.[642] This payment was made six months after the due date in December 1890.

Two days before making the final licence payment, Thomas applied to the Lands Department for a lease covering his 224 acre selection. In this application, he declared that he had paid all fees due and went on to state that £504/7/6 worth of improvements had been made on the selection. He also stated that he had 'complied with all the other conditions of the said licence'. In response to the question 'Where does your family reside?' Thomas answered that he was 'Just married'. Although Thomas had signed his marriage certificate, he did not sign this application and instead he marked it with an X.[643]

The Lands Department office in Ararat approved Thomas's selection lease application and on 21 July the application was approved by the Lands Department in Melbourne.[644] Soon after this approval was granted, a further £7/12/6 was paid. Within two months of his marriage to Catherine, £13 had been paid to the Lands Department[645] and Thomas now had secure tenure over his 224 acre selection.

# 29   Married Life in Stawell

After their marriage, Thomas and Catherine continued to live in Stawell. On 15 June 1891, Thomas took out a miner's right on a block measuring 66 feet by 165 feet in Fisher Street.[646] The taking out of this miner's right did not indicate that Thomas was going to work as a miner but it gave Thomas and Catherine the right to live in a house on this block of land near the Quartz Reefs mining area.

In August Catherine decided to go back into farming and she purchased a twenty-five acre block of land on Commercial Road at Illawarra from Remigio Zala[647] with a straight cash transaction. This block was around five kilometres to the west of Stawell. A small creek ran through the block that had been one of the first parcels of land near Stawell opened up for farming in the 1860s. This land appears to have been suited to running a few head of livestock, growing a few acres of vegetables and perhaps having a small orchard. There was also a house on this land but it does not appear as if Catherine and Thomas lived there on an ongoing basis.

At the start of 1892, Thomas sold the 224 acres of land at Jallukar that he held under a selection lease to Dr William Symes, the Stawell surgeon to whom he had earlier sold the sixty-seven acre block.[648] It is not surprising that he moved to sell the 224 acres so soon after securing the lease. To achieve full ownership of this land, the selection lease provisions required him to work the land and progressively pay it off over the next fourteen years. This meant continuing to work the land until 1905, when he would be in his seventy-ninth year.

The key reason why Thomas would have been happy to sell the selection lease at this time was the high value of land. In June 1891 Catherine's son, John, had sold a block of land at Jallukar for £4/5/- an acre.[649] While Thomas still owed the Lands Department over £140 on the selection lease and although the land had suffered considerable bushfire damage in early 1891, it is clear that he would have received a reasonable sum on making this sale.

In 1893 and 1894, Thomas appeared on the Stawell Shire Council records as the rate payer for the twenty-five acre block of land at Illawarra that Catherine had purchased in August 1891. In fact the 1894 council records identified him as a farmer who was the owner of this twenty-five acre block of land. At this time, the annual rates on the block were eight shillings and four pence. Thomas paid the rates in 1893 but he did not pay them in 1894.[650]

In 1894 or 1895, Catherine's son James returned to Stawell with Mary and their children.[651] By this time there was a major recession in Melbourne and there was much less work available in the building and construction industry. In Stawell James was able to get work as a miner and they lived in Wimmera Street, about half a kilometre down the hill from the Quartz Reefs.

The 1895 Stawell Shire rate records no longer showed Thomas as the owner of the block of land at Illawarra. Catherine May, a farmer, was now listed as the owner of this land. These rate records gave Catherine's address as C/o Thomas Green, Canning Street, Stawell[652]—the home of her daughter and son-in-law.

In the same year, the Stawell rate records show Thomas and Catherine had moved from Fisher Street to Lower Clemes Street where they were the occupiers and owners of a house on which Thomas paid three shillings in rates. This street was very near to Patrick Street and just down the hill from the Quartz Reefs. The rate records list him as a farmer.[653]

Thomas continued to pay rates on this property in 1896 and 1897,[654] and during this period Catherine continued to be listed as the farmer owner of the twenty-five acres of land at Illawarra. For both these years, consistent with past practice, she paid no rates on her land. Her address on the rate records was simply given as Stawell.[655]

Sometime in 1897 or 1898, Catherine was faced with the no doubt very unwelcome news that James and his family and Hannah and her family were leaving Stawell and moving to Western Australia. This move involved a journey of around 3500 kilometres to the Western Australian goldfields. By 1897, the goldmining industry in Stawell was in serious decline. Some Quartz Reefs mines were closing because of poor gold returns and, with the Victorian economy in recession, other mines closed due to lack of available capital for their development.[656] In 1892 and 1893, major gold rushes had occurred at Coolgardie and Kalgoorlie in Western Australia. These rushes were more than 600 kilometres to the east of Perth. Large numbers of miners from Stawell, and particularly the young and more entrepreneurial amongst them, decided to make the move to the west. James and Hannah were in fact doing the same thing their parents had done forty years earlier when they left Tasmania and crossed Bass Strait to live in Victoria. The two families saw limited opportunities for themselves at Stawell and they were chasing a secure and prosperous future.

When Hannah, James and their families made the long trek to Western Australia, Catherine surely despaired of ever seeing them again. However, John, Jane and their family were still in the colony of Victoria. They were living at Balmoral, ninety kilometres to the west of Stawell, and in the late 1890s three of their children—Catherine and John Robert who were in their early twenties, and Jane who was in her late teens—were at an age where they may have wanted to stay with Catherine and experience the excitements of Stawell.

On 20 March 1898, Thomas was called to attend the Police Court in Stawell.[657] It was more than fifty-eight years since his first court appearance at

Lewes, near Brighton, but this time he was a witness for the prosecution. The case was reported in the *Stawell News and Pleasant Creek Chronicle* and it involved a charge of using 'insulting words'. Naomi Bass, the wife of the publican of the Caledonian Hotel in Patrick Street, had brought this charge 'against a young man named James Davis, a miner'. Mr Rowan, the Police Magistrate and two local Justices of the Peace heard the case.[658]

As the first witness, Naomi Bass told the court that on the afternoon of Saturday 11 March, James Davis accompanied by two other men entered the bar of the Caledonian Hotel at 4.20 pm and they 'called for drinks'. Naomi told the court that she refused to supply Davis with drink because 'he was very much under the influence of liquor'. She told the court that at this the defendant 'became very abusive; making use of abominable expressions'. She would not repeat these 'abominable expressions' in the courtroom and instead the words were written down on a piece of paper and handed up to the bench.[659]

Thomas was the next witness and he was called to give 'collaborating evidence'. Thomas told the court that he was in the hotel at the time of the incident and he confirmed to the court that James Davis was 'very drunk at the time'. However, he then went further and told the court that in his opinion Davis 'did not know what he was saying'.[660]

Mr Grano, who was appearing in the proceedings for the defendant, would have been delighted to hear what he considered to be mitigating evidence assisting his client given by the prosecution witness. Mr Grano highlighted the evidence that Davis was 'so drunk that he did not know what he was doing' and told the court that 'They must take the evidence being given as being true, and although Davis must be punished for behaving in such a manner, he asked the bench to take into consideration the circumstances of the case'.[661]

Although James Davis was found guilty, he was only fined £1/8/6.[662] Thomas had appeared in the witness box to assist the prosecution but, by presenting the classic drunk's defence to the court, he ended up assisting the defence. Perhaps Thomas looked at young James Davis in the dock, recalled his own experiences at Lewes and then decided that he would rather not help the prosecution gain a conviction. Perhaps he just did not know when to stop talking.

In 1899, Catherine May was still listed in the Stawell Shire rate records as the farmer who owned the twenty-five acre block at Illawarra and she had still failed to pay the rates on this land.[663] In that year the Stawell Borough rate records show that the name Thomas May was crossed out as the occupier of the house in Lower Clemes Street and instead the occupier was listed as a James Battania.[664] Thomas still appears to have been the owner of this house. In 1899, a person or persons with the surname May are listed in these records as occupying a house in Fisher Street. Almost certainly this was Catherine and Thomas.

\*\*\*

The year 1900 was one of significant change for Catherine and Thomas. On 28 June Thomas became the owner of a store located in Patrick Street, Stawell,[665] just down from the Quartz Reefs mining area and a few blocks from St Patrick's Catholic church. It was opposite the Caledonian Hotel which we know Thomas had patronized in the past and where he no doubt still liked to have a drink.

The Mays purchased the store from Daniel Hadfield, a twenty-three-year-old[666] who had owned the store since April 1898.[667] There had been a general store run on this block of land since at least as early as 1877. In 1877, the Quartz Reefs were at peak production and no doubt there was plenty of custom from the miners and their families. However, by 1900 custom at the store would not have been as strong because of the decline in mining and the reduction in population that had occurred in Stawell over the previous five years.

It is easy to understand why Catherine and Thomas purchased this store. In 1900, they were both seventy-three years of age and no doubt it was getting more difficult to travel the five kilometres to Illawarra and farm the twenty-five acres of land. Owning and operating the store would mean neither of them had to travel out to Illawarra and they could live on the premises. As they aged they would always be in easy reach of the health and other services that were available in town.

Thomas almost certainly took pride in becoming a storekeeper. As a boy on the back streets in Brighton, he lived near the shops on James Street that serviced the needs of the working people. He would have looked enviously at the goods in these stores that he had no means of owning. Now he owned such a store and all its goods.

The store specialized in groceries, with a few household hardware items also in stock. The shelves were stacked with large amounts of jam, cheese, tea, tinned meat and Worcester sauce.[668] These items clearly had a significant place in the diet of the Quartz Reefs miners and their families. A large supply of candles was also kept in stock. With no electricity in people's homes, candles were an important part of everyday life in Stawell. Many of their customers would appear to have been the wives of the miners working on the Quartz Reefs. Catherine would have known quite a few of these women.

When they took over the store, Thomas and Catherine apparently decided to employ Daniel Hadfield's brother Harry to help them with the heavier tasks and to provide assistance with the paperwork associated with the business. Both had very limited literacy skills and Catherine had no children left in town to help her with this work. There is no available evidence to show any significant connection between Thomas and Harry Hadfield prior to Thomas buying the store.

In June 1900, Harry Hadfield was a twenty-six-year-old bachelor. He had been born in Landsborough thirty kilometres to the east of Stawell and was the illegitimate son of a woman identified as Ellen Hayes. Harry claimed that his father was Thomas Hadfield, a watchmaker in Stawell in the 1870s and 1880s. On Harry's 1873 birth certificate, Thomas Hadfield did not acknowledge that he was the father but, in reporting the birth, he described himself as the 'Authorised Agent'.[669] In the 1870s, Ellen Hayes had at least two other illegitimate children who identified Thomas Hadfield as their father.[670] In 1887, Thomas Hadfield at fifty-nine years of age married thirty-seven-year-old Emma Shoulder[671] and he apparently put the association with Ellen Hayes into the past. On Thomas Hadfield's death in 1891, Harry was not acknowledged as his child.[672]

Soon after the purchase of the Patrick Street store, Catherine moved to stop farming the land at Illawarra. The block was not sold but leased out. On 29 April 1901, Catherine paid £1/19/- to the Stawell Shire Council,[673] which meant she was now up to date with the rate payments due on the block. As the wife of a store owner, it may have been considered foolish not to be prompt in the payment of your own accounts. It could set a bad example to your customers.

At around the time that Thomas purchased the store Catherine's son John and his family left Balmoral. They also headed off to a gold rush, but this rush was far closer to Stawell than Western Australia. In late June 1900, gold was discovered by the Emmett brothers on the south-east slopes of Mount William in the Grampian ranges. This gold strike was, as the crow flies, only about ten kilometres from the selections under Redman Bluff that Catherine had farmed in the 1870s and 1880s. John and his family moved to the gold rush town of Mafeking that had been established close to the strike. It appears they did well at the Mafeking field because they stayed there for four and a half years working as tribute miners.[674] A tribute miner was someone who paid a fee or a 'tribute' to the holder of a mining claim or lease and then received whatever was the value of the minerals extracted from that claim or lease.

At this time, the move to Western Australia appears to have been successful for Catherine's other two children Hannah and James. In June 1900, Hannah Green had her ninth child while they were living at Coolgardie in the Western Australian goldfields[675] but by 1901 or 1902,

Hannah and Thomas and their children had left the goldfields and taken up a farm at Lion Mill in the Darling Range, forty kilometres east of Perth.[676] In 1901, James and his family were living at Menzies, 130 kilometres north of Kalgoorlie.[677] James was working on the Menzies goldfield primarily as a skilled tradesman manufacturing and repairing metal implements. These were skills in demand in the goldfields and he appears to have been doing well.

In May 1901, the first general election occurred for the parliament of the new Commonwealth of Australia. In this election both Hannah Green and her sister-in-law, Mary Copley, had their first experience of being entitled to vote in an election. At this time women had the vote in Western Australia and South Australia, but not in any other state. This situation changed in June 1902 when the Commonwealth Franchise Act passed the national parliament and became law. Under this act Australia became the first country in the world to give women the same right as men to vote and stand for election to the national parliament. When Catherine McMahon was born in Ireland in 1827, extensive restrictions applied on the right to vote and stand for parliament and at that time it was not even contemplated that these rights should extend to women. Now at seventy-five years of age, Catherine finally had the right to vote.

# 30 Rather a Peculiar Will

In late July 1903, Thomas May became ill with heart problems and two months later he was diagnosed as having a 'senile heart'.[678] This meant that his heart was not adequately pumping blood. As a consequence of these problems, he developed dropsy and the soft tissues in his body began to swell.

At around the same time, life was changing for Harry Hadfield, the storeman who to the best of our knowledge still worked in the Patrick Street store. September 16, 1903 was his wedding day. He was married at St Patrick's Catholic church in Stawell to Mary Walter, a widow.[679] We do not know whether Thomas was well enough to attend this wedding. Harry was thirty years of age at the time of this marriage and although Mary gave her age as forty, she was in fact forty-four.[680] Mary was the widow of James Walter, a farmer at Callawadda, twenty kilometres north of Stawell,[681] who had died in January of that year.[682] Walter had farmed 262 acres of freehold land and he held leases covering another 490 acres,[683] so this was certainly a financially advantageous marriage for Harry.

Twelve days later, on 28 September 1903, Thomas died at Patrick Street of the heart problems that had caused his illness over the previous two months.[684] The death of a seventy-six-year-old man with heart problems would normally only be noted in passing by all but his nearest and dearest, but the death of Thomas May caused somewhat of a sensation in Stawell.

It was Thomas's 'last Will and Testament' that both shocked and surprised and no doubt gave rise to much scandalous gossip. The will dated 1 July 1901 read as follows:

> This is the last will and testament of me Thomas May of Stawell in the State of Victoria made this 1st day of July one thousand nine hundred and one. I give devise and bequeath unto Harry Hadfield of Stawell all my real and personal estate goods and chattels of any sort whatever belonging to me with the exception of one shilling which I bequeath to my wife Catherine May and direct that all my just debts & funeral & testamentary expenses shall be paid as soon as conveniently after my decease and hereby appoint John Webster of Stawell Telegraph Operator and Walter Stanton of Stawell Letter Carrier Executors of this my will. In witness whereof I have hereunder set my hand this 1st July of in the year of our Lord one thousand nine hundred and one signed Thomas May.[685]

The will was witnessed by J. Webster and W. Stanton.[686] On 1 July 1901, when this will was signed, Thomas May was seventy-four years of age, John Webster was thirty-three,[687] and Walter Stanton was twenty-nine.[688]

We do not know what had occurred during the twelve years of marriage that led Thomas to make this will. We can only speculate about what caused him to treat Catherine in this way and deprive her of her legitimate inheritance. Was it extreme bitterness even hatred for Catherine, an obsessive interest in Harry Hadfield, or an outward symptom of some form of senile dementia? Regardless of why the will was written in this way, its effect on Catherine was profound.

On 29 September 1903, the death of Thomas was formally reported to the Register of Births, Deaths and Marriages by Harry Hadfield. In reporting the death, Harry identified himself as the 'Authorized Agent'.[689]

The death of Thomas was reported in the *Stawell News and Pleasant Creek Chronicle* on 29 September in the following terms: 'A very old resident, in the person of Mr Thomas May of Patrick Street, died last night at the advanced age of 88 years. The funeral will leave deceased's late residence at 3.30 tomorrow afternoon.' In fact Thomas was seventy-six years of age, not eighty-eight. Illness must have aged him prematurely as it appears he was thought to be a very old man.

On Wednesday, 30 September 1903 at 3.30 pm, Thomas's funeral cortege left his Patrick Street home. He was buried in the Roman Catholic section of the Stawell cemetery.[690]

Harry Hadfield wasted no time in seeking to implement the terms of Thomas May's last will and testament. Four days after Thomas's death, the executors of the will gave public notice in the *Stawell News and Pleasant Creek Chronicle* of their intention to apply for probate. The following notice appeared in the paper:

> Estate of Thomas May, late of Stawell, Storekeeper, deceased. All persons having any Claims against the Estate of the above-named deceased are requested to send particulars of same to us before the 8th instant.
>
> Wettenhall & Lewers, Victoria Place, Stawell. Solicitors of the Estate.[691]

After the validity of the will was established, the next issue was to identify the 'real and personal estate goods and chattels of any sort whatever belonging' to Thomas. By September 1903, Catherine and Thomas had been married for more than twelve years and it would have been an extremely difficult task to determine who owned what. Both Thomas and Catherine had limited literacy skills and therefore there was probably very little paperwork to neatly spell out ownership.

The Patrick Street store was known as Thomas May's store, and both the Stawell Borough rate records and the property transaction records showed Thomas as the owner of the store, land and building that had been purchased from Daniel Hadfield in 1900. Regardless of the source of the money used to purchase this property, the physical real estate of the store was clearly recorded as belonging to Thomas.

Harry Hadfield may well have claimed that the twenty-five acre block of land at Illawarra had been the property of Thomas. The Stawell Shire rate records, the only available record concerning property ownership available in the town at the time of Thomas May's death, showed Thomas as the owner of this property for the two years immediately after it was purchased from Remigio Zala in 1891. This suggests that Thomas purchased the property.

It would have been very difficult to establish ownership of a wide range of property in the May household. Who owned the horses, drays, carts, household furniture and equipment and any money in the house? Catherine may have been able to argue that the fixtures in the shop had been purchased by her and that some or all of the working capital used to run the business had been hers.

On 15 October 1903, John Webster and Walter Stanton, the two men identified as the executors in the 1 July 1901 Thomas May will, signed two applications for probate to be declared on this will.[692]

In the first application, John Webster and Walter Stanton declared that the value of Thomas May's 'REAL AND PERSONAL ESTATE' was £509/3/3. In this application, the beneficiaries of the will were listed as 'Catherine May—Widow' and 'Harry Hadfield—No Relation'.

This application contained detailed information concerning what made up the personal estate component of this figure. It tells us that twenty-five people owed various sums of money to Thomas May from 'W. Ewers', who allegedly owed four shillings and eleven pence, to 'J. Williams' and 'Mrs Dooling' who each allegedly owed £10. It claimed that in total these twenty-five people had owed £95/18/11 to Thomas on his death.[693] It appears that most of these people were customers of the May store who had allegedly made purchases on account.

This application also contained a detailed audit of the stock in the store. There were ninety-one different products listed in this audit and they varied greatly in value. There was one shilling worth each of sago, fruit ciders and baking powder but £42/12/8 worth of jam. The people living at the Quartz

Reefs clearly loved their jam! The audit stated that the stock in hand in the store had a total value of £193/19/8.[694]

In the second application, John Webster and Walter Stanton declared that 'The said deceased left property in Victoria not exceeding in value the sum of £583/14/4 consisting of real estate of the value of £240 and personal estate of the value of £343/14/4'. In this application, they provided no details concerning what constituted the £240 of real estate.

When we look at the value of the real estate that was claimed in both these applications for probate, it strongly suggests that the executors were leaving open the option of claiming that Harry Hadfield was now the rightful owner of the twenty-five acres of land at Illawarra. The second application claimed that the value of the real estate component of Thomas May's estate was an amount not exceeding £240. The first application did not have a specific figure concerning the value of the real estate, but it claimed that the total value of the estate was worth just over £509 and specific details were provided of personal estate matters that amounted to just under £290. This leaves the strong impression that there was considered to be a real estate component to the estate that was valued at around £220.

While we cannot be certain of the true value of the store, there is strong evidence that it was worth considerably less than £220. In 1897, six years earlier, this same store was subject to probate when the then owner Theresa Shea died and her daughter Alice inherited it. This declaration of probate held that the store had a value of £50.[695] The six years between 1897 and 1903 in Stawell were years of continuing economic decline, with the nearby Quartz Reefs mines closing or reducing the size of their operations. This would have been a negative factor in terms of the available return from the store. While the 1897 store valuation might have been deliberately on the low side in a non-controversial probate to minimize tax, it is not plausible that six years later, given the circumstances in Stawell, the store had more than quadrupled in value. In 1903, the twenty-five acre block at Illawarra would have had a value of around £4 an acre[696] and this, when combined with the 1897 shop value, starts to provide a basis for the real estate value in excess of £200.

Harry Hadfield and the executors of the will would have been keen to obtain probate as soon as possible, so that Harry could get access to the money and the real estate. Additionally, the grocery products left in the store, while mainly long lasting, would lose value if they were just left sitting on the shelves and furthermore, the prospects of getting full payment from customers with outstanding store accounts would have been maximized by being able to press them for payment without delay. No doubt these are the reasons why the probate application had been lodged promptly, but the application had been constructed in such a way that if, after further investigations, it was found that claims for other property could be substantiated, then the executors would be free to pursue them.

The sum total of what both applications meant was that as things stood Catherine was going to receive one shilling from the estate of her husband, Thomas, and Harry Hadfield was apparently going to receive at least £500. Catherine must have been devastated by this situation.

\*\*\*

While Catherine was struggling to come to terms with Thomas's will and facing an uncertain future, preparations were under way for a national federal parliamentary election in Australia covering all seats in the House of Representatives and half the seats in the senate. The date for this election had been set as Wednesday, 16 December 1903. In Victoria, with a casual vacancy to be filled in the Senate, four Senators would be elected. This was to be the first election where women in all Australian states had the vote on the same basis as men, and women also had the right to stand for election to the parliament.

On 15 October in Portland in the south-west of the State, Miss Vida Goldstein opened her campaign to be elected to fill one of the four available Senate positions.[697] Vida Goldstein was the first woman in Australia to nominate for election to the federal parliament. On this day, the following article appeared in the *Stawell News and Pleasant Creek Chronicle*:

> For the first time in the history of Stawell a lady candidate for a seat in the Parliament will address the electors on Tuesday next, when Miss Vida Goldstein who is seeking election to the Senate will explain her political views in the Town Hall. The ladies have hitherto displayed some reluctance in attending political gatherings even though specially invited, but on this occasion a considerable number have signified this intention of being present. Under these circumstances a lady can go to the meeting with full knowledge that she will find there a fair proportion of her own sex.

30. 1902 photograph of Vida Goldstein who campaigned successfully in Stawell during the 1903 federal election.

In 1903, Vida Goldstein was thirty-four years of age and she was one of the leading women's rights campaigners in the world. In the 1890s, she came to the view that the fundamental right that women needed was the right to vote and that this political power would produce improved social and economic conditions.[698] In August 1900, Vida was appointed the Secretary of the Victorian United Council for Women's Suffrage and she became the leading women's rights campaigner in Victoria. In 1902, Vida, as the Australian delegate, attended an International Women Suffrage Conference in Washington DC. While there, she met President Theodore Roosevelt and addressed committees of the Congress.

On 20 October, another story appeared in the *Stawell News and Pleasant Creek Chronicle* concerning the Vida Goldstein election campaign meeting that was due to be held that evening.

> An address to the electors will be given in the Town Hall this evening by

Miss Vida Goldstein who is a candidate for a seat in the Senate at the forthcoming elections. Needless to say the advent of a lady candidate for parliamentary honors has aroused a great deal of interest and it is safe to prophesy that the Town Hall will be filled to overflowing. There will be a large number of ladies present, and special arrangements have been made for their accommodation.

Unfortunately Vida missed her train, so the meeting was rescheduled for the evening of 22 October.

\*\*\*

On the same day as the rescheduled meeting, the two applications for probate on the will of Thomas May, signed by John Webster, telegraph operator, and Walter Stanton, letter carrier, were lodged in the Supreme Court of Victoria.[699]

Two days later, the *Stawell News and Pleasant Creek Chronicle* reported on both this application for probate and the Vida Goldstein campaign meeting. Most unusually, the newspaper commented on the Thomas May will. The article read:

> Rather a peculiar will from Stawell was lodged for probate on Thursday. It was that of the late Thomas May, storekeeper of Patrick Street. The will was sworn at £583 and the will was as follows:
> 
> 'I give devise and bequeath to Harry Hadfield, Stawell, all my real and personal estate goods and chattels, with the exception of one shilling which I bequeath to my wife Catherine May and direct that all my just debts & funeral & testamentary expenses shall be paid as soon as conveniently after my decease.'

In researching this story, we have reviewed more than six years of editions of the *Stawell News and Pleasant Creek Chronicle*. This covered the periods both before and after the death of Thomas May. The newspaper regularly reported on the terms of wills that had been submitted for probate. In all this time, the Thomas May will was the only one where any sort of comment or judgment about the terms of the will was made by the newspaper. In describing this will as 'peculiar', the newspaper was breaking longstanding practice. Undoubtedly it saw this will as a story that would interest its readers but it also seems to be drawing attention to the apparent unfairness of the will. After all, Vida Goldstein had raised the issue of rights for women at her meeting two days earlier and aroused much discussion, and no newspaper could fail to see the relevance of the will to the current debate.

The report on Vida's election campaign meeting was extremely detailed. Headlined as 'Monster Gathering in the Town Hall', the report stated 'The Town Hall was packed to the doors'. The reporter noted that a large proportion of those at the meeting were ladies 'and for their comfort the front part of the hall was reserved for them'.

The meeting opened with remarks from the Mayor of Stawell, Councillor Napthine. The newspaper then reported that Miss Goldstein was received with applause and she tendered an apology for not fulfilling her engagement two days earlier. She told the meeting that it was a very sore point with her, as it was the very first time she had ever failed to keep a public engagement and she suspected that some people would say, 'Of course it is just what might be expected from a woman'. However, she then assured the meeting that it was actually the fault of a slow driving cabman that she had missed the train that was to take her to Stawell. The audience responded with laughter and applause. She was a polished speaker and she had the audience on her side.

Vida spoke about the importance of the vote to women, especially now that so many of them had to go out in the world to earn their own living. She suggested that it was a matter of simple justice that women should have a vote to protect their interests.

She directly confronted the argument that women should not have the right to vote or go into parliament because they could not fight for their country. She said she believed women could fight but hoped they never would and suggested that by giving women the vote and enabling them to go into parliament they would be hastening the cessation of hostilities. She believed that most women would agree with Benjamin Franklin that 'There never was a good war or a bad peace'. She would have struck an immediate accord with the majority of her female audience when she said that 'Every time a soldier was born into the world a woman risked her life that that soldier might be born'.

The idea of equal pay for equal work was strongly supported and Vida argued that with the increasing number of women in employment, it was necessary to have equal pay for equal work or women would become a serious menace to organized labour.

Vida also spoke about the injustice of the existing laws and she suggested that women who said they did not want the vote did not know what their legal status was. She raised the issues of marriage and divorce laws and laws relating to the guardianship of children and the disposal of a man's property. She informed her audience that a married woman had no legal right to her own child and she told them that a husband had the right to will away every bit of property he had and leave his wife and children destitute. At this point there must have been people in the audience who thought of the situation in their own town where Catherine May had been left only one shilling in her husband's will. Gossip in a community the size of Stawell would have ensured that Catherine's plight was known long before anything appeared in the paper. Vida went on to stress that the only countries in which these laws had been changed were those in which women had got the vote.

Vida was reported as concluding her address by appealing to the women in the audience to take their share of public work and try and make the country better than it was. She was roundly applauded. She had made a big impact on Stawell and the newspaper commented that at the meeting Miss Vida Goldstein had justified her candidature for the Senate.

We do not know whether Catherine attended the meeting. Given her personal difficulties at the time it appears unlikely. However, throughout her life Catherine had shown that she could make hard decisions, take risks, fight for her rights and stand up for her family. She now found herself humiliated by her late husband's will and left with very little in terms of personal wealth. She would surely have strongly supported Vida: a woman who so articulately opposed such treatment and stood up for the rights of women.

Following Vida's address in Stawell, support continued to be shown in the *Stawell News and Pleasant Creek Chronicle* for her election to the Senate. In the 27 October edition, a letter to the editor by 'J.I.B' noted how Miss Goldstein in her address had shown 'tact, intelligence and judgement' and 'intellectual ability'. The writer congratulated Vida for raising 'the social questions of our Commonwealth' and concluded by stating, 'I ask the ladies of Stawell to do the best they can for the candidate by voting for her and their own interests'. Vida's candidacy was being treated seriously in Stawell and her election address continued to generate discussion in the weeks leading up to the election.

\*\*\*

While Vida Goldstein was making an impact in Stawell, progress continued to be made in having the terms of Thomas May's will accepted. On 7 November, probate was granted to John Webster and Walter Stanton.[700]

Some time prior to 16 December, Catherine's daughter-in-law, Mary and three of her six children arrived in Stawell.[701] The children were Mary's two youngest sons, eleven-year-old Ernest and seven-year-old Stanley, and either twenty-year-old Elizabeth or eighteen-year-old Mary. James stayed in Menzies with the rest of his family. Catherine had not seen Mary or any of her children since they left for Western Australia five or six years earlier. If they could afford it, it was common for men and/or their families who had originally come from Victoria to return to that State for a break or holiday. This normally occurred at the start of the summer months and it provided people with an escape from the searing heat on the Western Australian goldfields. James' work as a blacksmith was obviously sufficiently lucrative for him to be able to afford to send his family back to Stawell.

We do not know whether this journey had been planned before Thomas May's death or prompted by the death and the contents of the will. James and his sister, Hannah Green, would have received reports of the death and of the will and they were no doubt worried about what was happening to their mother and to her share of the property in Patrick Street.

While in Stawell, Mary was registered on the 1903 federal election voting roll as living in Wimmera Street.[702] This is the street where she and her family had lived prior to their move to Western Australia. Mary's presence in Stawell would not only have been of great comfort to Catherine but it would also have given her significant moral support in dealing with the public attention, and practical help in dealing with the issues arising from her husband's will.

We do not know where Catherine lived immediately after the death of Thomas. In this period, when probate had not been granted on the will, the two executors had no legal right to remove her from the Patrick Street store and home. However, when probate was granted on 7 November the executors became legally responsible for the store and home and at this time, they could have directed Catherine to leave the building.

By 16 December 1903 Catherine was no longer living in the home attached to the store. In the electoral roll for the federal election that was conducted on this day, she was listed as residing at Meagher Street, Stawell, and her occupation was listed as home duties.[703] She did not have far to move, as Meagher Street is immediately behind Patrick Street.

Catherine's treatment under Thomas May's will was undoubtedly the subject of much discussion for many Stawell residents in the lead-up to the 1903 December federal election, especially since the town's newspaper had labelled the will 'peculiar'.[704] Catherine would have been well known to many in the town, especially those who shared her Catholic faith and those who had patronized the Patrick Street store. She had first lived in Stawell in the 1860s and then returned there, as a widow of means, after the sale of her 240 acre Jallukar selection. While Thomas May had been the registered owner of the Patrick Street store, quite a number of people would have known or assumed that Catherine had made a major contribution to its establishment. As the story of the one shilling will and Catherine's loss of her home did the rounds, it would surely have made many female voters more receptive to Vida Goldstein's message of women's rights.

In reporting on the federal election, the *Stawell News and Pleasant Creek Chronicle* stated that this was 'the first time the ladies had the privilege of exercising the franchise and they availed themselves of it in very large numbers'. A Miss Fawcett had the honour of being the first woman to vote in Stawell. The newspaper reported that: 'From ten o'clock until twelve the ladies trooped in crowds and Patrick Street never perhaps in its history presented a gayer appearance. Voting to the ladies assumed the importance of a social function and they dressed in their very best.'[705] Not only did the women of Stawell vote in their fashionable best, but at this election they voted in substantial numbers. Although voting was not compulsory, approximately 650 women voted and 433 men. This vote in Stawell, where 60 percent of voters were women,[706] contrasted markedly with the Victoria wide vote where 48.7 percent of voters were women.[707]

The voting system for the Senate election in 1903 was significantly different to the system used in Australia today. In this election, there were eighteen candidates standing for four Victorian Senate seats and, unlike today, each elector had four votes. Each elector voted for the four candidates that they wanted to see fill the Senate seats. The seats were then filled on the basis of a first past the post system, where the four candidates with the highest number of votes went into parliament.

When the Senate votes cast in Stawell were counted, the results were a stunning endorsement of Vida Goldstein, who received 380 votes[708]. This is 35.75 percent of the people in Stawell who voted. Among the eighteen candidates for the Senate, she achieved the third highest vote in Stawell and if this vote had been repeated state wide she would have easily been elected.

However, the vote for Vida Goldstein across Victoria was nowhere near as good. She got 16.83 percent of the votes cast, which positioned her as fourteenth out of the eighteen candidates and consequently she was not elected.[709]

The election result would have meant little to Catherine as she struggled with the fact that probate had been granted to executors John Webster and Walter Stanton, who were proceeding to implement the terms of Thomas's will. Catherine was now facing a very difficult future and some hard decisions would have to be made.

# PART SEVEN
# CATHERINE'S FINAL YEARS

## 31 A Difficult Decision

By February 1904, as the end of summer approached, it was time for Catherine's daughter-in-law Mary and her three children to head back to join James on the Western Australian goldfields. Although the Thomas May will had still not been finalized, Catherine had to decide what she was going to do in the future. There was a lot to consider.

If she stayed in Stawell after Mary departed, she would be left with no family in the town. If she remained alone in Stawell, the executors of the will and Harry Hadfield could continue to raise and press further property claims upon her. Also, she must have felt that in Stawell she would always be known as the wife who was left a single shilling in her husband's will. This was a humiliation to be avoided and Catherine decided that she did not want to remain in Stawell.

The next decision to make was where she would go. At this time John was the only one of her three children living in Victoria. He was still based at Mafeking on the south-west slopes of Mount William. However, in early 1904 the Mafeking goldfields were in decline and the town had only a few hundred residents remaining and no great amenities. In winter, it was sometimes cut off from the outside world by wet and impassable roads and the weather could get so cold that snow fell. There was very little to recommend Mafeking as a place to live for anyone, much less for a woman in her late seventies. Additionally, at Mafeking she would still be within easy reach of continuing enquiries from the executors of the will and Harry Hadfield.

A move to Western Australia to join either James and Mary or Hannah and Thomas was her second option. This would have been a giant step for the seventy-six-year-old Catherine to contemplate and there were several issues to be considered before a decision could be made. The first was the length of the journey itself. It involved a 460 kilometre train trip from Stawell to Adelaide and then a boat voyage of around five days to Albany on the south-west coast. The inventory of passenger departures from Melbourne to Fremantle at the start of the twentieth century shows that very few people in their sixties, much less their seventies, made the ship voyage to Western Australia.[710] After arriving in Albany, there would have been a further train trip of approximately 400 kilometres to Northam, a hundred kilometres east of Perth. An additional sixty kilometres would take her to the home of Hannah and Thomas but, if she were to stay with James and Mary, it would involve travelling a further 600 kilometres.

The second issue was the climate in Western Australia. While Stawell could have hot weather in summer, Western Australia and particularly Menzies was a far hotter and more hostile environment in which to live. The statistics since temperatures were first recorded show that the average summertime maximum temperature for Stawell is 27.5°C.[711] The average summer time maximum temperature for Menzies is 34°C.[712] While Catherine and Mary did not have access to these statistics, her family would have told Catherine that Menzies was far hotter, drier and dustier than Stawell.

The third issue was where she would live if she went to Western Australia. Her daughter Hannah had ten children and does not appear to have been as well off as James. It appears that there would have been little room for Catherine if she were to live on an ongoing basis with her daughter. Alternatively, James had six children and two of these were near-adult women. It would have been more practical for Catherine to live with James and Mary.

By early March 1904 the decision was made—Catherine was going to leave Stawell and travel to Western Australia with Mary and the children. Before leaving Stawell she would have arranged her affairs as best she could. No doubt some items of property were given to John, while other items may well have been sold and the money put towards her trip. With the will not yet finalized, Harry Hadfield and the executors would have been concerned in case Catherine was disposing of property that belonged originally to Thomas May and therefore now, in their eyes, to Harry. There was little they could do to stop this without a court order and it would have looked terrible to be taking to court the widow who had been left one shilling.

The one item of property that Catherine did nothing about was the twenty-five acre block of land at Illawarra.[713] She made no move to sell this land and it continued to be leased out. By this time, she would have made sure that the Titles Office in Melbourne had her listed as the registered owner of this land, thus ensuring that the executors had no hope of substantiating a claim on it.

We do not know the precise date, but prior to 15 March Catherine left Stawell for the last time.[714] It was Catherine Copley who boarded the train to Adelaide, not Catherine May. For the rest of her life Catherine was to be known as Mrs Copley.

On 15 March 1904, at Port Adelaide, a party that was identified as 'Mrs Copley and family' boarded the SS *Buninyong* for the voyage to Albany. The shipping records identify that this party was made up of three adult females and two male children.[715] The ship carried cargo as well as passengers and it left port the next morning at 5.30 am.[716]

The *Buninyong* was a totally different ship to the barque *Australasia* that transported Catherine from Ireland to Hobart Town nearly fifty-five years earlier. The *Buninyong* had a steel hull and it weighed 2070 tons. It was eighty-five metres in length and was powered by three coal-fired boilers.[717] It had electric lighting throughout, and a music room and card room for the comfort and entertainment of the passengers.[718] In contrast, the *Australasia*

31. A picture card promoting the SS *Buninyong*.

was a wooden sailing ship with no amenities that weighed 485.3 tons and was thirty-five metres in length.[719]

The 2000 kilometre voyage from Adelaide to Albany took five days and the *Buninyong* arrived at 2.40 pm on 20 March.[720] Upon disembarking, Catherine, Mary and the three children joined the Great Southern Railway for the trip to Northam.

We cannot be certain what Catherine did after reaching Northam. Mary was no doubt keen to return to Menzies to be reunited with James and her remaining three children. Perhaps before travelling to Menzies, Catherine visited her daughter Hannah and her son-in-law Thomas at their Lion Mill farm. There she would have seen their ninth child, Mervyn, who had been born in October 1900,[721] and their tenth and last child Norman who had

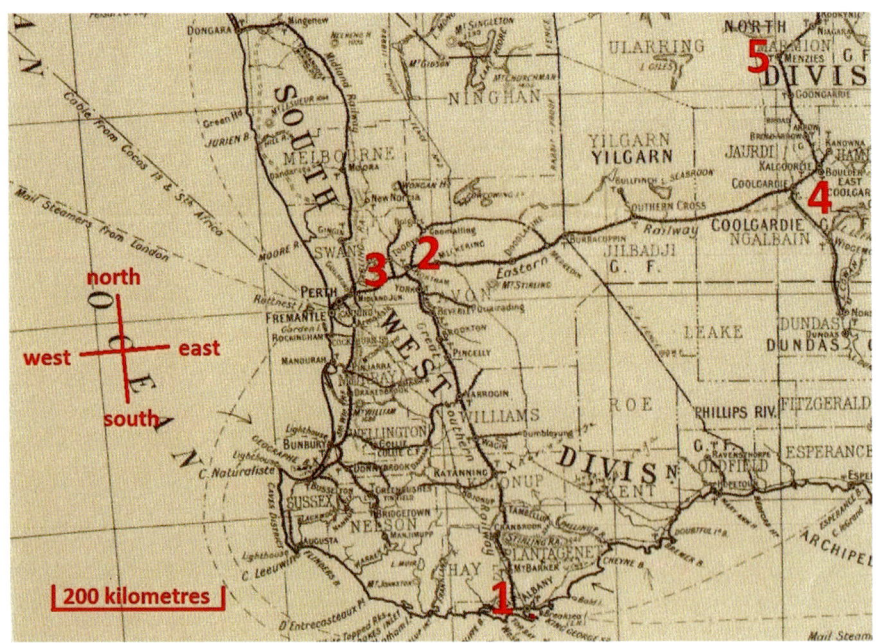

32. Taken from 1902 map of Western Australia with the following locations marked: 1. Albany; 2. Northam; 3. Lion Mill; 4. Kalgoorlie; and 5. Menzies. (Map reproduced courtesy of the Barr Smith Library of the University of Adelaide [Daisy Bates Special Col./86, Western Australia Dept. of Lands and Survey, map of Western Australia (1902–1903)])

been born in June 1903.[722] Today Lion Mill is known as Mount Helena.

Catherine did not live on an ongoing basis with Hannah and in due course she made the trip to Menzies. First this involved travelling more than 550 kilometres by train to Kalgoorlie on a line that had been constructed in 1896. For much of the way Catherine would have travelled alongside the goldfields water pipeline that had only opened in 1903. This pipeline carried desperately needed water from the Darling Ranges near Perth to the dry goldfields. In the 1830s, many people had considered the chain pier in Brighton that went 320 metres out into the English Channel to be one of the wonders of the world. As an engineering achievement, the chain pier paled into insignificance when compared to this pipeline constructed by the legendary Irish-born engineer, Charles Yelverton O'Connor. It was 550 kilometres in length and 760 mm in diameter. With its eight pumping stations it lifted the water over 300 metres elevation before it flowed into a reservoir near Kalgoorlie.

Kalgoorlie was a gold town like Stawell but on a completely different scale. Gold was first found in the region by an Irishman, Paddy Hannan, and just five years after his find, the nearby Boulder mining leases had produced £24 million worth of gold. By 1904, Kalgoorlie had proven to be the richest goldmining centre in Australia. Catherine was very familiar with the features and sounds of goldmining towns, but even she may have been a little daunted by the size and scale of the operations in Kalgoorlie.

From Kalgoorlie, Catherine headed north on the final 130 kilometre leg of her rail journey to Menzies on a section of line that had opened in 1898. She was nearing the end of a journey of more than 3500 kilometres. She was about to arrive at a mining town that was starting to enter a long period of gradual decline. Goldmining had reached its peak around 1900 and by 1904 mines were starting to close down.

Gold was first discovered in Menzies in 1894[723] and the pattern of development that followed was typical of all gold rushes—a rapid expansion in population, substantial investment of capital, construction of mining infrastructure, and construction of town facilities and amenities.

33. The Menzies railway station where in 1904 Catherine Copley completed her long journey from Stawell. The station closed many years ago but the line is still used today for mining industry work.

When Catherine arrived in 1904 she found a town that had all the usual human infrastructure and amenities of the time including a town hall, railway station, a number of pubs, breweries, churches for the main religious denominations, and a wide range of shops. One feature of Menzies that she would have found both new and strange was the Afghan camel drivers' camp that was located near the end of Webb Street, where James and Mary had their house.[724] The camels were known as the ships of the desert and the Afghan camel drivers took the goods that were delivered by train to outlying settlements not connected to the railway. Catherine would not have seen anything like these camels in Ireland, Van Diemen's Land or Victoria.

The climate and the landscape in and around Menzies would have made the biggest impact on Catherine. In summer on average, the temperature reached 40°C or more on one day a week.[725] The average annual rainfall in Menzies was around 250 mm,[726] compared to 530 mm at Stawell.[727] Due to the harshness of the climate, there was hardly a tree of any size and the landscape was made up of red soil, rocks and small scrubby bushes. Most buildings and houses had corrugated-iron walls that heated up during hot days but cooled at night. In following the gold rushes in western Victoria and living at Jallukar and Stawell, Catherine had known hot and unpleasant environments, but the climate in Menzies was considerably harsher than anything she would have previously experienced.

\*\*\*

Meanwhile, back in Stawell a further step was taken in the implementation of the terms of Thomas May's will. On 2 December 1904, the Land Titles Office in Melbourne registered that the ownership of the store in Patrick Street Stawell had been taken over by Harry Hadfield.[728] It is not clear why it took nearly twelve months for this to occur, but once the title was in his name it did not take long for Harry to decide that he did not want to re-open and operate the store. At the start of January 1905, after actually owning the store for only one month, Harry sold it. The *Ararat Chronicle* newspaper contained the following report concerning this sale:

> Mr P.A. Pola, who has for a considerable time past conducted business at Mount William has purchased the premises in Patrick Street, Stawell, formerly owned by the late Mr. T. May, opposite the Caledonian Hotel and intends to carry on business there as a general storekeeper. Mr Pola will take possession next week and will open as soon thereafter as possible.[729]

It took Pietro Pola around two months to get the Patrick Street store ready and stocked for opening. When it re-opened in March, the following advertisement appeared in the *Stawell New and Pleasant Creek Chronicle*:

> IMPORTANT ANNOUNCEMENT!
> MR. P.A. POLA OF MOUNT WILLIAM
> BEGS TO ANNOUNCE THAT HE HAS
> PURCHASED THE PREMISES IN
> PATRICK ST. FORMERLY OCCUPIED
> BY THE LATE MR. T. MAY AND HAS
> OPENED A GENERAL STORE.
> THE BEST OF GOODS WILL BE
> SUPPLIED AT LOWEST PRICES[730]

While Harry Hadfield was selling the store and Pietro Pola was establishing his identity as its new owner, Catherine and her family were moving to sell off the twenty-five acre block at Illawarra. On 30 December 1904, the Land Titles Office in Melbourne recorded that Catherine May no longer owned the block and that Jane Copley, her daughter-in-law, was now the owner of this land. On 16 February 1905, the Land Titles Office in Melbourne recorded that Jane Copley had sold this block back to Remigio Zala.[731]

In selling this land, Catherine was cutting her final link with Stawell and Victoria. By this stage, she appears to have realized that she would spend her final days in Western Australia.

# 32    The Heat of Summer

In the first half of 1906, Catherine turned seventy-nine years of age. She had reached milestones in her life that she had probably never contemplated achieving. She now had twenty-two grandchildren and had just become a great-grandmother. This first great-grandchild, a boy, was born to her first grandson John Robert Copley and his wife Mary Franklin. Predictably the baby was given the name John.[732] By now Catherine must have been starting to feel her age.

On Wednesday, 3 October 1906, Catherine shared in a significant family celebration—the marriage in Menzies of her granddaughter Mary Catherine Copley to Daniel O'Brien, a blacksmith who lived at Kanowna on the Western Australian goldfields.[733] Perhaps at this wedding, Catherine recalled her own marriage to a blacksmith in Hobart Town fifty-four years earlier. The occupation of the groom was about the only similarity between the two weddings, with Mary Catherine's father, James, turning the event into a statement of his family's success.

The 6 October edition of the *North Coolgardie Herald* carried a detailed report of the O'Brien–Copley wedding under the headline 'Orange Blossoms'. It told its readers that 'The Roman Catholic Church, Menzies was the scene of a very pretty wedding'. A local Catholic priest, Father Fagan, 'officiated at the ceremony, which was followed by a Nuptial Mass. Although the ceremony took place at the early hour of 8 am, the church was crowded to its utmost holding capacity with friends and well-wishers of the contracting parties.'

It stated that the bride 'looked charming in a dress of cream silk, trimmed with Paris lace and goffered frills, with the usual wreath and veil, also carrying a white ivory prayer book, inlaid with mother of pearl, the gift of Father Fagan' and it went on to describe the dresses of the two bridesmaids, Bessie and Florence, Mary Catherine's two sisters.

No detail was overlooked and it was reported that 'After the ceremony the wedding party repaired to the residence of the bride's parents, where a splendid wedding breakfast was in readiness' and where 'thirty or forty friends of the happy couple sat down, and after ample justice had been done to the good things provided' a number of toasts were proposed that the guests 'drank in bumpers of champagne'.

The article concluded with a list of the presents given to the bride and groom. These presents were described as being 'numerous and costly' and they included a marble clock from the father of the bride. Catherine must have felt both proud and happy as she watched her granddaughter marry with considerable style, expense and respectability.

\*\*\*

At the start of December Catherine faced another full summer of baking heat. By this time, she had lived through two such summers in Menzies, but familiarity would not have made the experience any easier.

The first week in December 1906 was the first week of summer both in terms of the official calendar and the actual weather. It was later noted in the *North Coolgardie Herald* that the weather at this time in Menzies had 'been decidedly hot and sultry'.[734] Often the hardest part of summer to cope with is the heat in the first hot spell and struggling to cope with the first heat of summer appears to be what broke Catherine's health. A general breakdown of the systems in her body followed. On Thursday 6 December the maximum temperature in Menzies reached 39.7°C and on Friday it was still 37.2°.[735] James and Mary called in a doctor D. Hussey to help Catherine,[736] but unfortunately nothing could be done beyond trying to keep her as cool as possible in the heat.

On Saturday 8 December at around 10 pm,[737] after the heat of the day had gone, Catherine's struggle ended and she died at the home of her son in Webb Street.[738] Although the heat of Menzies almost certainly hastened her death, she had died surrounded by her family and this would surely have given her great comfort.

James wasted no time after his mother's death and Catherine's funeral was arranged for the next day.[739] Sunday was a typical Menzies summer day with the temperature reaching 37.3°C.[740] In the afternoon, the coffin with Catherine's body was taken to the Menzies cemetery,[741] one kilometre north of the town, where the Roman Catholic priest, Father Graham, officiated at the graveside.[742] The *North Coolgardie Herald* reported that the funeral 'was largely attended'.[743]

In officiating at this service, Father Graham was burying a woman whose life had seen great changes. Catherine had lived in a number of very different places ranging from the green hills of County Clare to the hot dry Menzies goldfield. In Ireland, her family had only a tenuous hold on ten acres of land. At Jallukar, she had secure tenure on her own 240 acre farm. In the early 1850s she had been a transported convict with nothing, and by the 1890s she had achieved what should have been lifetime financial security in Stawell. At the time of her birth in 1827, no member of her family had the vote or any say in the political process, but in 1903 she herself had gained the right to vote in an election where women in Stawell fully and actively participated in the political process.

Father Graham was burying a woman who met the challenges of life head-on and seized opportunities when she saw them. Stealing Darby Rogers' sheep was an opportunity for much-needed food. In March 1852 she married John Copley, a man she believed would offer her new opportunities. With John she risked the move from Van Diemen's Land, judging that the penalties of the Vandemonian law were outweighed by the opportunities of the goldfields. She met the challenges of giving birth and raising a family both in the convict system and on the Victorian goldfields. When land was opened up in Victoria for working people to take up selections, she took up the challenge first with John and then, after his death, as a successful selector in her own right.

It appears that Catherine saw her marriage to Thomas May as an opportunity for support and companionship in the final years of her life. This marriage was her greatest failure. Nevertheless, it was her preparedness to meet challenges and to seize opportunities that had allowed her to live such an interesting and successful life.

Catherine Copley, the woman who was born in 1827 in the McMahon family home in Ireland, now lies in the dry, red desert soil of Menzies, Western Australia. She deserves to be remembered.

# EPILOGUE

# What Happened to...

## The Thomas May Will

At the time of Catherine Copley's death in Menzies in 1906, more than three years after the death of Thomas May, the executors had still not finalized their management of his will and estate. They were still leaving open their options to pursue Catherine for funds and property that they may have been able to claim belonged to Harry Hadfield. In fact, it was May 1909 before the executors completed their management of the estate.[744]

A major reason for this delay was that the inheritance from Thomas had proven to be nowhere near as lucrative for Harry Hadfield as was anticipated in October 1903. Although Harry received and sold the title to the Patrick Street store, it is clear that he inherited considerably less than the more than £500 that was suggested in the original assessment.

In the final report of the executors of the will that was submitted to the Supreme Court in May 1909, a set of accounts prepared in December 1904[745] showed that the price received for the groceries that were in stock in the store at the time of Thomas's death was only £67/11/6; considerably less than the value of £191/19/8 that had been given to this stock in the original application for probate.

This set of accounts also showed that only limited success had been achieved in getting payment from the debtors who, in the original probate application, were alleged to owe £95/18/11 to Thomas. The accounts show that only £41 had been received from these alleged debtors.

In fact when the necessary monies had been paid to the executors of the estate and the lawyers, Harry Hadfield was left with only £12/12/9 in cash from the Thomas May estate.

The final report issued in May 1909 contains no record of Catherine or her children ever receiving the one shilling that Thomas left for Catherine in his will.

## The Copley Family in Yorkshire

Probably the biggest frustration in writing this story is that we were able to find out so little about John Copley's first wife Mary. We were not able to discover what happened to Mary after John was convicted of sheep stealing at the York Assizes in March 1840.

We do know that at the time of the April 1841 census, Mary no longer lived in the house she had shared with John on Scholes Lane. In fact, the 1841 census has no record of Mary living in either Scholes or nearby Thorpe Hesley. The 1841 census contained around 110 women who had the name Mary Copley. The vast majority of these due to their age and marital situation were clearly not John's wife, and further research into the background of the remaining women failed to satisfy us that any of them were possibilities.

What can be said is that, following John's conviction and transportation, Mary almost certainty experienced a punishment just as great, if not greater than her husband. Not only was she left with three young children to support, she also had to live with the stigma of being the wife of a convict. It would be fascinating to know what happened to her and the three children after John was transported to Van Diemen's Land.

John's father, also named John Copley, continued to live in Thorpe Hesley after his son was transported. The April 1861 England census showed this John Copley living in Sough Hall in Thorpe Hesley and at seventy-two years of age he was still working as a nailor.[746] On 8 May 1861, John Copley senior died of 'Decay of Nature' and was buried in the church yard of the Holy Trinity Anglican church in Thorpe Hesley.[747]

## James Fraser

After James Fraser was banished from Hobart Town in July 1851, he lived the rest of his life in the north of the colony. He received his ticket-of-leave on 26 September 1854, a month and a half after John Copley. On 11 June 1855 he was convicted in Launceston of being drunk and he was fined £1. He received a conditional pardon on 23 September 1856.[748] This was two months after John received his conditional pardon.

The convict authorities repeatedly rejected requests for James to be given permission to marry his long-time partner Marie Matthews but they eventually married in 1859.[749] James died of peritonitis on 13 April 1871 at Longford in the north of Tasmania. He was working as a gardener at the time of his death.[750]

## Norfolk Island

The penal settlement on Norfolk Island was closed down in 1855, only four years after John Copley was taken off the island.[751] The British authorities had decided that there was no future for such a place of brutal, unrelenting punishment.

The walls around the nail making and blacksmith shop on the edge of Slaughter Bay, where John worked between 1847 and 1851, still stand. Today, this area is used as a base for the maintenance workers who have the job of maintaining the historic remains of the Norfolk Island penal settlement area. In August 2010, the historic significance of this area was recognized when UNESCO gave it World Heritage listing as a place of special cultural and physical significance.

Even though more than 160 years have passed since the whale boat was upset on the evening of 12 April 1848, whale boats are still used today to move goods onto Norfolk Island from ships anchored offshore. These whale boats are towed by smaller motorized boats. There is still no safe harbour on Norfolk Island.[752] No one today, even with motorized towing boats, would dream of trying to land a whale boat laden with goods or people in the dark of night.

## Matthew Walker

The Walker family did not escape from Norfolk Island unscathed. On 11 June 1849, Matthew and Jane Walker's twenty-six-day-old daughter, Matilda, died on the island, and on 30 December 1850 Elizabeth, aged four and a half, also died.[753] Both were buried in the Norfolk Island cemetery and today an appropriately small headstone, carved by a convict stonemason, still marks the grave of these young girls. Matthew Walker stayed on Norfolk Island until the last convict left in 1855.[754] At this time he was the most senior official on the island, holding the position of Superintendent of Convicts.

In March 1864, Matthew was appointed to a position in the NSW prison service and for most of the 1870s he was the Governor of the Goulburn gaol.[755]

Matthew lived for a further thirty-four years after he was rescued from the rough surf off Norfolk Island in 1848. He died at Liverpool, twenty kilometres west of Sydney, on 13 August 1882.[756]

## Point Puer

When Thomas May arrived at the juvenile establishment at Point Puer in August 1842 it held around 800 boy convicts.[757] From that time on, the number steadily declined and by 1844 when Thomas left there were only 162 boys in residence there.[758] By the late 1840s, the British authorities no longer used transportation as a punishment for convicted juvenile offenders and, as a consequence, Point Puer was abandoned in 1849 and the few remaining juvenile inmates were removed to the Government Farm at New Town near Hobart.[759]

Both the materials and the construction methods that had been used to build the Point Puer juvenile establishment were of poor quality. These buildings soon decayed, collapsed and disappeared. There is little trace of them and the baking oven area used by the boy convicts is the only remaining physical feature of the establishment. Today you can walk through the area at Point Puer where Thomas May learnt to grow vegetables and crops. From this area, you can look across the bay at the remains of the Port Arthur convict settlement and visit the Isle of the Dead that lies just offshore.

## Cascades Female Factory

In October 1851, when Catherine completed her last stint in the Cascades Female Factory, it was experiencing a major overcrowding problem with more than 1000 female convict inmates.[760] This situation did not last. In April 1853, the last transportation vessel carrying female convicts arrived in Hobart Town and after this the number of inmates at the Factory rapidly declined.

By January 1865, the Cascades Factory and all the staff had become the responsibility of the Tasmanian colonial government. At this time, the Factory held female offenders convicted of offences in Tasmania and only a handful of women transported from England and Ireland.[761] In 1877 it ceased to be a prison for convicted female prisoners.[762] In the latter part of the nineteenth century, parts of the site were used as a depot for female invalids, a depot for male invalids, a boy's reformatory and a contagious diseases hospital. The last of these facilities closed in 1896 and the Cascades Factory site was left untenanted.[763]

Today the Cascades Female Factory area is a site of historic significance. There are no major buildings still standing but the walls that imprisoned Catherine and thousands of other transported female convicts still surround the site. Large stone wash tubs that convicts like Catherine slaved over during sentences of hard labour can be seen in the memorial garden on the site. In August 2010, the Cascades Female Factory was listed as a UNESCO World Heritage site.

## Lamplough

The town of Lamplough entered a period of rapid decline after thousands of diggers and their families abandoned the town in December 1860. In April 1861, 469 people lived at Lamplough but by 1905 the population had dwindled to fifty. Today only one family lives on the site of the town[764] and a sign on the Sunraysia Highway five kilometres south of Avoca is all that remains to show us where Lamplough was located.

## William O'Callaghan

After his election to the Victorian parliament in February 1880, William O'Callaghan had a gruelling three years as a member for the seat of Wimmera. In 1880, this seat covered the area in western Victoria from Mildura and Swan Hill in the north to farmland south of Horsham. In visiting his constituents, William travelled for hundreds of kilometres, relying largely on horse-drawn transportation. At this time there were only limited rail services in the north-west of the colony.

In 1882, Skibbereen-born William was at the centre of a major controversy when he, along with four other members of the Victorian parliament, signed a document entitled the 'Grattan Centenary Address' from 'the Irish in Victoria to the Irish in Ireland'. This address referred to the British imperial government of Ireland as 'foreign despotism' and spoke with pride of the struggle for Irish independence and home rule. William and the other four members of parliament were strongly criticized. Public meetings across Victoria 'emphatically denounced' them.[765]

In February 1883, William stood for re-election as a member for the seat of Wimmera. He cited the success of representations he had made to the Minister for Lands that resulted in the maximum amount of land a selector could take up being increased from 320 acres to 640 acres and he reminded the electors of the 170 kilometres of new rail line and nine new state schools that had been constructed by the government in the Wimmera electorate since his election in 1880.[766]

He pledged that if re-elected to the parliament he would push for married women to be given the right to select and take up farm land.[767] This reform was needed to allow women like Catherine Copley to be able to retain land they owned under selection leases if they remarried. In the early 1880s in Victoria, married women had no right whatsoever to own any property.

The Wimmera electorate was not impressed. William was soundly defeated in the 1883 election, as were another two of the four MPs who signed the Grattan Centenary Address.

William O'Callaghan died on 26 June 1891. He was seventy-three years of age.[768] Soon after his death, the *Seymour Express* newspaper described him as 'a public man in every sense of the word … a genial, kindly citizen' and 'a sterling friend'.[769] Undoubtedly Catherine would have agreed with this description.

# Daniel Sullivan

Daniel Sullivan's contribution to knowledge of the flora of the Grampian Mountains was recognized in 1884 when he was elected as a Fellow of the Linnaean Society in London. The Linnaean Society is a leading international organization that encourages debate and research into the biological sciences. In early 1895, Daniel made his final contribution as a botanist when the record of his work in the Grampians was published in the book, *A Complete Census of the Flora of the Grampians and Pyrenees* (Victoria).[770]

Daniel died in June 1895.[771] On his death, his estate that included his botany collection only had a financial value of £55.[772] Today thousands of people every year visit the Grampian mountain ranges to admire and enjoy the wild flowers that he first identified in the 1870s and 1880s.

## David Gaunson

After helping Catherine to secure the leases covering her Jallukar selections, David Gaunson was defeated at an election for the seat of Ararat in July 1881. One can only wonder whether his leading role in the defence of the infamous bushranger Ned Kelly worked against him in this rural electorate. In the following twenty-five years, Gaunson repeatedly stood for election to the Victoria parliament.[773] He was re-elected on several occasions but failed to make the same impact he had made in the 1870s and early 1880s. In the mid-1890s, he became the legal adviser to John Wren, the Melbourne gambling identity and entrepreneur who was immortalized in the Frank Hardy book *Power Without Glory*. Gaunson died in 1907 and John Wren was one of the pallbearers.

## Jallukar

After Catherine sold her Jallukar selections in 1888, the area continued to develop. A key landmark in the establishment of any Australian community occurred on 22 November 1895 when a public meeting at the state school determined to establish the Jallukar cricket club.[774] By the year 1900, virtually all of the land in the district had been taken up by selectors.

By 1906, 400 to 500 people lived at Jallukar. Most families owned their own farms. A government-funded school educated the children of these farmers and it was a requirement in law that all children attend. In the first decade of the twentieth century, an annual magazine was published by the Jallukar community titled *Red Man's Review*, named after the Grampians peak that towered over John and Catherine's selection. The *Red Man's Review* featured local news for the previous year and contained stories and poetry written by community members.[775] At this time, Jallukar had a debating society that competed with other debating groups from surrounding areas. The important issues of the time were debated in the community hall and these debates were major social events.

After the First World War, the Jallukar community entered a period of gradual and continual decline. As the land-holdings of individual farmers became bigger, the population decreased. Transportation improved and the farmers who stayed in the area used either Moyston to the south or Pomonal to the north and the bigger centres of Ararat and Stawell as their service and social centres. In 1946, a public meeting voted to disband the Jallukar cricket club.[776]

Today, while it is marked on most maps, there is not even a signpost on the Moyston to Pomonal road to indicate you are passing through Jallukar. While Jallukar has disappeared, it will always be a place where in the second half of the nineteenth century numerous people, most of them born in England or Ireland, worked relentlessly to establish their own farms and to provide a far better life for themselves and their children.

## The Copley Selections Under Redman Bluff

Ronald MacMaster from Lake Bolac, who purchased Catherine's two selections in 1888,[777] retained ownership of the land until 1911. In that year he sold this land to Harrie Banfield,[778] then the editor of the *Ararat Advertiser*, who used the 240 acres under Redman Bluff as a weekend retreat. When on the property, he stayed in Mountain Hut, originally

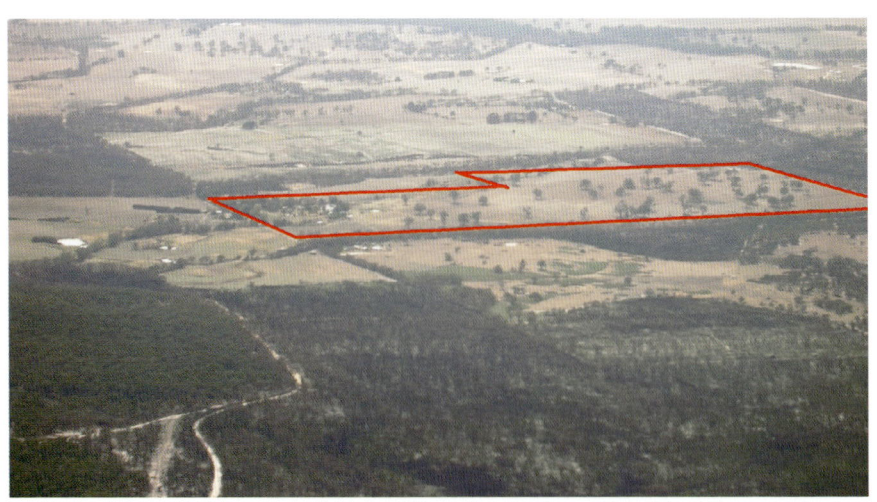

34. Photo taken in 2006 from top of Mount William showing the outline of the 240 acres of land that John Copley selected in 1875/76.

constructed by the Copleys in the 1870s and 1880s as their family home. This house was destroyed in the 1939 Black Friday bushfires that devastated the Grampian ranges and resulted in the loss of seventy-one Victorian lives. Harrie Banfield cleared much of the land and ran cattle on the 240 acres.

Today, it is still possible to appreciate the dimensions of John and Catherine's 240 acre selections by climbing Mount William. Looking to the north-east from the top of the mountain, a patch of mostly cleared land can be seen that is largely surrounded by bushland. The outline of this patch of land roughly reflects the boundaries shown on the Copley's 1876 land selection maps.

The 240 acres of land that John and Catherine selected are still owned by the Banfield family. On this land, the Banfields operate a tourist park with the wholly appropriate name Grampians Paradise. With the stunning backdrop of Mount William and Redman Bluff, this park is surely a place of true peace and beauty.

In the last twenty-five years, the Banfields have carried out extensive work to turn the land into parkland featuring a wide range of native flora and fauna. They have worked to re-establish the Redman Bluff Wetland on the property and this has included the construction of lakes of various sizes and depths. There are now eight species of frogs in the wetland, including the endangered growling grass frog,[779] and the park has an abundance of wild flowers, native birds and animals.

John and Catherine selected this land because they recognized its fertility and its potential to grow crops and vegetables and support livestock to feed hungry miners and their families. After the close confinement of convict life, they must have felt at times that this was a place where you could believe you were the only people in a tranquil world. When you walk this land today, you share this feeling.

## Vida Goldstein and Elections in Stawell

At the 1906 federal election that was held four days after Catherine died in Menzies, there was no female candidate for the citizens of Stawell to vote for. Vida Goldstein did not stand for election. The attitude of the citizens of Stawell to female involvement in the political process was totally different at this 1906 election and the press reflected this. At the 1903 election, the *Stawell News and Pleasant Creek Chronicle* reported extensively on women having the vote and female involvement in the political process. The only comment this newspaper made prior to the 1906 election in relation to women voting was that 'women should avoid voting at times when men will rush booths'.[780]

In 1910 Vida Goldstein again stood in Victoria for election to the Senate, but this time she did not have a campaign meeting in Stawell. When the election results for the Stawell electoral subdivision were announced, Vida only received seventy-five votes, or 5.2 percent of the vote. This contrasts starkly with the more than 30 percent vote she received in 1903. Across the state of Victoria, Vida received 16 percent of the vote.[781] This state-wide vote was virtually identical to the percentage of the vote she received in

1903 and again she fell well short of being elected to the parliament.

In researching this book, we were surprised that there seemed to be little or no appreciation in Stawell of the significant historical landmark that the town had achieved in 1903 in voting to elect a woman to the federal parliament. After all, this woman was Vida Goldstein, Australia's leading women's rights campaigner, and this vote happened forty years before the first woman was actually elected to the Australian federal parliament. Further, while we do not claim to have extensively researched the matter, we could find no reference to any other Victorian community that at the 1903 election voted to elect a woman to the parliament.

The reason for this lack of appreciation of the 1903 Stawell vote for Vida no doubt lies with the stand she took in relation to the First World War. In 1914, on the declaration of war, Vida publicly stated that: 'The time has come for women to show that they, as givers of life, refuse to give their sons as material for slaughter, and that they recognize that human life must be the first consideration of nations'.[782] This stand was totally consistent with the position Vida had enunciated at the Stawell Town Hall public meeting in October 1903 when she stated 'there never was a good war or a bad peace',[783] and throughout the war Vida was an active anti-war campaigner.

In 1917, Vida again stood for election to the senate but this time she stood on an anti-war policy platform. While Vida should be admired for her preparedness to stand up for her long-held belief, in 1917 Stawell there was no support for this view. In this Senate election only twenty-two people in the Stawell electoral sub-division voted for Vida.[784] In May 1917, the *Stawell News and Pleasant Creek Chronicle* that had so strongly supported her in 1903 commented:

> A notable feature about the Senate elections is the severe rebuff electors in the State have given the independent candidate, Vida Goldstein. In no part of the State was she favoured with a decent vote, thus showing that her views were in no way acceptable. Her deposit is almost certain to enrich the consolidated revenue.[785]

Vida Goldstein was correct in her statement at the start of the First World War that it would turn into a slaughter. Between 1914 and 1918, more than 60,000 Australian men died in this war and from the Stawell district alone there were 134 deaths.[786] At the May 1917 election, the voters in Stawell strongly rejected Vida because they just could not contemplate much less accept that there was no adequate justification for the death of all these men. After the war, the Stawell community was apparently not at all keen to recognize or remember that in 1903 it had actually voted to elect this woman to the federal parliament.

After the 1917 election, Vida retired from active involvement in politics. She died in August 1949.[787]

# Harry Hadfield

Harry Hadfield continued to live in Stawell after he sold the Patrick Street shop to Pietro Pola in January 1905. In the same year, Harry's wife Mary gave birth to a son, Joseph.[788] Mary Hadfield died in May 1912.[789] In July 1913 Harry Hadfield married a widow, Agnes Ewers,[790] and in September of that year eight-year-old Joseph died.[791]

Harry Hadfield died on 29 September 1953. This was fifty years and one day after the death of his benefactor Thomas May. He died in a Salvation Army Men's Eventide Home in the Melbourne suburb of Blackburn. The death certificate identified him as 'Henry Joseph Hayes, known as Henry Joseph Hadfield'. He was buried with his first wife in the Stawell cemetery.[792]

# Hannah Green (daughter of John and Catherine)

In 1907, Hannah and her husband Thomas Green gave up farming at Lion Mill, thirty-five kilometres east of Perth.[793] When Hannah died on

9 January 1925 she was living at 119 Goslin Street in Subiaco, a suburb of Perth. She was sixty-four years of age. Her husband Thomas had died before her. At Hannah's death, nine of her ten children were still living.[794]

## Mary and James Copley

In either 1915 or early 1916, Mary and James Copley moved from the eastern goldfields in Western Australia to live in Fremantle, near Perth.[795]

1916 must have been a dreadful year for both Mary and James. On 5 April their eldest son, twenty-seven-year-old James Joseph, joined the Australian Army and commenced training to fight on the Western Front in France.[796] On 26 May their youngest son, nineteen-year-old Stanley, also enlisted.[797] Just one week after Stanley enlisted to fight, their middle son, twenty-four-year-old Ernest, died. As a sad illustration of the unpredictability of life, Ernest died when he fell off a cart while working as a grocer at Leonora, a hundred kilometres north of Menzies, in the Western Australian goldfields.[798] Then near the end of the year, Mary and James had to farewell both their remaining sons as they left Fremantle on troop ships to fight on what had become the killing fields of the Western Front.

James Copley died on 17 September 1927 at the family home at 30 Forrest Street in Fremantle.[799] Mary Copley died at the same family home on 23 August 1941.[800]

## John Copley (son of John and Catherine)

In April or May 1905, John Copley, along with the rest of his family, moved from Mafeking in the Grampian mountains to Yarram in South Gippsland, Victoria.[801] In Yarram, the Copleys ran a carting business. In 1915, John,

Jane and their four unmarried children (one son and three daughters) moved back to western Victoria and lived at Ararat,[802] where John worked as a labourer on the railways.[803] Jane died in 1921,[804] and John on 18 March 1934.[805] Both are buried in the Copley family grave in the Catholic section of the Ararat cemetery.

## Denis McMahon (Catherine's Brother)

Some time after his marriage to Susan in May 1856, Denis McMahon moved from Hobart Town to the north of Tasmania. In December 1858, Denis lived in a house on Westbury Road, Westbury,[806] but by December 1860 he had moved onto a twenty acre farm at Selborne, fourteen kilometres northeast of Westbury.[807] In the late 1850s and early 1860s, it appears that Denis lived not far from his brother William.

In September 1860, Denis became a father and this child, a son, was named James.[808] In February 1862, Susan gave birth to a second son, Michael.[809]

It appears that some time after the birth of Michael, Denis and his family moved across Bass Strait to Victoria, where they lived on Little Leichhardt Street in Melbourne.[810] On 25 March 1868, Susan gave birth to a daughter whom they named Catherine. Baby Catherine died four days after her birth.[811]

Susan McMahon died on 14 June 1881 in Melbourne.[812] Either before or soon after the death of his wife, Denis moved back to Tasmania, where he died in Launceston on 2 November 1889. He was listed as a labourer at the time of his death.[813]

## William McMahon (Catherine's Brother)

After completing his ten year transportation sentence, William McMahon stayed in Tasmania and married Mary Anne Keane on 8 May 1862.[814] Mary Anne had been born in Tulla in County Clare only twenty kilometres to the south-west of William's birthplace at Cappabane. Mary Anne and William had five children; four sons and one daughter. After his marriage, William worked first as a farm labourer and then as a tenant farmer near Deloraine in the north of Tasmania. In 1890, William and his son William Patrick first leased and then purchased a 148 acre farm at Quamby bordering the Meander River near Westbury, ten kilometres east of Deloraine.[815] William died on 4 April 1905, twenty months before his sister Catherine Copley.[816]

## The McMahons at Cappabane

After Catherine, Denis and William McMahon were convicted of sheep stealing and transported to Van Diemen's Land, members of the McMahon family continued to live at Cappabane and we know that in 1855, Catherine's brother Michael leased land there.[817] We have not been able to discover what happened to Catherine's mother Margaret or her three remaining brothers, James, Patrick and John.

In the 1850s Michael McMahon married and he brought up his family at Cappabane. In April 1901, Michael's son, Patrick, and his family lived on and farmed this land. By this time Patrick was forty-two years of age and he lived with his wife Mary and their family of one son and five daughters. Patrick spoke both Irish and English but his children did not speak Irish.[818]

Today, Paddy Joe McMahon and his wife Una continue to live at Cappabane. Paddy Joe is the great-grandson of Catherine's brother Michael. In early September 2007, we were able to visit Paddy Joe and Una at their home.

Like us, it was only in the last few years that Paddy Joe and Una heard of the conviction and transportation of Catherine, Denis and William in the middle of the nineteenth century. It appears that the branches of the family on different sides of the world had decided to try to forget and put these traumatic events behind them. Paddy Joe told us that the conviction and transportation of the three McMahon siblings helped to explain to him why previous generations of McMahons hated the English with such great passion and intensity. He understood that the struggle for Irish independence justifiably generated very strong feelings, but it seemed to him that the conviction, transportation and loss of three members of one family in the terrible circumstances of the Irish potato famine could only add to the intensity of this feeling.

During our visit, Paddy Joe showed us the location of the old McMahon family home that in February 1849 Catherine and two of her brothers saw for the last time when they left for their fateful visit to Darby Roger's sheep field. We visited the Mass Rock and we also took in the magnificent view to the east looking across Lough Derg to the hills of northern Tipperary.

## Catherine's Final Resting Place

When we visited Paddy Joe and Una McMahon at their home in Ireland, the one major part of Catherine's story we still had not discovered was the location and time of her death. We did not yet know that Catherine had moved to Western Australia after the death of Thomas May in 1903. However, because two of her children had moved to Western Australia, we had checked a register of deaths in that state, but Catherine's death was not contained in this register. We could find no death certificate for her in Victoria. We searched under both May and Copley but to no avail. We spent many days in the Victorian State Library in Melbourne checking every edition of the *Stawell News and Pleasant Creek Chronicle* from 1903 to 1908 hoping to find some reference that would tell us what had happened to Catherine. We spent fruitless days walking through cemeteries in western Victoria in the hope that we would stumble upon a headstone engraved with her name.

Our visit to her birthplace in County Clare inspired us to try again and in January 2008 we found a new listing for the death of a Catherine May in Menzies, Western Australia, on 8 December 1906. In no time, we obtained a copy of the death certificate and it verified that we had finally found Catherine.[819] On the day we received this certificate, we determined to visit her grave in the Menzies cemetery.

In August 2008 we made this visit to Menzies. Menzies today is a faint shadow of the town that Catherine lived in from 1904 through to her death in December 1906. Only around a hundred people live there today. The Menzies Town Hall built in the late 1890s during the peak of the gold boom is the most substantial building left in the town. Webb Street where Catherine lived with her son James and his family still exists, but there are only three houses in it. The rest of the street is a sandy, red desert landscape. We found it very hard to picture the October 1906 wedding celebration in Webb Street where Catherine and the rest of the family toasted the bride and groom with bumpers of champagne.

We found the grave of Catherine Copley in the Roman Catholic section of the Menzies cemetery. We believe we may have been the first people in more than ninety years to visit her grave.

35. Catherine Copley's grave in the Roman Catholic section of the Menzies cemetery.

We had a very special task to perform during this visit. Paddy Joe McMahon had sent us a piece of grey slate that had been part of the old McMahon family home at Cappabane and he wanted us to place this stone on Catherine's grave. Catherine now lies in her remote Western Australian grave with a lasting link to her early life in Ireland. Her Irish and Australian relatives salute her.

# Acknowledgments

This book could not have been written without access to the resources and information held by numerous libraries, archive centres, museums and local history and genealogical groups both in Australia and overseas. These organizations vary from major national libraries to small volunteer-run community groups. All these organizations play a vital role because they are repositories of the information that helps us explain and understand our past. We thank all these organizations and their staff members for their invaluable assistance.

We gratefully acknowledge the help and support given by Hans and Jennifer Schroeder during the writing and finalizing of this manuscript. Their input was greatly appreciated.

We also wish to thank Anne McMahon, a descendant of Catherine's brother William. Anne gave us access to some primary source material and references that have been invaluable in writing the book. Additionally, we appreciated Anne's review of the manuscript.

# List of Illustrations

1. Places of significance in the story of Catherine McMahon. This map taken from: d-maps.com/carte.php?lib=ireland_map&num_car=2295&lang=en.

2. The view today from the site of Catherine McMahon's childhood home.

3. 1842 Ordnance Survey map covering the Scarriff and Cappabane region with places of significance highlighted. Reproduced with permission from the Clare County Library, Ennis, Co. Clare, Ireland.

4. 1820 painting of the Ennis Courthouse (right) by William Turner de Lond titled 'The marketplace and court-house, Ennis, Co. Clare'. Reproduced with permission from Tony Honan, Honan Antiques, Ennis, County Clare, Ireland.

5. The *Anson* moored at Queen's Domain near Hobart Town. Reproduced with permission from the Tasmanian Archive and Heritage Office (PH30-1-1980).

6. The Cascades Female Factory in 1880. Reproduced with permission from the Tasmanian Archive and Heritage Office (NS1013/1/46).

7. Map of England showing places of significance in the story of John Copley. This map was taken from: d-maps.com/carte.php?lib=england_map&num_car=5579&lang=en.

8. York Court House where in 1840 John Copley was convicted and sentenced.

9. The Hobart Town Supreme Court (left) where John Copley was convicted of house burglary in April 1847. Reproduced with permission from the Tasmanian Archive and Heritage Office (PH52/1/9/17).

10. Part of a sketch of the convict establishment at Kingston on the south coast of Norfolk Island with significant features marked. Reproduced with permission from the Tasmanian Archive and Heritage Office. Taken from (PH30-1-8644).

11. The Norfolk Island jetty. Photo courtesy of the Norfolk Island Museum.

12. The headstone on the grave of Alfred Essex Baldock with its inaccurate and puzzling quotation from the book of Matthew.

13. The pentagonal gaol at Kingston, Norfolk Island (the new gaol) where convicts served punishment sentences for breaches of discipline. Reproduced with permission from the Tasmanian Archive and Heritage Office (PWD266-1-1891).

14. St David's Church in Hobart Town where Catherine McMahon and John Copley married in March 1852. Reproduced with permission from the Allport Library and Museum of Fine Arts, Tasmanian Archive and Heritage Office (AUTAS 001139592646).

15. 1858 view from St David's Church looking down Murray Street, Hobart Town. Reproduced with permission from the Tasmanian Archive and Heritage Office (NS1013/1/1124).

16. Section of the 1858 Jarman map of Hobart Town showing the area around Sullivan's Cove. Reproduced with permission from the Tasmanian Archive and Heritage Office (Taken from map of Hobart Town drawn and engraved by R. Jarman 1858 AUTAS 001131821787).

17. Map of western Victoria. Based on (Hughes, William 1817-1876, Victoria [cartographic material] 1865–1875, MAP NK 2456/140) contained in the National Library of Australia Maps Collection.

18. Map of south-east England showing places of significance in the story of Thomas May. This map taken from: d-map.com/carte.php?lib=south_east_england_map&num_car=16357&lang=en

19. A small part of King George IV's Royal Pavilion.

20. 1899 map of Brighton, England. Part of the following map owned by the State Library of Victoria (Taken from Map Brighton, England Maps 216.7 ATU 1917 [1840 – Sussex No 66 Edward Stanford 12,13 & 14 Long Acre WC, Geographer to the King, Sussex {East} Sheet LXVI = Second Edition 1899]).

21. Part of 1840s map of the Point Puer Boy Convict Settlement. Reproduced with permission from the Tasmanian Archive and Heritage Office and taken from PWD266-1-1846 'Plan – Tasman Peninsula – Point Puer – New Gaol and Settlement'.

22. View of the Grampian Mountains from the Copleys' eighty acre selection block.

23. March 1875 Lands Department drawing of the sixty-seven acre Thomas May Jallukar selection and the bordering forty acre selection held by the younger John Copley. Drawing reproduced with permission from the Victorian Department of Sustainability and Environment (PROV, VPRS 626/P, Unit 87, File 2452/19.20 'Mason/Smith/Copley', May/Copley selection drawing).

24. 1884 map of Stawell, Ararat and Grampians mountain area. Part of the (Sands & McDougall Limited Victoria [cartographic material] 1884 MAP RM 3865) contained in the national Library of Australia Maps Collection.

25. May 1876 land selection drawing showing the two Copley selections located near Redman Bluff. Drawing reproduced with permission from the Victorian Department of Sustainability and Environment (PROV, VPRS 626/P, Unit 71, File 286 'Copley/McMaster', Copley selection drawing).

26. Mountain Hut beneath Redman Bluff, taken around 1911. Photo reproduced with permission

from Tom Banfield, Grampians Paradise Camping and Caravan Parkland.

27. William O'Callaghan, MP for Wimmera from 1880 to 1883. The Victorian Parliamentary Library, Parliament of Victoria, Melbourne is the source for this image.

28. David Gaunson, the MP for Ararat from 1875 to 1881. The Victorian Parliamentary Library, Parliament of Victoria, Melbourne is the source for this image.

29. Stawell in 1880 from the top of the Quartz Reefs. Photo reproduced with permission from the Stawell Historical Society.

30. 1902 photo of Vida Goldstein. Reproduced with the permission of Meredith and Diana Creightmore.

31. A picture card promoting the SS *Buninyong*. This image is owned by the State Library of Victoria (H92.302/20).

32. Taken from 1902 map of Western Australia. Map reproduced courtesy of the Barr Smith Library of the University of Adelaide [Daisy Bates Special Col./86, Western Australia Department of Lands and Survey, map of Western Australia (1902–1903)].

33. The Menzies railway station where in 1904 Catherine Copley completed her long journey from Stawell.

34. Mount William showing the outline of the 240 acres of land that John Copley selected in 1875/76.

35. Catherine Copley's grave in the Roman Catholic section of the Menzies cemetery.

36. Stone on Catherine McMahon's grave.

# Bibliography

## Archival Sources

*Ireland*
1825 Tythe Applotment for Parish of Moyne, Townland of East Shean
1855 Griffith Land Valuation, Parish of Moyne, Townland of Cappaghabaun Park
1855 Griffith Land Valuation, Parish of Tomgraney, Townland of Augrim
1901 Ireland Census, County Clare, Cappabane
National Archives of Ireland, Dublin, Document Reference TR 7, p. 100, Record 528 of 567, McMahon, William: http://www.nationalarchives.ie/cgi-bin/naisearch01
National Archives of Ireland, Dublin, Outrage Papers 5/279, 1849

*England*
1841 England Census
1851 England Census
1861 England Census
British Vital Record, LDS FHL 1067107 Dates 1826-1836 (Thomas May christening)
Essex Record Office ('ERO'), Lewes, Calendar of Prisoners, QCR1/EW6/1
ERO, Lewes, QS Midsummer Case No 15 Ref QR/E862
ERO, Lewes, QS Roll, Trial Indictment, December 1841
ERO, Lewes, QS Midsummer QCR 1/4/E6
ERO, Lewes, QCR 1/4/E7
Sheffield and Rotherham Red Book 1868, Sheffield Archive
St Mary's Church Ecclesfield, Yorkshire births, marriages and deaths registers
UK National Archives, Kew, ASSI 44/156, Court Notice of Convictions
UK National Archives, Kew, HO8/65 and 66 (June–December 1840)
UK National Archives, Kew, HO8/70, Register of Prisoners on the Hulks

*Tasmanian Archive and Heritage Office*
AE 764/1/71 John Copley Insolvency File
CON 14/1/5 John Goss, Identification, convict record
CON 14/1/8 John Copley, Identification, convict record
CON 14/1/16, Thomas May, Identification, convict record
CON 14/1/16 Thomas Sargent, Identification, convict record
CON 14/1/43 Denis McMahon and William McMahon, Identification, convict record
CON 15/1/6 Catherine McMahon, Identification, convict record
CON 18/1/26 John Copley, Description List, convict record
CON 31/1/14 James Fraser, Conduct Record, convict record
CON 33/1/6 John Copley, Conduct Record, convict record
CON 33/1/11 Alfred Essex Baldock, Conduct Record, convict record
CON 33/1/25 Thomas May, Conduct Record, convict record
CON 33/1/25 Thomas Sargent, Conduct Record, convict record
CON 33/1/100 Denis McMahon and William McMahon, Conduct Record, convict record
CON 37/1/3 James Fraser, Conduct Record, convict record
CON 41/1/24 Catherine McMahon, Conduct Record, convict record
CON 52/3 and CON 52/5 Convict Applications to Marry
CSO 50 – 19 to 27 Government Blue Books from 1844 to 1850
SC32 – Minutes of Proceedings in Criminal Cases various centres, including Norfolk Island; SC 32/1/6 – Hobart, Oatlands January 1847 – December 1851
Tasmanian Archives, Tasmania Colonial Family Index
Tasmania Westbury Valuation Rolls for 1858 and 1860

## Victoria
*State Library of Victoria*
1869 Land Selection Act
General Report on the State of the School at the Settlement Norfolk Island—State Library of Victoria
Ledcourt Station Cash Book – State Library of Victoria (Manuscript Collection—MS Box 914/1-2)
Redman's Review, State Library of Victoria(SLTF 052 R24J)
*Public Record Office Victoria (PROV)*
Public Record Office Victoria, Daniel Sullivan will and probate 59*434 1895
Public Record Office Victoria, Theresa H Shea will and probate 65/376 1897 (North Melbourne)
Public Record Office Victoria, James Walter letters of administration 86.86 1903 (North Melbourne)
Public Record Office Victoria, Thomas May will and probate 88.857 1903 (North Melbourne)
CRS K269, Roll 14—Passenger Arrivals Western Australia (North Melbourne)
VPRS 625/P, Unit 106, File 5707, Thomas May selection file (PROV—Melbourne)
VPRS 626/P, Unit 71, File 273/20, Copley/McMaster selection file (PROV—Melbourne)
VPRS 626/P, Unit 71, File 286, Copley/McMaster selection file (PROV—Melbourne)
VPRS 626/P, Unit 87, File 2452/19.20, Mason/Smith/Copley selection file (PROV—Melbourne)
VPRS 626/P, Unit 95, File 3125, Thomas May selection file (PROV—Melbourne)
VPRS 626, Parish of Jallukar, Land selection file 2084/19.20
VPRS 01677/P/0000, Unit 000011, Type V2, Ararat Court Minute Book (PROV—Ballarat)
VPRS 1103, Units 8 to 14, Stawell Borough Rate Records (PROV—Ballarat)
VPRS 3506, Melbourne Outward Passenger Departures (PROV—North Melbourne)
VPRS 3770, Units 3 to 20, Stawell Shire Rate Records (PROV—Ballarat)
VPRS 12991/P/0001, Unit 3, Type V2, Ararat Shire Council Minute Book (PROV—Ballarat)
VPRS 13753/P/001, Ararat Section 19 and 20 Land Act 1869, Unit 001, Type V3, (PROV—North Melbourne)
VPRS 15206/P0001 Ararat Shire Rate Book Units 3 to 23 (PROV—Ballarat)
VPRS 15250/P/001, Ararat Shire Letter Book (PROV—Ballarat)
*Other Victorian Archive References*
Avoca Historical Society, website, Lamplough name index
Melbourne National Archives, Consign No B 5846/1
Victorian Land Title, Parish of Illawarra, Crown Allotment 45A
Victorian land Title Records for Parish of Stawell, section 44, crown land allotment 14A
Stawell Genealogical Group Record of Admissions to Stawell Hospital

## New South Wales
Aaron Price Diary on Norfolk Island, Dixson Library

## Western Australia
Western Australia Post Office Directories 1901 to 1916
Shire of Menzies web site (www.menzies.wa.gov.au)
State Library of Western Australia – Harry P. Woodward, Geological Map of Menzies, North Coolgardie, 1905—Call No. 4730/14/(37/15)

### Articles and Papers
Baxter, John L., 'Early Chartism and Labour Class Struggle: South Yorkshire 1837–1840', appeared in *Essays in the Economic and Social History of South Yorkshire*, edited by Sidney Pollard and Colin Holmes, South Yorkshire County Council, 1976
Cooper, Stephen, 'Burglars and Sheepstealers', appeared in *Crime and Criminals in a South Yorkshire Village in the 19th Century*, 1992
Cooper, Stephen, 'The Stirrings in Thorpe Hesley on Saturday Night', appeared in *Aspects of Rotherham*, edited by Melvyn Jones, Wharncliffe Publishing, 1995
Dalkin, Nixon R., *Colonial Era Cemetery of Norfolk Island – Entry 23 Baldock, A.E.*, Pacific Publications, 1891
Enright, Flannan P., *Transportation from the Clare Spring Assizes of 1849*
Jenks, Doctor, *Report on the Sanitary State of the Town of Brighton and on the Causes and Prevention of Fever*, 5 April 1840
Jones, Melvyn, *The People of Thorpe Hesley and Scholes*, 1990
Jones, William H.B., *Surgeon Superintendent on Elphinstone(4) report on transportation voyage*, 18 August 1842
Kilroy, Alexander, *Surgeon Superintendent on Australasia report on transportation voyage*, 12 October 1849

McMahon, Anne, 'The Anson as Female Reformatory Hulk', *Tasmanian Ancestry*, March 2009
McMahon, Anne, and Owen, K.M., *Transported to Life in Australia: The Story of William McMahon – Convicted at the Clare Spring Assizes 1849 and Sentenced to Ten Years Transportation to Van Diemen's Land*
Price, Aaron, *Diary on Norfolk Island*
Strangeman, Denis, *The Gold Rush to Lamplough*, Avoca and District Historical Society Inc. web site (This paper with some modifications appeared in the journal *Familia* published by the Ulster Historical Foundation, Vol. 2, No. 3, 1987, pp. 3–21; and the *Victorian Historical Journal*, Vol. 60, No. 1, March 1989, pp. 3–26)
Wylie, Robert, *Surgeon Superintendent on Lady Raffles report on transportation voyage*, 17 March 1841

**Newspapers**
*The Adelaide Register*
*Ararat Advertiser*
*Ararat Chronicle*
*The Argus* (Melbourne)
*Brisbane Courier*
*Clare Journal*
*Colonial Times and Tasmanian*
*The Dimboola Banner*
*Goulburn Herald*
*Hobart Advertiser*
*Hobart Courier*
*Hobart Mercury*
*Hobart Town Courier*
*Hobart Town Gazette*
*Kalgoorlie Miner*
*Melbourne Herald*
*North Coolgardie Herald*
*Pleasant Creek News and Stawell Chronicle*
*Pleasant Creek News and Wimmera Advertiser*
*Seymour Express*
*Sheffield and Rotherham Independent*
*Stawell News and Pleasant Creek Chronicle*
*Stawell Times and Wimmera Advertiser*
*Sussex Express*
*The Western Australian*

**Books**
Aldous, Richard, *The Lion and the Unicorn: Gladstone vs Disraeli*, Pimlico, London, 2007
An Emigrant Mechanic (Alexander Harris?), *Settlers and Convicts or Recollections of Sixteen Year's Labour in the Australian Backwoods*, Melbourne University Press, 1964
Armer, Isabel, *A Range of Views of Jallukar and Bellellen*, 1996
Banfield, Lorna, *Like the Ark: The Story of Ararat* (revised edition), Longman Cheshire, Melbourne, 1986
Barry, John Vincent, *The Life and Death of John Price: A Study of the Exercise of Naked Power*, Melbourne University Press, 1964
Billis, R.V., and Kenyon, A.S., *Pastoral Pioneers of Port Phillip*, Macmillan, Melbourne, 1932
Bomford, Janette M., *That Dangerous and Persuasive Woman: Vida Goldstein*, Melbourne University Press, 1993
Boyce, James, *Van Diemen's Land*, Black Inc, Melbourne, 2008
Brand, Ian, *Port Arthur, 1830–1877*, Regal Publications, Launceston, 1990
Britt, M.G., *The Commandants: The Tyrants who Ruled Norfolk Island*, Herron Publications Pty Limited, Queensland, 1980
Cooper, Stephen, *A House Divided: The Life and Death of John Billam of Thorpe Hesley*, Bridge Publications, Penistone, England, 1987
Cowley, Trudy Mae, *A Drift of Derwent Ducks*, Research Tasmania, Hobart, 2005
Daniels, Kay, *Convict Women*, Allen & Unwin, Sydney, 1998
Derrincourt, William, *Old Convict Days*, edited by Louis Becke, T.F. Unwin, London, 1899
Dixson, Miriam, *The Real Matilda: Women and Identity in Australia, 1788–1975*, Pelican Books, Melbourne 1976

Duckworth, Jeannie, *Fagin's Children: Criminal Children in Victorian England*, Hambledon and London, London, 2001
Evans, A.G., *C.Y. O'Connor: His Life and Legacy*, University of Western Australia Press, 2001
Female Factory Research Group, *Women at Cascades Female Factory*, Research Tasmania, 2009
Fines, Ken, *A History of Brighton and Hove*, Phillimore & Co. Ltd, West Sussex, England, 2002
Finlay, Henry, *To Have and Not to Hold*, Federation Press, Annandale, 2005
Frost, Lucy, *Footsteps and Voices: A Historical Look Into the Cascades Female Factory*, Female Factory Historic Site, 2004
Gilbert, Edmund M., *Brighton: Old Ocean's Bauble*, Flare Books, Sussex, 1975
Grey, Peter, *The Irish Famine*, Thames & Hudson, London, 1995
Hall's Gap and Grampians Historical Society Inc., *Golden Days of Mount William Mafeking Centenary Celebration June 1900: June 2000*,
Hall's Gap and Grampians Historical Society Inc., *Victoria's Wonderland: A Grampians History*, 2006
Hazzard, Margaret, *Punishment Short of Death: A History of the Penal Settlement at Norfolk Island*, Hyland House, Melbourne, 1984
Healey, Justin, *Women's Rights*, The Spinney Press, Thirroul, NSW, 2005
Howard, Patrick, *To Hell or to Hobart*, Kangaroo Press, Kenthurst, NSW, 1993
Jones, Joan and Mel, *Images of England: In and Around Thorpe Hesley and Wentworth*, Tempus Publishing Limited, Gloucestershire, 2001
Kinealy, Christine, *This Great Calamity: The Irish Famine, 1845–52*, Gill & McMillan Ltd, Dublin, 2006
*King James 1611 New Testament Bible*, owned by Sgt E.W. Copley: printed by British & Foreign Bible Society
Kingston, Robert, *Good Country for a Grant: A History of the Stawell Shire*, Shire of Stawell, 1989
Lord, Richard, *The Shot Tower and its Builder, Joseph Moir, Hobart 1870*, Richard Lord & Partners, Tasmania, 1980
Madden, Ger, *A History of Tuamgraney and Scariff, Since Earliest Times*, East Clare Heritage, Tuamgraney, County Clare, 2000
McClaughlin, Trevor, *Irish Women in Colonial Australia*, Allen & Unwin, Sydney, 1998
Moore, James F.H., *The Convicts of Van Diemen's Land*, V.D.L. Publications, Sandy Bay, Tas., 1995
Murray, Robert, and White, Kate, *The Golden Years of Stawell*, Lothian Publishing Company, Port Melbourne, 1983
National Trust of Australia (Tasmania), *The Penitentiary Chapel and Criminal Courts*, 1998–
Nicholson, Ian, *Shipping Arrivals and Departures Tasmania, 1834–1842, and Gazetteer*, Roebuck, 1985
O'Farrell, Patrick, *The Irish in Australia*, New South Wales University Press, Kensington, NSW, 1987
O'Gorman, Michael, *A Pride of Paper Tigers: A History of the Great Hunger in the Scariff Workhouse Union from 1839 to 1853*, East Clare Heritage, Tuamgraney County Clare, 1994
O Murchadha, Ciaran, *Sable Wings Over the Land: Ennis, County Clare, and its Wider Community During the Great Famine*, Clasp Press, Ennis County Clare, 1998
O'Toole, Sean, *The History of Australian Corrections*, UNSW Press, Kensington, NSW, 2006
O'Tuathaigh, Gearoid, *Ireland Before the Famine, 1798–1848*, Gill & Macmillan, Dublin, 2007
Poirteir, Cathal, *The Great Irish Famine*, Mercier Press, Dublin, 1995
Pridmore, Walter B., *Point Puer and the Prisons of Port Arthur*, W.P. Pridmore, Murdunna, Tas., 2005
Pridmore, Walter B., *Richmond and the Coal River Valley*, W.P. Pridmore, Murdunna, Tas., 2003
Pridmore, Walter B., *Van Diemen's Land to Tasmania ... 1642–1856*, W.P. Pridmore, Collinsvale, Tas., 2008
Pybus, Cassandra, and Maxwell-Stewart, Hamish, *Yankee Political Prisoners in an Australian Penal Colony, 1839–1850: American Citizens, British Slaves*, Melbourne University Press, 2002
Rayner, Tony, *Female Factory Female Convicts*, Esperance Press, Dover, Tas., 2004
Roberts, Stephen, *The People's Charter: Democratic Agitation in Early Victorian Britain*, The Merlin Press Ltd, London, 2003
Robertson, Elizabeth, *Elizabeth Robertson's Diary, Norfolk Island 1845*, Printed by Newey & Beath, 1999
Robson, Lloyd, *A History of Tasmania, Volume 1: Van Diemen's Land from the Earliest Times to 1855*, Oxford University Press, Melbourne, 1983
Rodgers, Pat, and Brenda, *No Sign of the Time: A Collection of Stories of the Menzies District*, Shire of Menzies and Hesperian Press, 1992
Rooney, Kevin (assisted by Peter Hawkridge), *Rooktown: A History of Scholes Rotherham*, Clifton Local History Group, 2004
Savill, Vanda, *Mount William Gold Rush*, V. Savill, Heywood, Vic., 1982
Sayers, C.E., *Shepherd's Gold: The Story of Stawell*, F.W. Cheshire, Melbourne, 1966

Smith, Coultman, *Shadow Over Tasmania*, Hobart, Tas., 1941
Smith, Nan, *Convict Kingston*, Photopress International, Norfolk Island, 1997
Smith, Yvonne, *Taking Time: A Women's Historical Data Kit*, Union of Australian Women, Melbourne, 1988
Strickland, Barry, *Golden Quest Discovery Trail Guide Book*, Golden Quest Trails Association Inc., 2003
Timbury, Cheryl, *The Plain People: John Marsden and his Children Jane, John and Thomas With Robert Stonehouse*, Cheryl Timbury, Ocean Grove, 1996
Underwood, Eric, *Brighton*, B.T. Batsford Ltd, London, 1978
Wesley, Jane, *A Street Guide Quality Row, Kingston Norfolk Island*, Norfolk Island Museum, Kingston, 1994
Wettenhall, Gib, *The People of Gariwerd: The Grampian's Aboriginal Heritage*, Aboriginal Affairs Victoria, 1999
Woodham-Smith, Cecil, *The Great Hunger: Ireland, 1845-1849*, Penguin Books, London, 1991

# Notes

## Chapter 1
1. Tasmanian Archive and Heritage Office [TA] CON 15/6 and CON 41/24 Catherine McMahon Convict Record
2. 1825 Tythe Applotment for Parish of Moyne, Townland of Eastern Shean
3. 1891 Victorian, Stawell marriage certificate Catherine Copley/Thomas May No. 3347
4. 1901 Ireland Census, County Clare, Cappabane McMahon family (Shows first language of Patrick McMahon, grandchild of James and Peggy McMahon, was Irish)
5. 1825 Tythe Applotment for Parish of Moyne, Townland of Eastern Shean
6. Paddy McMahon Cappabane, Scarriff, County Clare
7. 1825 Tythe Applotment for Parish of Moyne, Townland of Eastern Shean

## Chapter 2
8. TA CON 41/24 Catherine McMahon Convict Record
9. Ibid.
10. Paddy McMahon believes that at this time McMahon holding would have been around 10 acres
11. Griffith 1855 Land Valuation record for Parish of Moyne, Townland of Cappaghabaun Park
12. O'Gorman, Michael *A Pride of Paper Tigers: A History of the Great Hunger in the Scariff Workhouse Union from 1839 to 1853*, Chapter 1, p. 1
13. Christine Kinealy, *The Great Calamity: The Irish Famine 1845–52*, p. 32 (quote taken from *Gardener's Chronicle and Horticultural Gazette*, 16 September 1845)
14. O'Gorman, p. 6
15. O'Gorman, p. 17
16. O'Gorman, p. 17
17. Advice from Paddy McMahon that in early twentieth-century McMahons tracked rabbits and hares in snow on Cappabane
18. This calculation is based on wage and food prices details in *A Pride of Paper Tigers* by Michael O'Gorman, pp. 22–23
19. O'Gorman, p. 28
20. O'Gorman, p. 19 (quote from *Limerick Chronicle*, 6 January 1847)
21. O'Gorman, p. 30
22. O'Gorman, p. 35
23. TA CON 33/100, Denis McMahon Convict Record
24. O'Gorman, p. 51

## Chapter 3
25. In TA CON 15/6 Catherine McMahon convict record has no mention of father James McMahon. This means he was dead at time of Catherine's conviction and transportation
26. *Clare Journal*, 12 February 1849
27. 1855 Griffith Land Valuation record for Parish of Tomgraney, Townland of Aughrim shows Jeremiah Rogers leasing 222 acres
28. National Archives of Ireland, Dublin, Outrage papers 5/279, 1849
29. Ibid.
30. 1825 Tythe Applotment for Parish of Moyne, Townland of Eastern Shean
31. National Archives of Ireland, Dublin, Outrage papers 5/279, 1849
32. Ibid.
33. Ibid.
34. Ibid.
35. Ibid.
36. *Clare Journal*, 5 February 1849
37. Flannan P. Enright, *Transportation from the Clare Spring Assizes of 1849*, p. 2
38. Enright, p. 1
39. Ibid.
40. Ibid.
41. Ibid.
42. Ibid.
43. National Archives of Ireland, Outrage papers 5/279, 1849
44. Ibid.
45. Ibid.
46. TA, CON 41/24, CON 15/6, CON 33/100, CON 14/43 Convict Records for Catherine, William and Denis McMahon

47 Ibid.
48 Enright, p. 1
49 *Clare Journal*, 1 March 1849

## Chapter 4

50 Ciaran O Murchadha, *Sable Wings Over the Land: Ennis, County Clare and its Wider Community During the Great Famine*, pp. 225–26 (Taken from *Limerick Examiner*, 28 March 1849)
51 Ibid.
52 The National Archives of Ireland, Document References TR 7, p 100, Record 528 of 567, McMahon, William, http://www.nationalarchives.ie/cgi-bin/naisearch01
53 TA, CON 33/100, Convict Records for Denis McMahon and William McMahon
54 Trudy Mae Cowley, *A Drift of Derwent Ducks*, Chapter 7, 'The Facts, Catherine McMahon'
55 Cowley, pp. 143–44
56 TA, CON 41/24, Convict Record for Catherine McMahon
57 Cowley, pp. 97–98
58 Cowley, pp. 99–100
59 Cowley, pp. 97, 100
60 Alexander Kilroy, Surgeon Superintendent on *Australasia*, report, dated 12 October 1849
61 Ibid.
62 Ibid.
63 TA, CON 41/24, Convict Record for Catherine McMahon
64 TA, CON 41/24, Convict Record for Catherine McMahon
65 Cowley, p. 113
66 Ibid.
67 Anne McMahon and K.M. Owen, *Transported to Life in Australia: The Story of William McMahon, Convicted at the Clare Spring Assizes and Sentenced to Ten Years Transportation to Van Diemen's Land*, p. 2
68 Anne McMahon, 'The Anson as Female Reformatory Hulk', *Tasmanian Ancestry*, March 2009, p. 225
69 Cowley, p. 133
70 Tony Rayner, *Female Factory Female Convicts*, p. 171
71 *Hobart Town Gazette*, 3 October 1829—Rules and Regulations for the management of the House of Corrections for Females, General Regulations, p. 221
72 Cowley, Chapter 7, 'The Facts, Catherine McMahon'
73 TA, CON 41/24, Convict Record for Catherine McMahon
74 Ibid.
75 *Hobart Town Gazette*, 3 October 1829—Rules and Regulations for the management of the House of Corrections for Females, p. 220
76 Ibid.
77 Cowley, Chapter 7, 'The Facts, Catherine McMahon'
78 Ibid.
79 Ibid.
80 Ibid.
81 Cowley, Chapter 7, 'The Facts, Bridgett Crotty'
82 Cowley, p. 123
83 TA, CON 14/8 and CON 33/6, Convict Record for John Copley

## Chapter 5

84 St Mary's Church, Ecclesfield, Yorkshire, Baptism Register for 1812, PR 54/5, p. 35
85 Age taken from 1861 John Copley death certificate Reg. District Rotherham, Sub-district Kimberworth, County of York, No. 339
86 Stephen Cooper, *The Stirrings in Thorpe Hesley on Saturday Night*, Notes and References Point 3
87 St Mary's Church, Ecclesfield, Yorkshire, Baptism Register for 1812, PR 54/5, p. 35
88 Stephen Cooper, *Burglars and Sheep Stealers, Crime in a South Yorkshire Village in the Nineteenth Century*, p. 78
89 Cooper, p. 85
90 St Mary's Church, Ecclesfield, Yorkshire, Burials Register for 1826, PR 54/34, f4, p. 234
91 St Mary's Church, Ecclesfield Yorkshire, Baptism Register PR 54/7 fiche 2, pp. 62, 63
92 St Mary's Church, Ecclesfield, Yorkshire, Burials Register for 1826, PR 54/34, f4, p. 234
93 All Saints Church, Rotherham, Yorkshire, Marriage Register for 1827, PR 87/28, fiche 4, p. 225
94 Richard Aldous, *The Lion and the Unicorn: Gladstone vs Disraeli*, p. 157
95 John L Baxter, *Early Chartism and Labour Class Struggle: South Yorkshire 1837–1840*, p. 144
96 Ibid., pp, 144–45
97 Ibid., p. 135
98 Ibid., p. 145
99 Tasmanian Archive and Heritage Office [TA], CON 33/6 and CON 14/8, John Copley Convict Record

100  TA, CON 14/8, John Copley Convict Record
101  TA, CON 33/6, John Copley Convict Record

## Chapter 6
102  Baxter. pp. 148–50
103  *Sheffield and Rotherham Independent*, 18 January 1840
104  1841 Census, Yorkshire, Registration District Rotherham, Township Thorpe Wath Upon Deane Wentworth, (RG HO 107, Piece 1329, Book/Folio 13/2, p. 16)
105  *Sheffield and Rotherham Independent*, 18 January 1840
106  Sheffield and Rotherham Red Book 1868, p. 83
107  *Sheffield and Rotherham Independent*, 18 January 1840
108  Ibid.
109  Ibid.
110  TA, CON 33/6, John Copley Convict Record
111  *Sheffield and Rotherham Independent*, 28 March 1840, p. 3
112  1851 Census, Yorkshire, Registration District Rotherham, Township Kimberworth (HO 107 2344)
113  *Sheffield and Rotherham Independent*, 28 March 1840, p. 3
114  UK National Archives, ASSI 44/156, Court Notice of Convictions

## Chapter 7
115  UK National Archives, Kew, H08/65 and 66 (June–December 1840)
116  Wikipedia, List of British prison hulks.
117  Based on William Derrincourt, *Old Convict Days*, edited by Louis Becke, Chapter 8, Part One, 'Dark England, Chapter VIII – I am sent to the hulks at Woolwich', p. 27. William Derrincourt was a convict on the *Justitia* in 1839.
118  UK National Archives, Kew, H08–65 and 66 (June–December 1840)
119  Derrincourt, pp. 27, 28
120  Derrincourt, p. 28
121  Wikipedia Online, HMS *Trafalgar*
122  Derrincourt, p. 28
123  Ibid.
124  UK National Archives, Kew, H08/65 and 66 (June–December 1840)
125  Report of Robert Wylie, Surgeon Superintendent on Lady Raffles, 24/10/1840 – 17/3/1841 (AJCP 3200)
126  Ian Nicholson, CBE, *Shipping Arrivals and Departures Tasmania Volume II 1834–1842*, p. 192
127  Report of Robert Wylie, Surgeon Superintendent on Lady Raffles, 24/10/1840 – 17/3/1841 (AJCP 3200)
128  Ibid.
129  *Colonial Times and Tasmanian*, 23 March 1841, Shipping News
130  Report of Robert Wylie, Surgeon Superintendent on Lady Raffles, 24/10/1840 – 17/3/1841 (AJCP 3200)
131  Ibid.
132  TA, CON 33/6 and CON 18/26, John Copley Convict Record
133  *National Trust Guide to The Penitentiary Chapel and Criminal Courts*, p. 1
134  Ibid., p. 8
135  Tasmanian Archive and Heritage Office [TA], CON 33/6, John Copley Convict Records
136  Ibid.
137  Ibid.
138  Ibid.
139  Ibid.
140  Ibid.
141  Ibid.
142  *Colonial Times and Tasmanian*, 13 April 1847
143  Richard Patterson story 22/9/1825 to 9/2/1891 Tasmanian Convict and Stonemason (www.timelions.com/richard.html)
144  *Colonial Times and Tasmanian*, 9 April 1847 (3 April 1847 Convict Department Notice from Comptroller-General's Office)

## Chapter 8
145  *Hobart Advertiser*, 23 April 1847
146  Ibid.
147  Tasmanian Archive and Heritage Office [TA] CON 37/3, CON 31/4, CON 18/20, CON 16/3, James Frazier Convict Record
148  *Hobart Advertiser*, 23 April 1847
149  Ibid.
150  Ibid.
151  Ibid.

152  *Colonial Times and Tasmanian*, 23 April 1847
153  *Colonial Times and Tasmanian*, 13 and 23 April 1847; *Hobart Advertiser*, 23 April 1847
154  *Colonial Times and Tasmanian*, 13 April 1847
155  *Colonial Times and Tasmanian*, 13 April 1847
156  *Hobart Advertiser*, 23 April 1847
157  Refer to Tuesday, 6 April 1847 edition of *Colonial Times and Tasmanian*, p. 2 for notice specifying 'This Journal is published on the Evening of every Tuesday and Friday…'
158  *Colonial Times and Tasmanian*, 9 April 1847, p. 4
159  TA, SC 32/1/6 Hobart, Oatlands January 1847 – December 1851, Minutes of 20 April 1847 Hobart Supreme Court Proceedings
160  Minutes of 20 April 1847 Hobart Supreme Court Proceedings
161  Lloyd Robson, *A History of Tasmania, Volume 1: Earliest Times to 1855*, pp. 470–71
162  Minutes of 20 April 1847 Hobart Supreme Court Proceedings
163  *Australian Dictionary of Biography*, online edition: Abbott, Edward (1801–1869)
164  *Hobart Advertiser*, 23 April 1847
165  Ibid.
166  Ibid.
167  Ibid.
168  Ibid.
169  Ibid.
170  *Hobart Town Courier*, 24 April 1847
171  *Colonial Times and Tasmanian*, 23 April 1847
172  TA CON 33/6, John Copley convict record; TA CON 37/3, James Frazier convict record

# Chapter 9
173  *Aaron Price Diary on Norfolk Island*, Dixson Library NSW, MSQ 247, 248 249
174  M.G. Britts, *The Commandants: The Tyrants Who Ruled Norfolk Island*, p. 147
175  Margaret Hazzard, *Punishment Short of Death: A History of the Penal Settlement at Norfolk Island*, p. 111
176  Rev. Rogers, *Correspondence Relating to the Dismissal of Rev Rogers from Norfolk Island*, p. 110
177  John Vincent Barry, *The Life and Death of John Price*, p. 54
178  John Vincent Barry, pp. 53, 54
179  TA, CON 33/11, Convict Record for Alfred Balduck
180  *Aaron Price Diary on Norfolk Island*, Dixson Library NSW, MSQ 247, 248, 249
181  *General Report on the State of the School at the Settlement Norfolk Island*, for period from June–September 1847, Mitchell Library, Melbourne State Library
182  Ibid.
183  *Aaron Price Diary on Norfolk Island*, Dixson Library NSW, MSQ 247, 248, 249
184  TA, CSO 50/19-1844
185  *Hobart Town Courier*, 22 May 1848—article identifies that Mathew Walker had three children on arrival in Van Diemen's Land
186  Time and date web site (www.timeanddate.com)
187  *Aaron Price Diary on Norfolk Island*, Dixson Library NSW, MSQ 247, 248, 249
188  Ibid.
189  *Aaron Price Diary on Norfolk Island*, Dixson Library NSW, MSQ 247, 248, 249, refers to 'Mr. Walker had a very narrow escape' and 'Mr. Walker was picked up by one of the prisoner'. TA, CON 33/6, John Copley Convict Record, refers to John being 'Recommended for good conduct on the occasion of whaleboat upsetting 14/4/1848' and on 14/2/1854 this was described as 'meritorious conduct'
190  Ibid.
191  TA, CON 33/6, John Copley Convict Record
192  King James 1611 New Testament Bible owned by Sgt E.W. Copley; Printed 1938 by British and Foreign Bible Society
193  TA, CON 37/3, James Frazier Convict Record
194  Rev. Rogers, *Correspondence Relating to the Dismissal of the Rev. Rogers from Norfolk Island*
195  TA, CON 33/6, John Copley Convict Record
196  Tasmanian Archive and Heritage Office [TA], CON 33/6, John Copley Convict Record
197  Ibid.
198  Rev. Rogers, *Correspondence Relating to the Dismissal of the Rev. Rogers from Norfolk Island*, p. 58
199  Margaret Hazard, *Punishment Short of Death: A History of the Penal Settlement at Norfolk Island*, p. 226
200  TA, CON 33/6, John Copley Convict Record
201  Ibid.
202  Ibid.
203  Ibid.
204  TA, CON 31/14, James Frazier Convict Record

205 Ibid.
206 Margaret Hazzard, *Punishment Short of Death: A History of the Penal Settlement at Norfolk Island*, p. 239
207 TA, CON 33/6, John Copley Convict Record
208 TA, CON 37/3, James Fraser Convict Record
209 TA, CON 33/6, John Copley Convict Record

## Chapter 10
210 Ibid.
211 First news of gold discovery appeared in *Launceston Examiner*, June 4, 1851
212 TA, CON 37/3, James Frazier Convict Record
213 Ibid.
214 Ibid.
215 Ibid.
216 TA, CON 37/3, James Frazier Convict Record
217 TA, CON 33/6, John Copley Convict Record
218 *Hobart Town Courier*, 24 April 1847
219 Ibid.
220 TA, CON 33/5, CON 14/5, John Goss Convict Records
221 Ibid.
222 Cowley, Chapter 7, 'The Facts: Bridgett Crotty'
223 Ibid.

## Chapter 11
224 Based on birth of son, John Copley, on 27 July 1852. See Cowley, Chapter 7, 'The Facts: Catherine McMahon', footnote 'c'
225 Refer to Henry Finlay, *To Have and Not to Hold*, Federation Press 2005, p. 30
226 TA, CON 41/24, Catherine McMahon Convict Record
227 Ibid.
228 Tony Rayner, *Female Factory Female Convicts*, p. 157
229 TA, Convict Applications to Marry: CON 52/5, p. 56, RGD37/11-1852/487: CON 52/3, p. 87 – CON 52/5, RGD37/11-1852/487
230 Lucy Frost, *Foot Steps and Voices: A Historical Look Into the Cascades Female Factory*, p. 17
231 Ibid.
232 TA, CON 33/6, John Copley Convict Record
233 TA, RGD 37/11-1852/487, Catherine McMahon/John Copley marriage
234 Ibid.

## Chapter 12
235 TA, CON 41/24, Catherine McMahon Convict Record
236 Cowley, Chapter 7, 'The Facts: Catherine McMahon'
237 TA, CON 41/24, Catherine McMahon Convict Record
238 TA, 1852 Register for Births in Hobart Town, John Copley No. 1638
239 Cowley, Chapter 7, 'The Facts: Catherine McMahon'
240 Ibid.
241 TA, 1852 Register of Births in Hobart Town: John Copley No. 1638
242 TA, 1853 Register of Births in Hobart Town: Catherine Copley No. 2531, shows that in August 1853 Catherine and John Copley living at New Wharf
243 TA, CON 41/24, Catherine McMahon Convict Record
244 TA, 1853 Register of Births for Hobart Town, Catherine Copley No. 2531
245 Cowley, Chapter 7, 'The Facts: Catherine McMahon'
246 TA, 1853 Register of Births in Hobart Town, Catherine Copley No. 2531
247 Ibid.
248 Ibid.
249 TA, 1853 Register of Deaths in Hobart Town, Catherine Copley No. 317
250 Ibid.
251 TA, CON 33/100, Denis McMahon Convict Record
252 TA, CON 33/100, William McMahon Convict Record
253 TA, CON 33/6, John Copley Convict Record
254 John Vincent Barry, p. 60
255 TA, CON 33/6 John Copley Convict Record
256 TA, CON 41/24, Catherine McMahon Convict Record
257 TA, CON 33/6, John Copley Convict Record
258 Cowley, Chapter 7, 'The Facts: Catherine McMahon'

259   TA, John Copley Insolvency File, AE 764/1/71, address for George Rex taken from statement by Martin Dumphy, law writer, concerning where John Copley insolvency papers sent
260   TA, John Copley Insolvency File, AE 764/1/71, Statement of Receipts from February 1855 to January 1856
261   *Hobart Courier*, 1 September 1855 (p. 4), Advertisement for let of premises 'lately occupied by John Copley'

## Chapter 13
262   TA, CON 33/100, William McMahon Convict Record
263   TA, John Copley Insolvency File, AE 764/1/71, Statement of Receipts from February 1855 to January 1856
264   TA, John Copley Insolvency File, AE 764/1/71, Statement of Payments from February 1855 to January 1856
265   TA, John Copley Insolvency File, AE 764/1/71, Statement of Receipts from February 1855 to January 1856
266   TA, John Copley Insolvency File, AE 764/1/71, Statement of Receipts from February 1855 to January 1856; and *Hobart Mercury*, 7 March 1856, Insolvency Court Report
267   TA, John Copley Insolvency File, AE 764/1/71, Statement of Receipts from February 1855 to January 1856, shows that early in the twelve month period John Copley received £25 to £27 for chaise carts from Mr Mills, Mr Clements and Mr Holmes
268   *Hobart Mercury*, 7 March 1856, Insolvency Court Report
269   TA, John Copley Insolvency File, AE 764/1/71, Statement of Receipts from February 1855 to January 1856, calculation based on payments received for carriage and metal trades work over this period
270   TA, John Copley Insolvency File, AE 764/1/71, Statement of Payments from February 1855 to January 1856; and *Hobart Mercury*, 7 March 1856, Insolvency Court Report
271   *Hobart Mercury*, 7 March 1856 Insolvency Court Report
272   TA, John Copley Insolvency File, AE 764/1/71, Statement of Receipts from February 1855 to January 1856
273   TA, John Copley Insolvency File, AE 764/1/71, Statement of Payments from February 1855 to January 1856
274   TA, John Copley Insolvency File, AE 764/1/71, Statement of Payments from February 1855 to January 1856
275   TA, John Copley Insolvency File, AE 764/1/71, Statement of Payments from February 1855 to January 1856
276   TA, CON 33/6, John Copley Convict Record
277   Ibid.
278   TA, John Copley Insolvency File, AE 764/1/71, List of John Copley Creditors on Insolvency and Statement of Payments from February 1855 to January 1856
279   TA, John Copley Insolvency File, AE 764/1/71, Statement of Receipts from February 1855 to January 1856
280   TA, John Copley Insolvency File, AE 764/1/71, Statement of Payments from February 1855 to January 1856
281   TA, John Copley Insolvency File, AE 764/1/71, Statement of Payments for 12 months from February 1855 to January 1856
282   TA, John Copley Insolvency File, AE 764/1/71 – 23/1/1856 John Copley application to be declared insolvent

## Chapter 14
283   Ibid.
284   Ibid.
285   Ibid.
286   Ibid.
287   *Hobart Courier*, 7 February 1856
288   Ibid.
289   Ibid.
290   TA, John Copley Insolvency File, AE 764/1/71, Fielding Brown Order declaring John Copley insolvent
291   *Hobart Mercury*, 22 February 1856
292   *Hobart Mercury*, 7 March 1856
293   TA, John Copley Insolvency File, AE 764/1/71, Statement of Receipts for 12 months from February 1855 to January 1856; and *Hobart Mercury*, 7 March 1856
294   *Hobart Mercury*, 7 March 1856
295   Ibid.
296   Ibid.
297   *Hobart Mercury*, 14 March 1856
298   *Hobart Courier*, 12 March 1856
299   *Hobart Mercury*, 14 March 1856
300   *Hobart Mercury*, 24 March 1856
301   TA, John Copley Insolvency File, AE 764/1/71, Statements of Receipts and Payments for 12 months from February 1855 to January 1856
302   *Hobart Courier*, 27 March 1856
303   Ibid.
304   Ibid.
305   TA, John Copley Insolvency File, AE 764/1/71, Fielding Browne Order discharging John Copley from insolvency

## Chapter 15
306    22 September 1856 Register of Birth of William Copley No. 1675 gives Sandy Bay as Copley place of residence
307    TA, CON 33/100, Denis McMahon Convict Record
308    28 May 1856 Register of Marriage of Denis McMahon and Susan McMahon in the District of Hobart No. 220 3346
309    Ibid.
310    22 September 1856 Register of Birth of William Copley in Hobart District No. 1675
311    Cowley, Chapter 7, 'The Facts: Catherine McMahon'
312    John Vincent Barry, *The Life and Death of John Price*, pp. 69–72
313    Ibid.
314    Barry, p. 71
315    *Hobart Courier*, 7 April 1855, p. 3
316    John Vincent Barry, p. 65
317    *Hobart Town Daily Courier*, 10 March 1857
318    TA, CON 41/24, Catherine McMahon Convict Record
319    *Hobart Town Daily Courier*, 31 March 1857
320    *Hobart Town Courier*, 2 March 1857 (advertisement)

## Chapter 16
321    *Launceston Examiner*, 7 March 1857 p. 5
322    C.E. Sayers, *Shepherd's Gold: The Story of Stawell*, p. 24
323    Denis Strangman, article *The Gold Rush to Lamplough*, pp. 2, 4. (Article can be found on Avoca and District Historical Society Inc. Victoria Australia web site.)
324    Strangman, p. 9, taken from paragraph starting 'There were hundreds of "paddocks"...'
325    Strangman, p. 3, taken from paragraph starting 'In one of the few non journalist accounts...'
326    Strangman, p. 13, taken from paragraph starting 'Ironically, just as the miners...'
327    Hannah Copley Lamplough birth certificate 1860, No. 15683
328    Strangman, p. 12, paragraph starting 'There are references in R.E. Johns' diaries...' refers to Father Fennelly visiting Lamplough
329    William Copley 1860 Lamplough death certificate No. 67
330    Hannah Copley Lamplough birth certificate 1860, No. 15683
331    Strangman, pp. 6, 8
332    William Copley 1860 Lamplough death certificate No. 67
333    Strangman, pp. 12, 13
334    Strangman, p. 13
335    Lorna Banfield, *Like the Ark: The Story of Ararat*, p. 81
336    *The Argus*, 'Missing Friends Messages' section, 17, 18 and 21 October 1865
337    Catherine McMahon, Victorian birth and death certificates (Birth – 1868/No. 4350 and Death – 1868/No. 2009) show father Denis McMahon living in South Melbourne
338    *The Argus*, 19 September 1864
339    TA, CON 18-1-21, p. 177, and CON 31-1-38, p. 317, James Shirley Convict Record
340    Public Record Office Victoria (PROV), Ballarat (B), VPRS 3770, Unit 3, 1867–1969, Stawell Shire Rate Records
341    *Hobart Mercury*, 1 December 1866, p. 3, and 10 December 1866, p. 3
342    *The Argus Melbourne*, 10 July 1867, p. 3
343    PROV, B, VPRS 3770, Unit 3, 1867–1869, Stawell Shire Rate Records
344    PROV, North Melbourne (NM), VPRS 13062/P/001: Unit 1, Type V3, License 2084 and VPRS 12028/P/1, Application 2084 ( John Copley 80 acre selection)
345    *The Major Mitchell Trail* published in 1990 by the Community, Education and Information Branch and National Parks and Wildlife Division Department of ConserPROVtion and Environment, Melbourne, Victoria, p. 44
346    Gib Wettenhall, *The People of Gariwerd: The Grampians' Aboriginal Heritage*, p. 6
347    Wettenhall, map on p. 3
348    Wettenhall, p. 18
349    R.V. Billis and A.S. Kenyon, *Pastoral Runs of Port Phillip*, Part One, p. 34 – Clarke, Wm., John, Turner
350    *Australian Dictionary of Biography* online edition: Clarke, William John Turner (1805–1874)
351    PROV, NM, VPRS 13753/P/001, Unit 001, Type V3, Application 2084

## Chapter 17
352    British Vital Records LDS FHL 1067107 Dates 1826–1836 (Thomas May christening)
353    Ibid.
354    Dr Jenks, *Report on the Sanatory State of the Town of Brighton and on the Causes and Prevention of Fever*, 5 April 1840, p. 6
355    Edmond M. Gilbert, *Brighton: Old Ocean's Bauble*, p. 105

356  Tour the authors did of the Royal Pavilion Brighton in October 2007
357  Gilbert, pp. 108–09
358  1851 English Census, Brighton registration district, St. Peters sub-district, Egremont Street, Household Schedule No. 85
359  1841 English Census, Brighton registration district, St. Peters sub-district, Egremont Street
360  Ibid.
361  Ibid.
362  Dr. Jenks, p. 6
363  Gilbert, p. 124
364  Gilbert, p. 129
365  East Sussex Records Office, Lewes QS Midsummer, Case No. 15 Ref QR/E862
366  1841 English Census, Borough of Brighton, Parish of Brighthelmston, p. 24, PRO HO 107/1123/1
367  East Sussex Records Office, Lewes QS Midsummer, Case No. 15 Ref QR/E862
368  Ibid.
369  East Sussex Records Office, Lewes QS Midsummer, QCR 1/4/E6 (Return of all persons committed or bailed for trial or indicted – 1 July 1839)
370  Jeanine Duckworth, *Fagin's Children*, p. 41
371  East Sussex Records Office, Lewes QS Midsummer, Case No. 15 Ref QR/E862
372  East Sussex Records Office, QCR/EW6/1
373  Duckworth, p. 54

## Chapter 18
374  Gilbert, p. 139
375  Eric Understood, *Brighton*, p. 106
376  East Sussex Records Office, QCR 1/4/E7
377  1841 English Census, Borough of Brighton, Parish of Brighthelmston, St. James Garden
378  *Sussex Express*, 4 December 1841
379  Thomas Dix age being 14 rather than 13 based on entry for Thomas Dicks in 1841 English Census, Registration District of Brighton, sub-registration district of St Peters, Bread Street.
380  1841 English Census, Borough of Brighton, Parish of Brighthelmston
381  1841 English Census, Borough of Brighton, Parish of Brighthelmston, St James Garden
382  *Sussex Express*, 4 December 1841
383  East Sussex Records Office, QCR1/4/E7
384  Tasmanian Archive and Heritage Office [TA], CON 33/25 and CON 14/16, Thomas Sargent Convict Record
385  1841 English Census, Borough of Brighton, Parish of Brighthelmston, Bread Street
386  1841 English Census, Borough of Brighton, Parish of Brighthelmston, Egremont Street
387  *Sussex Express*, 4 December 1841
388  East Sussex Records Office, Lewes Quarter Sessions Roll, December 1841
389  East Sussex Records Office, QCR 1/4/E7
390  1841 English Census, London, District of the Inner Temple, No. 8 Kings Bench Walk
391  East Sussex Records Office, Lewes Quarter Sessions Roll, Trial Indictment, December 1841
392  1841 English Census, District of Brighton, Parish of Brighthelmston, Kensington Garden
393  East Sussex Records Office, Lewes Quarter Sessions Roll, Trial Indictment, December 1841
394  1841 English Census, Borough of Brighton, Parish of Brighthelmston, Warrick Street
395  East Sussex Records Office, Lewes Quarter Sessions, Trial Indictment, December 1841
396  East Sussex Records Office, Lewes Quarter Sessions, Trial Indictment, December 1841 and 1841 English Census, Borough of Brighton, Parish of Brighthelmston
397  *Sussex Express*, 4 December 1841
398  Ibid.
399  East Sussex Records Office, QCR1/4/E7, 1/12/1841 Session

## Chapter 19
400  East Sussex Records Office, Calendar of Prisoners, QCR1/EW6/1
401  Duckworth, p. 83
402  Duckworth, p. 94
403  Duckworth, p. 89
404  Wikipedia, HMS *Euryalus*
405  Duckworth, p. 85
406  Duckworth, p. 89
407  East Sussex Records Office, Calendar of Prisoners, QCR1/EW6/1
408  English National Archives Kew, H08/70, Register of Prisoners on the Hulks
409  Duckworth, p. 84
410  TA, CON 33/25, CON 14/16, Thomas May Convict Record

411  English National Archives Kew, H08/70, Register of Prisoners on the Hulks
412  TA, CON 33/25, CON 14/16, Thomas May Convict Record
413  Report by William Jones, Surgeon Superintendent Elphinstone (4), AJCP PRO 3194
414  Ibid.
415  Ibid.
416  TA, CON 33/25, CON 14/16, Thomas May Convict Record
417  TA, CON 33/25, CON 14/16, Thomas May Convict Record
418  Report by William Jones, Surgeon Superintendent, Elphinstone (4), AJCP PRO 3194
419  Ibid.
420  Ian Brand, *Port Arthur*, p. 43–44
421  Brand, p. 44
422  TA, CON 33/25, Thomas May Convict record and 11/9/1853 Hobart Town registration of death of Thomas Fredrick May, RGO 35/4, 420/1853
423  Brand, p. 45
424  TA, CON 33/25, Thomas May Convict Record
425  Ibid.
426  Ibid.

## Chapter 20
427  11/9/1853 Hobart Town registration of death for Thomas Fredrick May, RGO 35/4, 420/1853
428  TA, RGD 37 399/1852 Thomas May/Anne Bottrell marriage
429  TA, 11/9/1853 Hobart Town registration of death of Thomas Fredrick May, RGD 37 399/1852
430  TA, Hobart Town registration of birth of Thomas Fredrick May, RGD 33/4, 2533/1853
431  11/9/1853 Hobart Town registration of death for Thomas Fredrick May, RGO 35/4, 420/1853
432  1891 Catherine Copley/Thomas May Stawell Marriage Certificate No. 35
433  Melbourne State Library, Ledcourt State Cash Book
434  Robert Kingston, *Good Country for a Grant*, p. 20
435  C.E. Sayers, *Shepherd's Gold*, p. 7
436  Melbourne State Library, Ledcourt Station Cash Book
437  Avoca Historical Society Website, Lamplough Name Index, Two letters to Thomas May at the Lamplough Post Office were not picked up in February and March 1860
438  Stawell Genealogical Group Record of Admissions to Stawell Hospital
439  Ibid.
440  Sayers, p. 64
441  Stawell Genealogical Group Record of Admissions to Stawell Hospital

## Chapter 21
442  PROV, NM, VPRS 625/P, Unit 106, File 5707, Thomas May selection – Ararat Lands Department file note headed 'Land Act 1869' concerning Thomas May application for selection licence
443  PROV, NM, VPRS 13753/P/001, Unit 1, Type V3, Rent Roll Ararat Selections 19 and 20 Land Act 1869, p. 106
444  PROV, Ballarat (B), VPRS 15206/P0001/Unit 4, Ararat Shire Rate Book 1870–1874
445  Isabel Armer, *A Range of Views of Jallukar and Bellellen*, p. 83 – 'Admissions to the Stawell Hospital During the 1880s of People from Bellellen and Jallukar'
446  C.E. Sayers, *Shepherds Gold – The Story of Stawell*, p. 65
447  Isabel Armer, p. 83 – 'Admissions to the Stawell Hospital During the 1880s of People from Bellellen and Jallukar'
448  PROV, B, VPRS 15206/P0001/Unit 4, Ararat Shire Rate Book 1870–1874
449  Lorna Banfield, *Like the Ark: The Story of Ararat*, p. 121
450  PROV, NM, VPRS 625/P, Unit 106, File 5707, Thomas May selection file, 19/11/1874 Application for Selection Lease
451  PROV, B, VPRS 15206/P0001/Unit 4, Ararat Shire Rate Book 1870–1874
452  Australian Bureau of Metrology website shows that the average rainfall for the Grampians mountains between 1961 and 1990 was over 800 mm. In the same period, the average annual rainfall both Stawell and Ararat was less than 600 mm (http://www.bom.gov.au/cgi-bin/climate/cgi_bin_scripts/annual_rnfall.cgi)
453  PROV, NM, VPRS 626/P, Unit 71, File 273/20, Copley/MacMaster – 26 February 1873 John Copley selection licence application sheet headed 'Application for licence under Part II of 'The Land Act 1869''
454  PROV. NM. VPRS 626/P, Unit 71, File 273/20, Copley/MacMaster – Ararat Lands Department file note headed 'Land Act 1869' with number 'No. 73/24271'.
455  1873 Copley/Stonehouse Marriage Certificate Ararat No. 36
456  Cheryl Timbury, *The Plain People – John Marsden and his children Jane, John and Thomas with Robert Stonehouse*, Chapter One – The Man John Marsden, pp. 2–4, 7, 8

457    PROV, NM, VPRS 137753/P/001, Unit 1, Type V3, Rent Roll Ararat Selections 19 and 20 Land Act, p. 106
458    1874 Catherine Copley birth certificate Ararat No. 49
459    PROV, NM, VPRS 13753/P/001, Unit 1, Type V3, Rent Roll Ararat Selections 19 and 20 Land Act, p. 304
460    PROV, NM, VPRS 625/P, Unit 106, File 5707, Thomas May selection – 19 May 1874 W. Matthew letter to Lands Department
461    PROV, NM, VPRS 625/P, Unit 106, File 5707, Thomas May selection – 19 May 1874 W. Matthew letter to Lands Department and VPRS 13753/P/00001, Unit 1, Type V3, Rent Roll Ararat Selections 19 and 20 Land Act 1869
462    PROV, NM, VPRS 625/P, Unit 106, File 5707, Thomas May selection – hand written file note by Lands Department officer
463    PROV, NM, VPRS 625/P, Unit 106, File 5707, Thomas May selection – schedule attached to 11 June 1874 Thomas May declaration
464    Taken from PROV, NM, VPRS 626/P, Unit 71, File 273/20, Copley/MacMaster – taken from document headed 'Land Regulations – Schedule III, Conditions of License Under 19, Part II, of "The Land Act 1869"', point 3. This requirement applied to all selectors, including Thomas May
465    PROV, NM, VPRS 625/P, Unit 106, File 5707, Thomas May selection – Department of Lands and Survey (Occupational Branch), District of Ararat file note, Consecutive Number 5025
466    PROV, NM, VPRS 625/P, Unit 106, File 5707, Thomas May selection – Mounted Constable Hornibrook report
467    PROV, NM, VPRS 625/P, Unit 106, File 5707, Thomas May selection – schedule attached to 11 June 1874 Thomas May declaration and Mounted Constable Hornibrook report
468    PROV, NM, VPRS 625/P, Unit 106, File 5707, Thomas May selection – hand written file note with 'Ararat' stamped on the top and VPRS 13753/P/00001, Unit 1, Type V3 – Rent Roll Ararat Selections 19 and 20 Land Act 1869
469    PROV, NM, VPRS 626/P, Unit 87, File 2452/19.20, Mason/Smith/Copley selection file
470    PROV, NM, VPRS 626/P, Unit 87, File 2452/19.20, Mason/Smith/Copley selection file
471    PROV, NM, VPRS 13753/P001, Unit 1, Type V3, Rent Roll Ararat Selections 19 and 20 Land Act, p. 104
472    PROV, NM, VPRS 626/P, Unit 71, File 273, Copley/MacMaster – taken from 27 October 1874 selection licence application sheet headed 'Schedule. Application for licence under Part II of "The Land Act 1869"'
473    1876 John Copley Stawell death certificate No. 2097
474    PROV, NM, VPRS 626/P, Unit 71, File 273, Copley/MacMaster – taken from 27 October 1874 selection licence application sheet headed 'Schedule Application for licence under Part II of "The Land Act 1869"'
475    PROV, NM, VPRS 625/P, Unit 106, File 5707, Thomas May selection – 18 November 1874 selection lease application, first sheet headed 'Land Regulations—Schedule IV'
476    PROV, NM, VPRS 625/P, Unit 106, File 5707, Thomas May selection – 18 November 1874 selection file note headed 'Ararat Sec 20 Land Act 1869'

## Chapter 22

477    PROV, NM, VPRS, 626/P, Unit 71, File 273, Copley/MacMaster – taken from 1 February 1875 Licence Certificate headed 'Licence under section 19 of the "The Land Act 1869"'
478    PROV, NM, VPRS 626/P, Unit 71, File 271, Copley/MacMaster – Taken from map titled 'Parish of Moyston, County of Borung'
479    PROV, NM, VPRS, 626/P, Unit 71, File 286, Copley/MacMaster – taken from 1/4/1876 Robert Allay, surveyor report
480    PROV, NM, VPRS 626/P, Unit 71, File 273, Copley/MacMaster, taken from 26/2/1878 application for selection lease
481    PROV, NM, VPRS 626/P, Unit 71, File 273, Copley/MacMaster – Last Will and Testament of John Copley
482    PROV, NM, VPRS 626/P, Unit 71, File 273, Copley/MacMaster – based on information taken from 26/2/1878 application for selection lease
483    PROV, NM, VPRS 13753/P001, Unit 1, Type V3, Rent Roll Ararat Selections 19 and 20 Land Act, p. 104
484    PROV, NM, VPRS 626/P, Unit 71, File 273, Copley/MacMaster – taken from 26/2/1878 application for selection lease
485    PROV, NM, VPRS 626/P, Unit 71, File 286, Copley/MacMaster – taken from 10/3/1876 selection licence application sheet headed '(Schedule II – Land Regulations 7/2/76) Application for licence under Part II of "The Land Act 1869"'
486    PROV, NM, VPRS 626/P, Unit 71, File 286, Copley/MacMaster – taken from Ararat Lands Department file note that contained 'District Surveyors Report' on 115 acre selection licence application
487    1876 John Robert Copley Stawell birth certificate No. 11294
488    Ibid.
489    PROV, NM, VPRS 626/P, Unit 71, File 273, Copley/MacMaster – taken from 26/2/1878 application for selection lease
490    PROV, NM, VPRS 626/P, Unit 71, File 286, Copley/MacMaster – taken from blank sheet file note headed '311 Ararat'
491    PROV, NM, VPRS 626/P, Unit 71, File 286, Copley/MacMaster – taken from 19.8.79 file note headed 'The

Land Act 1869'
492   Robert Murray and Kate White, *The Golden Years of Stawell*, p. 69
493   PROV, NM, VPRS 626/P, Unit 71, File 273, Copley/MacMaster – Last Will and Testament of John Copley
494   *Pleasant Creek News and Wimmera Advertiser*, 18 August 1876
495   1876 John Copley Stawell death certificate No. 2097
496   1876 John Copley Stawell death certificate No. 2097
497   1876 John Copley Stawell death certificate No. 2097
498   Stawell Cemetery Records held by Stawell Genealogical Group

## Chapter 23
499   1869 Land Selection Act, clause 28
500   PROV, NM, VPRS 13753/P001, Unit 1, Type V3, Rent Roll Ararat Selections 19 and 20 Land Act, p. 104
501   PROV, NM, VPRS 626/P, Unit 71, File 273, Copley/MacMaster, taken from 26/2/1878 selection lease application
502   PROV, NM, VPRS 626/P, Unit 71, File 273, Copley/MacMaster – taken from 26/2/1878 selection lease application
503   PROV, NM, VPRS 13753/P001, Unit 1, Type V3, Rent Roll Ararat Selections 19 and 20 Land Act, pp. 104, 105
504   PROV, NM, VPRS 626/P, Unit 71, File 273, Copley/MacMaster – taken from 26/2/1878 selection lease application
505   PROV, NM, VPRS 626/P, Unit 71, File 273, Copley/MacMaster – 4 February 1878 Lands Department letter addressed to John Copley sheet headed 'ARARAT Department of Lands and Agriculture'
506   PROV, NM, VPRS 626/P, Unit 71, File 273, Copley/MacMaster – 27 February 1878 selection lease application with first sheet headed 'Land Regulations—Schedule IV'
507   Victorian Parliament web site. 'A Data Base of all Victorian MPs since 1851' entry for William O'Callaghan (http://www.parliament.vic.gov.au/re-member/bioregfull.cfm?=618)
508   *Ararat Advertiser*, 7 January 1868
509   1854 Victorian Marine Register for Births, Entry for birth of William O'Callaghan states his father William O'Callaghan born in Skibbereen. Skibbereen Heritage Centre [SHC] records show William Callahan baptized in Skibbereen and Rath Parish on 21 November 1819. SHC records show William Callaghan and Julia Bird had three children (William, John and Jeremiah) in Skibbereen between 1850 and 1853. The names of these children and their birth dates correspond with the ages of three children with the same names shown on Julia O'Callaghan's (nee Bird) Victorian death certificate (1897, No. 25410). (Note: SHC considers 'Callahan' and 'Callaghan' to be the priest's spelling of 'O'Callaghan'.
510   Cecil Woodham-Smith, *The Great Hunger: Ireland 1845–1849*, p. 163
511   PROV, NM, VPRS 626/P, Unit 71, File 273, Copley/MacMaster – 27 February 1878 selection lease application with first sheet headed 'Land Regulations—Schedule IV', first page, point 7
512   PROV, NM, VPRS 626/P, Unit 71, File 273, Copley/MacMaster – Lands Department report of Catherine Copley lease application sheet headed 'The Land Act 1869, Section 20, No. 273, Date 26-2-78'
513   PROV, NM, VPRS 626/P, Unit 71, File 273, Copley/MacMaster – 2 April 1878 William O'Callaghan letter to Minister for Lands
514   PROV, NM, VPRS 626/P, Unit 71, File 273, Copley/MacMaster – Department file note headed 'ARARAT Reg. No. 11385'
515   In 11 June 1878 William O'Callaghan letter Catherine's surname was spelt 'Copely'. The basis to this spelling mistake appears to be William O'Callaghan using the spelling for the Copley surname in the 15 March 1852 Hobart Town marriage certificate for Catherine and John. This spelling mistake has been corrected here and in all other correspondence/documentation where it was used.
516   PROV, NM, VPRS 626/P, Unit 71, File 273, Copley/MacMaster – 11 June 1878 William O'Callaghan letter to Surveyor General
517   PROV, NM, VPRS 626/P, Unit 71, File 273, Copley/MacMaster – Lands Department file note headed 'Reg. No. 11621'
518   PROV, NM, VPRS 626/P, Unit 71, File 273, Copley/MacMaster – 9 August 1878 William O'Callaghan letter to Minister for Lands
519   PROV, NM, VPRS 626/P, Unit 71, File 273, Copley/MacMaster – file note on blank sheet, relePROVnt comment dated 16/10/1878
520   PROV, NM, VPRS 13753/P001, Unit 1, Type V3, Rent Roll Ararat Selections 19 and 20 Land Act, p. 104
521   PROV, NM, VPRS 626/P, Unit 71, File 273, Copley/MacMaster – 29 October 1878 William O'Callaghan letter to Minister of Lands
522   PROV, NM, VPRS 626/P, Unit 71, File 273, Copley/MacMaster – 29/10/1878 Office of Land and Survey File Note
523   PROV, NM, VPRS 626/P, Unit 71, File 273, Copley/MacMaster – 7 November 1878 'Department of Lands and Survey' letter to Catherine Copley
524   PROV, NM, VPRS 626/P, Unit 71, File 273, Copley/MacMaster – 21 December 1878 William O'Callaghan letter to Secretary for Lands

525　PROV, NM, VPRS 626/P, Unit 71, File 273, Copley/MacMaster – 21 December 1878 William O'Callaghan letter to Secretary for Lands
526　PROV, NM, VPRS 626/P, Unit 71, File 286, Copley/MacMaster – 15 August 1879 application for selection lease
527　PROV, NM, VPRS 626/P, Unit 71, File 273, Copley/MacMaster – 26 February 1878 'Application for lease or crown grant by licensee'
528　PROV, NM, VPRS 626/P, Unit 71, File 286, Copley/MacMaster – 15 August 1879 application for selection lease
529　PROV, NM, VPRS 626/P, Unit 71, File 273, Copley/MacMaster – date for Department letter to William O'Callaghan based on date cited in O'Callaghan 18 February 1879 letter in reply
530　PROV, NM, VPRS 626/P, Unit 71, File 273, Copley/MacMaster – 18 February 1879 William O'Callaghan letter to Secretary for Lands
531　PROV, NM, VPRS 626/P, Unit 71, File 273, Copley/MacMaster –file note headed 'Catherine Copely Widow of John Copely' reviewing Catherine Copley lease application
532　PROV, NM, VPRS 626/P, Unit 71, File 273, Copley/MacMaster –file note headed 'Catherine Copely Widow of John Copely' reviewing Catherine Copley lease application
533　PROV, NM, VPRS 626/P, Unit 71, File 273, Copley/MacMaster – date of Department letter to William O'Callaghan based on date cited in 30 April 1879 O'Callaghan letter in reply
534　PROV, NM, VPRS 626/P, Unit 71, File 273, Copley/MacMaster – 30 April 1879 William O'Callaghan letter to the Secretary for Lands
535　PROV, NM, VPRS 626/P, Unit 71, File 273, Copley/MacMaster – taken from 'Office of Land and Survey' file note that recorded 30 April 879 William O'Callaghan letter was received by the Office of Lands and Survey on 6 May 1879

## Chapter 24
536　PROV, B, VPRS 01677/P/0000, Unit 000011, Type V2, Ararat Court Minute Book
537　PROV, B, VPRS 15206/P00001/Units 6 and 7, Ararat Shire Rate Books
538　PROV, B, VPRS 15206/P00001/Units 6 and 7, Ararat Shire Rate Books
539　PROV, B, VPRS 15206/P00001/Unit 000011, Type V2, Ararat Court Minute Book
540　PROV, B, VPRS 15250/P/001, Ararat Shire Letter Book, p. 983
541　PROV, B, VPRS 15206/P/001/Unit 7, Ararat Shire Rate Book
542　Lorna Banfield, *Like the Ark – The Story of Ararat*, p. 110
543　PROV, B, VPRS 15206/P00001/Unit 7, Ararat Shire Rate Book
544　PROV, B, VPRS 12991/P/0001, Unit 3, Type V2, Ararat Shire Council Minute Book, p. 466
545　PROV, B, VPRS 12991/P/0001, Unit 3, Type V2, Ararat Shire Council Minute Book
546　PROV, B, VPRS 15250/P/001, Ararat Shire Letter Book, p. 983
547　PROV, B, VPRS 15206/P00001/Unit 7, Ararat Shire Rate Book
548　PROV, B, VPRS 12991/P00001, Type V2, Ararat Shire Minute Book and PROV, B, VPRS 15206/P00001/Unit 7, Ararat Shire Rate Book
549　1879 Copley/Green Stawell marriage No. 21

## Chapter 25
550　PROV, NM, VPRS 626/P, Unit 71, File 286, Copley/MacMaster – taken from 18 August 1879 Catherine Copley application for selection lease, Declaration upon oath by licensee, points 1 and 7
551　PROV, NM, VPRS 626/P, Unit 71, File 286, Copley/MacMaster, taken from 18 August 1879 Catherine Copley application for selection lease, Declaration upon oath by licensee, point 3 and section dealing with selection fencing
552　PROV, NM, VPRS 626/P, Unit 71, File 286, Copley/MacMaster – taken from 18 August 1879 Catherine Copley application for selection lease
553　PROV, NM, VPRS 626/P, Unit 71, File 273, Copley/MacMaster, taken from 18 August 1879 Catherine Copley application for selection lease, p. 2
554　PROV, NM, VPRS 626/P, Unit 71, File 286, Copley/MacMaster – taken from 18 August 1879 Catherine Copley application for selection lease, p. 2
555　PROV, NM, VPRS 626/P, Unit 71, File 286, Copley/MacMaster – 18 August 1879 Catherine Copley Application for selection lease where Catherine cites Wilson & Co.. as Lexington squatters and R.M. Billis and A.S. Kenyon, *Pastoral Pioneers of Port Phillip*, Part Two, p. 210 that states Alex Wilson and J. Williamson became Lexington squatters in February 1882. We have accepted that the change in Lexington squatter from Clarke family interests to Wilson & Co. occurred at time specified by Catherine rather than by Billis and Kenyon.
556　R.M. Billis and A.S. Kenyon, *Pastoral Pioneers of Port Phillip*, Part One, p. 141–42 – Alexander Wilson details pastoral leases held from 1849 to 1880s
557　PROV, B, VPRS 15206/P0001/Unit 7, Ararat Shire Rate Book
558　PROV, NM, VPRS 626/P, Unit 71, File 286, Copley/MacMaster – 19/8/1879 Department File note headed 'The Land Act 1869' reviewing Catherine Copley lease application
559　Ibid.

560   PROV, NM, VPRS 626/P, Unit 71, File 286, Copley/MacMaster – Department of Lands and Survey letter to Catherine Copley dated 10 September 1879
561   1895 Daniel SulliPROVn Death in District of Moyston, Reg. No. 6648
562   PROV, NM, VPRS 626/P, Unit 71, File 286, Copley/MacMaster – 26 September 1879 Statutory Declaration signed by 'Catherine Copley of Parish of Moyston'
563   1895 Daniel SulliPROVn Death in District of Moyston, Reg. No. 6648
564   *Victoria's Wonderland – A Grampians History* compiled by Halls Gap and Grampians Historical Society, pp. 91, 92
565   PROV, NM, VPRS 626/P, Unit 71, File 286, Copley/MacMaster – sheet headed 'Application by widow of deceased licensee for lease'
566   PROV, NM, VPRS 626/P, Unit 71, File 286, Copley/MacMaster – Office of Lands and Survey File Note Reg. No. 22837 (Date of Letter 26.9.79)
567   PROV, NM, VPRS 626/P, Unit 71, File 286, Copley/MacMaster – Secretary of Lands Department letter to Catherine Copley dated 20 October 1879
568   PROV, NM, VPRS 626/P, Unit 71, File 286, Copley/MacMaster – Copley children correspondence headed 'Moyston 7 Jan. 1880'
569   PROV, NM, VPRS 626/P, Unit 71, File 286, Copley/MacMaster – Lands Department file note headed 'Catherine Copely widow of John Copely'
570   PROV, NM, VPRS 626/P, Unit 71, File 273, Copley/MacMaster – 31/5/1880 Catherine Copely letter to David Gaunson MLA
571   PROV, NM, VPRS 626/P, Unit 71, File 273, Copley/MacMaster – 31/5/1880 Catherine Copely letter to David Gaunson MLA
572   *Victoria's Wonderland – A Grampians History* compiled by Halls Gap and Grampians Historical Society, refer to p. 90 for detailed example of Daniel SulliPROVn hand writing
573   PROV, NM, VPRS 626/P, Unit 71, File 273, Copley/MacMaster – 31/5/1880 Catherine Copely letter to David Gaunson MLA
574   PROV, NM, VPRS 626/P, Unit 71, File 273, Copley/MacMaster – Hand written note attached to Catherine Copley letter to David Gaunson
575   *Pleasant Creek News and Stawell Chronicle*, 2 March 1880
576   PROV, NM, VPRS 626/P, Unit 71, File 273, Copley/MacMaster and PROV, NM, VPRS 626/P, Unit 71, File 286, Copley/MacMaster – Both files contain the same sheet head 'Application to Surrender Lease (section 3, Land Act 1880)' with the same details concerning the need to transfer to section 3 of the Land Act 1880
577   PROV, B, VPRS 12991/P/0001, Unit 000003, Type V2 – Ararat Shire Minute Book
578   PROV, B, VPRS 15206/P0001/Unit 7 – Ararat Shire Rate Book
579   *Ararat Advertiser*, October to December 1880 Reports on Ararat Shire Council Meetings
580   *Ararat Advertiser*, 14 January 1879
581   *Ararat Advertiser*, early April 1881 report on Ararat Petty Sessions

# Chapter 26

582   PROV, NM, VPRS 626/P, Unit 71, File 286, Copley/MacMaster – 8 January 1881 Daniel O'Callaghan letter to the Secretary of the Lands Department
583   PROV, NM, VPRS 626/P, Unit 71, File 273, Copley/MacMaster – Hand written Ararat Branch of Lands Department hand written file note headed 'Ararat Catherine Copley 125 acres'
584   PROV, NM, VPRS 626/P, Unit 71, File 273, Copley/MacMaster – hand written note on Department File sheet headed 'Ararat'
585   PROV, NM, VPRS 626/P, Unit 71, File 286, Copley/MacMaster – hand written note on Department File sheet with the numbers '8 159' on top and headed 'Catherine Copley'
586   PROV, NM, VPRS 626/P, Unit 71, File 286, Copley/MacMaster – dates taken from 8 January 1881 Daniel O'Callaghan letter in this file
587   PROV, NM, VPRS 626/P, Unit 71, File 286, Copley/MacMaster – 8 January 1881 Daniel O'Callaghan letter to Secretary of Lands Department
588   PROV, NM, VPRS 626/P, Unit 71, File 286, Copley/MacMaster – 8 January 1881 Daniel O'Callaghan letter to Secretary of Lands Department
589   PROV, NM, VPRS 626/P, Unit 71, File 286, Copley/MacMaster – Office of Lands and Survey Melbourne File Note headed 'Reg. No. 28819', 'Date of Letter 8.1.81' – 'She can obtain lease on payment of rent arrears'
590   PROV, NM, VPRS 626/P, Unit 71, File 286, Copley/MacMaster – reference to two further letters of demand sent to Catherine contained in 2 March 1881 Daniel Callaghan letter to Secretary of Lands Department
591   PROV, NM, VPRS 626/P, Unit 71, File 286, Copley/MacMaster – detailed in Office of Lands and Survey Melbourne File Note headed 'Reg. No. 29015' 'Date of Letter 2.3.81'
592   PROV, NM, VPRS 626/P, Unit 71, File 286, Copley/MacMaster – 2 March 1881 Daniel O'Callaghan letter to Secretary of Lands Department
593   PROV, NM, VPRS 626/P, Unit 71, File 286, Copley/MacMaster –detailed in 'Office of Lands and Survey Melbourne' File Note headed 'Reg. No. 29015' 'Date of Letter 2.3.81'

594   PROV, NM, VPRS 626/P, Unit 71, File 286, Copley/MacMaster –detailed in 'Office of Lands and Survey Melbourne' File Note headed 'Reg. No. 29015' 'Date of Letter 2.3.81'
595   PROV, NM, VPRS 626/P, Unit 71, File 286, Copley/MacMaster – blank sheet of paper with handwritten notes and top of paper has words 'Endorse both leases'

## Chapter 27
596   PROV, NM, VPRS 13753/P/Unit 1, Type V3, Rent Roll Ararat Selections, 19 and 20 Land Act 1869
597   *Pleasant Creek News and Stawell Chronicle,* 3 September 1881
598   PROV, NM, VPRS 625/P, Unit 106, File 5707, Thomas May selection – Department File note on payments headed 'No. 5707 The undermentioned allotment of land has been PURCHASED under Section 20, "Land Act 1869"' (second last sheet in file)
599   1882 Copley/McGee Stawell marriage No. 39
600   PROV, B, VPRS 12991/P0001/Unit 4 – Ararat Shire Minute Book 1881–1885
601   PROV, B, VPRS 15206/P00001/Unit 8 – Ararat Shire Rate Records
602   PROV, NM, VPRS 13753/P/0001/Unit 1 Rent Roll Ararat Selections 19 and 20 Land Act 1869
603   Based on birth register records for birth of Mary Catherine Copley at Whittlesea in November 1884 (1885 Birth Reg. No. 6652)
604   Melbourne National Archives Consign No. B 5846/1
605   PROV, NM, VPRS 626/P, Unit 95, File 3125, Thomas May selection – refer to survey map on sheet headed 'Land Act 1869, Section 19 Part 2, Application of Thomas May' dated 19/1/1885
606   PROV, NM, VPRS 626/P, Unit 95, File 3125, Thomas May selection – sheet headed 'questions and statements referred to in the declaration'
607   PROV, NM, VPRS 626/P, Unit 95, File 3125, Thomas May selection – 19.1.1885 land survey report
608   PROV, NM, VPRS 626/P, Unit 95, File 3125, Thomas May selection – sheet headed 'Ararat. Section 2 Land Act'
609   Ibid.
610   PROV, NM, VPRS 13753/P/001, Unit 1, Type V3, Rent Rolls Ararat Selections 19 and 20 Land Act 1869
611   PROV, B, VPRS 15206/P0001/Unit 9 – Ararat Shire Rate Records
612   PROV, B, VPRS 15250/P/001 – Ararat Shire Letter Book
613   PROV, B, VPRS 15206/P0001/Unit 9 – Ararat Shire Rate Records
614   PROV, B, VPRS 15206/P0001/Unit 10 – Ararat Shire Rate Records
615   PROV, NM, VPRS 626, Parish of Jallukar, Land selection file 2084/19.20
616   Isabel Armer, *A Range of Views of Jallukar and Bellellen,* p. 42 (Bellellen selection map)
617   Based on birth certificate for James Copley, son of Mary and James Copley, born in Footscray in 1887 No. 3308
618   PROV, NM, VPRS 626, Unit 71, File 286, Copley/MacMaster – Sheet headed 'Names of Parties Thereof' 'Catherine Copley and Archibald Gray'
619   PROV, NM, VPRS 626, Unit 71, File 273, Copley/MacMaster – sheet headed 'Transfer of Leasehold' and VPRS 626, Unit 71, File 286, Copley/MacMaster – sheet headed 'Names of Parties Thereof' 'Catherine Copley and Archibald Gray'
620   PROV, NM, VPRS 13753/P/0001/Unit 1, Type V3 Rent Roll Ararat Selections 19 and 20 Land Act 1869
621   Based on discussion in 2006 with Tom Banfield current owner of the 240 acres of land that made up the Copley Redman Bluff selections
622   Major Mitchell diary 13 July 1836

## Chapter 28
623   PRO, B, VPRS 1103, Unit 8 – Stawell Borough Rate Records
624   PROV, B, VPRS 1103, Units 8 and 9 – Stawell Borough Rate Records
625   1891 Laurence Green Registration of birth at Stawell No. 7200
626   *Pleasant Creek News and Stawell Chronicle,* 16 August 1890
627   PROV, NM, VPRS 626/P, Unit 95, File 3125, Thomas May selection – the survey map headed 'Land Act 1869, Section 19 Part 2, Application of Thomas May' and dated 19/1/1885 – shows that on taking up the selection licence Thomas had to construct around 270 chains (5,420 metres) of fencing rather than more than 500 chains to enclose the full boundary of the selection
628   PROV, NM, VPRS 626, Unit 95, File 3125 – information taken from Thomas May 7/6/1891 application for selection lease, p. 2 – 'CultiPROVtion' section
629   PROV, B, VPRS 12991/P/0001, Ararat Shire Minute Book, September 1887 and November 1887 meetings
630   *Pleasant Creek New and Stawell Chronicle,* 4 April 1891
631   Ibid.
632   PROV, B, VPRS 15206/P0001/Units 11 and 12, Ararat Shire Rate Records – In the 1890 to 1891 period in the rate records the ownership of this land changed from Thomas May to Dr William Symes
633   PROV, NM, VPRS 13753/P/0001, Unit 1, Type V3, Rent Roll Ararat Selections 19 and 20 Land Act 1869
634   PROV, NM, VPRS 626, Unit 95, File 3125, Thomas May selection file – taken from 7/6/1891 application for selection lease, p. 2 – 'Building' section
635   *Ararat Chronicle,* 18 February 1891

636  *Ararat Advertiser,* 17 February 1891
637  1891 Catherine Copley/Thomas May Stawell marriage certificate No. 3347 – On this certificate Thomas gave Stawell as his usual place of residence (even though under his selection licence he supposed to live on the Jallukar selection)
638  1891 Catherine Copley/Thomas May Stawell marriage No. 35
639  Taken from 1924 Annie Doyle death certificate in Stawell No. 618
640  C.E. Sayers, *Shepherds Gold,* p. 183
641  PROV, NM, VPRS 626/P, Unit 95, File 3125, Thomas May selection file, information taken from Thomas May 7/6/1891 application for selection lease, p. 1 – it is noted that six year selection licence commenced on 1 June 1885
642  PROV, NM, VPRS 626/P, Unit 95, File 3125, Thomas May selection file – hand written note on plain piece of paper after 7/6/1891 application for selection lease
643  PROV, NM, VPRS 626/P, Unit 95, File 3125, Thomas May selection file – 7/6/1891 selection lease application
644  PROV, NM, VPRS 626/P, Unit 95, File 3125, Thomas May selection file – sheet headed 'Ararat, The Land Act 1869' concerning Lands Department review of 7/6/1891 application for a selection lease
645  PROV, NM, VPRS 13753/P/0001, Unit 1, Type 3, Rent Roll Ararat Selections 19 and 20 Land Act 1869

## Chapter 29
646  Stawell Historical Society Card Index, Thomas May Miners Right Application No. 7805 of 15.6.1891
647  Victorian Land Titles Records for Parish of Illawarra, Crown Allotment 45A
648  PROV, NM, VPRS 626/P, Unit 95, File 3125, Thomas May selection file – 'Transfer of Leasehold' memo dated 9/1/1892
649  *Ararat Advertiser,* 6 June 1891 and 20 June 1991
650  PROV, B, VPRS 3770, Units 11 and 12, Stawell Shire Rate Records
651  PROV, B, VPRS 1103, Unit 10, Stawell Borough Rate Records
652  PROV, B, VPRS 3770, Unit 13, Stawell Shire Rate Records
653  PROV, B, VPRS 1103, Units 10,11, and 12, Stawell Borough Rate Records
654  PROV, B, VPRS 1103, Units 10, 11, and 12, Stawell Borough Rate Records
655  PROV, B, VPRS 3770, Units 14 and 15, Stawell Shire Rate Records
656  Sayers, Chapter 19, 'Magdala'
657  *Stawell News and Pleasant Creek Chronicle,* 21 March 1898
658  Ibid.
659  Ibid.
660  Ibid.
661  Ibid.
662  Ibid.
663  PROV, B, VPRS 3770, Unit 17, Stawell Shire Rate Records
664  PROV, B, VPRS 1103, Unit 14, Stawell Borough Rate Records
665  Victorian Lands Title Records for Parish of Stawell, section 44, Crown Allotment 14A
666  Daniel Hadfield age taken from Daniel Hadfield/Annie McNamara marriage certificate St Patricks Melbourne 1917, No. 5551
667  Victorian Lands Title Records for Parish of Stawell, section 44, Crown Allotment 14A
668  PROV, NM, Thomas May will and probate 88.857 (List of shop contents in 1903)
669  Henry Hadfield Landsborough birth certificate 1873 (16 August)
670  Hannah Carter (Hadfield) death certificate 1960 No. 23489 and Daniel Hadfield/Annie McNamara marriage certificate St. Patricks Melbourne 1917 No. 5551
671  1887 Thomas Hadfield/Emma Shoulder Stawell marriage certificate No. 152
672  1891 Thomas Hadfield Stawell death certificate No. 8255
673  PROV, B, VPRS 3770, Unit 20, Stawell Shire Rate Records
674  PROV, B, VPRS 15206, Units 22 and 23, Ararat Shire Rate Records – 1902 to 1904; 1903 Electoral Roll for federal seat of Grampians, town of Mafeking; and John Robert Copley/Mary Franklin Mafeking (Ararat) marriage certificate No. 3
675  Western Australia (WA), 1900 Thomas Mervyn Green Coolgardie birth certificate No. 231
676  WA, 1903 Norman Green Perth birth certificate No. 751 and WA 1904 Post Office Directory, p. 195
677  1901 Electoral Roll for the federal seat of Coolgardie

## Chapter 30
678  1903 Thomas May Stawell death certificate No. 11501
679  1903 Harry Hadfield/Mary Walter Stawell Marriage Certificate No. 4772
680  1858 Mary Hunter Pleasant Creek birth certificate No. 18715
681  1912 Mary Hadfield Stawell death certificate No. 7749
682  1903 Harry Hadfield/Mary Walter Stawell Marriage Certificate No. 4772
683  PROV, NM, James Walter Letters of Administration 1903 86.86
684  1903 Thomas May Stawell death certificate No. 11501

685 PROV, NM, Thomas May will and probate 1903 88.857
686 Ibid.
687 Age taken from 1894 birth certificate for Ellen Webster, Stawell, No. 15804
688 Age taken from 1896 birth certificate for Annie Stanton, Stawell, No. 23580
689 1903 Thomas May Stawell death certificate No. 11501
690 *Stawell News and Pleasant Creek Chronicle*, 29 September 1903
691 *Stawell News and Pleasant Creek Chronicle*, 3 October 1903
692 PROV, NM, Thomas May will and probate 1903 88.857
693 Ibid.
694 Ibid.
695 PROV, NM, Theresa H Shea will and probate 1897 65/376 and Victorian Land Titles Records for Parish of Stawell, Section 44, Crown Allotment 14A
696 In 1891 Catherine's son, John Copley, received £4/5/- an acre for a block of land he sold at Jallukar – refer to *Ararat Advertiser*, 5 June 1891 and 20 June 1991 for details. In the following period, we found no evidence that the PROVlue of farming land around Stawell and Ararat dropped. In fact, it would appear to have increased in PROVlue.
697 Janette M. Bomford, *That Dangerous and Persuasive Woman – Vida Goldstein*, p. 59
698 Bomford, p. 20
699 *Stawel News and Pleasant Creek Chronicle*, 24 October 1903
700 PROV, NM, Thomas May will and probate 1903 88.857
701 Details for three children are based on 'Copley family' return trip Fremantle shipping arriPROVls on 24/3/1904 from S.S. Buninyong. Two male children under 12 years of age, (Ernest and Stanley both under 12 years of age) and three adult women, (Catherine, Mary and one of Mary's adult daughters). At 1903 federal election, Mary Copley was enrolled as living in Stawell in the seat of Grampians
702 1903 federal election roll for the seat of Grampians
703 1903 federal election roll for the seat of Grampians
704 *Stawell News and Pleasant Creek Chronicle*, 24 October 1903
705 *Stawell News and Pleasant Creek Chronicle*, 17 December 1903
706 Ibid.
707 *Stawell News and Pleasant Creek Chronicle*, 1 September 1906
708 *Stawell News and Pleasant Creek Chronicle*, 17 December 1903
709 *Stawell News and Pleasant Creek Chronicle*, 19 December 1903

## Chapter 31
710 PROV, NM, VPRS 3506, Melbourne Outward Passenger Departures
711 Bureau of Metrology web site for Stawell (http://reg.bom.gov.au/climate/averages/tables/cw_079042shtml)
712 Bureau of Metrology web site for Menzies (http://reg.bom.gov.au/climate/averages/tables/cw_012052shtml)
713 Victorian Land Title, Parish of Illawarra, Crown Allotment 45A
714 Based on Catherine departing Adelaide for Western Australia on the S.S. Buninyong on 15/3/1904
715 PROV, NM, CRS K269, Roll 14 (Note: *Albany Advertiser*, 23 March 1904, p. 3, identifies the Copley party as containing one adult and four children. We believe that the official ship record should be accepted and that it is reasonable to believe that Catherine travelled to Western Australia with Mary and children.)
716 *Albany Advertiser*, 23 March 1904, p. 3
717 *The Western Australian*, 29 May 1899 – p. 7 (taken from article on 'extensive alterations' to 'Steamer Buninyong'; and Victorian Ship's graveyard Wrecks web site (http://www.vicwrecks.com/control.html)
718 *The West Australian*, 29 May 1899 – p. 7 (taken from article on 'extensive alterations' to 'Steamer Buninyong')
719 Patrick Howard, *To Hell or to Hobart*, p. 118
720 *Albany Advertiser*, 23 March 1904, p. 3
721 1900 Mervyn Joseph Green Coolgardie birth certificate No. 231
722 1903 Norman Green Perth birth certificate No. 754
723 *Golden Quest Discovery Trial Guide Book*, p. 43
724 State Library of Western Australia – Harry P. Woodward, *Geological map of Menzies, North Coolgardie*, 1905 – Call No. 4730/14/(37/15)
725 Shire of Menzies web site (http://www.menzies.wa.gov.au/about_us/climate.html)
726 Bureau of Metrology web site for Menzies (http://reg.bom.gov.au/climate/averages/tables/cw_012052shtml)
727 Bureau of Metrology web site for Stawell (http://reg.bom.gov.au/climate/averages/tables/cw_079042shtml)
728 Victorian Lands Record for Parish of Stawell, section 44, crown allotment 14A
729 *Ararat Chronicle*, 7 January 1905
730 *Stawell News and Pleasant Creek Chronicle*, March and April 1905 editions
731 Victorian Land Records, Parish of Illawarra, Crown Allotment 45A

## Chapter 32
732    1905 John Fredrick Copley Yarram Yarram birth certificate No. 22747
733    1906 Copley/O'Brien North Coolgardie marriage certificate No. 35
734    *North Coolgardie Herald*, 8 December 1906
735    Ibid.
736    1906 Catherine May North Coolgardie death certificate No. 40
737    *Kalgoorlie Miner*, 11 December 1906
738    1906 Catherine May North Coolgardie death certificate No. 40
739    Ibid.
740    Ibid.
741    *North Coolgardie Herald*, 10 December 1906
742    1906 Catherine May North Coolgardie death certificate No. 40
743    Ibid.

## Epilogue
744    PROV, NM, Thomas May will and probate documentation 1903 88.857
745    Ibid.
746    1861 English Census, County of York, Parish of Kimberworth, Ecclesiastical District of Thorpe Hesley
747    1861 John Copley death, County of York, Sub-District of Kimberworth, Death No. 339
748    Tasmanian Archive and Heritage Office [TA], James Fraser Convict Record CON 37/3
749    TA, Applications Permission to Marry, CON 52/3 p. 151, CON 52/4, CON 52/6; TA, Tasmania Colonial Family Index, TASP 3777178
750    TA, RGD 35/40, Deaths in the District of Longford, 253/1274
751    Margaret Hazzard, *Punishment Short of Death – A History of the Penal Settlement of Norfolk Island*, p. 244
752    The authors visited Norfolk Island in June 2008
753    Headstone on Walker grave in Norfolk Island cemetery
754    *Goulburn Herald* (NSW), 15 August 1882
755    *The Sydney Morning Herald*, 14th August 1882 and *The Maitland Mercury and Hunter River General Advertiser*, 19 August 1882
756    1882 Matthew Walker NSW Death certificate Reg. No. 1882/007757
757    Coultman Smith, *Shadow Over Tasmania*, p. 74
758    Ian Brand, *Port Arthur, 1830–1877*, p. 45
759    Coultman Smith, *Shadow Over Tasmania*, p. 75
760    Tony Rayner, *Female Factory Female Convicts*, p. 171
761    Rayner, pp 177/179
762    Rayner, pp 180/182
763    Rayner, p. 183
764    Denis Strangeman, *The Gold Rush to Lamplough*, p. 13
765    *Brisbane Courier*, 19 June 1882, p. 3
766    *The Dimboola Banner*, 16 February 1883
767    Ibid.
768    1891 William O'Callaghan District of Richmond (in Melbourne) death certificate No. 8027
769    *Seymour Express*, 30 June 1891
770    *Victoria's Wonderland – A Grampians History* Compiled by Halls Gap and Grampians Historical Society, p. 92
771    1895 Daniel SulliPROVn District of Moyston death certificate No. 6648
772    PROV, NM, Daniel SulliPROVn will and probate 1895 59*434
773    *Australian Dictionary of Biography*, online edition: Gaunson, David (1846–1909) (http://adbonline.anu.edu.au/biogs/A040266b.htm?hilite=Gaunson)
774    Isabel Armer, *A Range of Views of Jallukar and Bellellen*, p. 55
775    *Red man's Review*, Melbourne State Library (SLTF 052 R24J)
776    Armer, p. 58
777    PROV, NM, VPRS 626, Unit 71, File 273, Copley/MacMaster – sheet headed 'Transfer of Leasehold' and VPRS 626, Unit 71, File 286, Copley/MacMaster –sheet headed 'Names of Parties Thereof' 'Catherine Copley and Archibald Gray'
778    Advice the authors received from Tom Banfield current owner of this land
779    Tom Banfield, *Grampians Paradise – Camping and CaraPROVn Parkland – A Walk Around our Parkland*
780    *Stawell News and Pleasant Creek Chronicle*, 11 December 1906, p. 3
781    *Stawell News and Pleasant Creek Chronicle*, 16 and 19 April 1910
782    *Melbourne Herald*, 3 August 1914, p. 12
783    *Stawell News and Pleasant Creek Chronicle*, 24 October 1903
784    *Stawell News and Pleasant Creek Chronicle*, 9 May 1917
785    *Stawell News and Pleasant Creek Chronicle*, 12 May 1917
786    Robert Kingston, *Good Country for a Grant – A History of the Stawell Shire*, p. 208

787   *The Argus*, 23 August 1949
788   1913 Joseph Hadfield Stawell death certificate No. 11412
789   1912 Mary Hadfield Stawell death certificate No. 7749
790   1913 Harry Hadfield/Agnes Ewers Stawell Marriage Certificate No. 8296
791   1913 Joseph Hadfield Stawell death certificate No. 11412
792   1953 Henry Joseph Hayes/Hadfield Stawell death certificate No. 11452
793   The 1907 Western Australia Post Office Directory (p. 202) showed Hannah and Thomas Green living at Lion Mill. The 1908 Post Office Directory entry for Lion Mill (p. 220) contained no listing for Hannah and Thomas
794   1925 Hannah Green death certificate No. 55
795   The 1915 Western Australia Post Office Directory contains the last entry for James Copley at Menzies (p. 244). The 1916 Post Office Directory entry for Menzies contained no listing for James Copley
796   Australian War Memorial web site, James Joseph Copley, Service No. 6255. Date Joined 24/4/1916; Date of Embarkation 18/9/1916 (http://www.awm.gov.au/research/people/nominal_rolls/first_world_war_embarkation/person.asp?p=178967)
797   Australian War Memorial web site, Stanley Joseph Copley, Service No. 2791. Date Joined 26/5/1916; Date of Embarkation 29/12/1916 (http://www.awm.gov.au/research/people/nominal_rolls/first_world_war_embarkation/person.asp?p=288163)
798   1916 Ernest John Copley Leonora death certificate No. 14
799   1927 James Copley Fremantle death certificate (died 17/9/1927)
800   1941 Mary Copley Fremantle death certificate No. 275
801   The April/May 1905 timing for the move from Mafeking to Yarram is based on John Robert Copley's marriage to Harriett Mary Franklin taking place at Mafeking in March 1905 and their first child being born at Yarram in June 1905 (birth of John Fredrick Copley 1905/No. 22747)
802   1915 Electoral Roll for the seat of Corangamite, sub-division of Ararat
803   1934 John Copley Ararat death certificate No. 12035
804   1921 Jane Copley Ararat death certificate No. 8050
805   1934 John Copley Ararat death certificate No. 12035
806   Tasmania, Westbury Valuation Roll for 1858
807   Tasmania, Westbury Valuation Roll for 1860
808   Tasmania Birth Records, James McMahon, Registration Place Westbury, Reg. No. 2302, RGD No. 33
809   Tasmania Birth Records, Michael McMahon, Registration Place Westbury, Reg. No. 1691, RGD No. 33
810   Catherine McMahon, Victorian birth certificate 1868/No. 4350
811   Catherine McMahon, Victorian death certificate 1868/No. 2009
812   Susan McMahon, Victorian death certificate 1881/No. 4920
813   1889 Deaths in District of Launceston, Denis McMahon, RGD 35/58 No. 899
814   1862, Marriages in Westbury District, William McMahon and Mary Keene, No. 637
815   Anne McMahon and K.M. Owen, *The Story of William McMahon – Convicted at the Clare Spring Assizes 1849 and Sentenced to Ten Years Transportation to Van Diemen's Land*
816   Tasmania, Registrar-General's Office, Extract on Search, No. 69699, Folio 820/05C (William McMahon died at Westbury on 4 April 1905)
817   1855 Griffiths Valuation, Parish of Moyne, Townland Cappaghabaun Park
818   1901 Census of Ireland, County Clare, Townland of Sheeaun
819   1906 Western Australia, North Coolgardie Catherine May death certificate No. 40

# Index

Abbott, Edward, 66, 67
Abel & Piggott, 106, 107
Adelaide, 256, 257
*Adolphus Yates*, 124
Afghan camel drivers, 260
Albany, 255, 256, 257
Alison, 17
All Saints Church, Rotherham, 46
Allen, James, 50
Amherst, 134
Anglican church tithe, 10
*Anson* (hulk), 33, 37, 41
Ararat, 124–126
   Court of Petty Sessions (see Court of Petty Sessions)
Ararat Shire Council, 164, 198–200, 205, 208–210, 217–218, 220–221, 223, 227
Armitage, Mr, 110
Aughrim townland, 20
Austin, John, 112, 115
*Australasia*, 31–32, 33, 41, 256–257
Avoca cemetery, 131

Bagnall, Sarah, 46
Baldock, Alfred Essex, 70–71, 72, 74–75
Ball, John, 84
Ballarat (also Ballaarat), 122, 126, 164
Ballooning, 266
Banfield
   family, 276
   Harrie, 275
Barry, Justice Sir Redmond, 210
Bass, Naomi, 235
Battania, James, 236
Beamont, John Henry, 113, 114
Bedford, Reverend, 91–92
Bellellen, 136, 222
Bennett, Constable, 51, 51–52
Bennett, Edward James, 180
Black, Alexander, 180
Black family, 11
Black Range, 135, 136, 164
*Black Swan* (steamer), 123

Blake, Margaret (see McMahon, Margaret)
Blencover, Robert Willis, 148, 150–151, 152
Bolen family, 11
Bonaparte, Napoleon, 43, 44, 45
Booth, Captain Charles O'Hara, 156
Bottrell, Anne (see May, Anne)
Boulder mining leases, 259
Boyd, James, 60
Brahn, Doctor George, 83
Brewer, W., 66, 66–67, 155
Brickfield Hiring Depot, 34, 35, 36, 89
Briggs, Robert, 161
Brighton (England), 139–143, 145, 146
   Chain Pier, 142–143, 258
   Egremont Street, 142, 147
   George Street, 143
   Nottingham Street, 139–140
   railway, 146
   Royal Pavilion, 140–141
   sea baths, 142
Brooks, Sir Arthur B., 13
Broughton, Bishop William, 59–60
Brown, Detective Constable, 64–65
Browne, Commissioner Fielding, 108, 109–110, 110–111, 113, 114, 115–116
*Buninyong*, SS, 256–257
Burgin, William, 51, 52
Burke, Mr, 159
bushfire, 194–195, 199, 202, 228–229, 276
Butcher, Charles, 45
Butcher, Thomas, 51, 53, 54
Butler, Doctor Thomas, 129

Caledonian Hotel, 235, 236, 261
Callawadda, 240
Campbell Town, 60, 61
Cappabane, 9, 10, 12–13, 17, 29, 222, 282–283
Cappaghabaun Mountain, 9
Capper, J.J., 153
Carfrae, Thomas, 161
Cascades Female Factory, 34, 35–40, 88, 90, 271–272
Chandler, John, 128

Chartism/Chartists, 46–49, 50, 52, 55–56, 127
Chatham (England), 152
Clare Spring Assizes, 23, 24–25
Clark, Mr (Bushy Plains), 158
Clarke, George F., 212–214
Clarke, Marcus, 70, 162
Clarke, Sir William, 203
Clarke, William, 136–137, 203
Clarkson, Constable, 63–64
Colleary, Constable, 22, 26
Collingwood, Admiral, 152
Collins family, 11
Colquhoun, Doctor Robert, 179, 180
Connell, Captain James, 30
convict diet
  *Australasia*, 31
  Cascades Female Factory, 38
  *Elphinstone (4)*, 155
  *Euryalus*, 154
  Grangegorman, 30
  Hobart Town domestic service, 34
  *Justitia*, 58
  Lewes prison, 145
convict rules and regulations
  Brickfields Depot, 34, 35
  Cascades Female Factory, 35–41
  *Elphinstone (4)*, 154–155
  *Euryalus*, 153–155
  Lewes prison, 145
  Norfolk Island tobacco regulations, 76–77
  permission to marry, 84, 89, 91, 269
  Point Puer, 157–158
Coolgardie, 234, 238
Copley, Catherine (also known as Margaret) (convicts' daughter), 94–96, 129
Copley, Catherine (convict) (see McMahon, Catherine)
Copley, Catherine (convicts' grand-daughter), 167–168, 234
Copley, Elizabeth (also known as Bessie) (convicts' grand-daughter), 250, 264
Copley, Ernest, 250, 280
Copley, Florence (convicts' grand-daughter), 264
Copley, Hannah (convicts' daughter also known as Annie and Joanna), 128–129, 174, 183, 184, 193, 195, 200–201, 225, 230, 234, 238–239, 251, 255, 257–258, 279–280
Copley, Hannah (mother of convict John), 44, 46, 129

Copley, Hannah (sister of convict John), 46
Copley, James, 99, 122, 128, 164, 183, 192, 193, 194–195, 201, 204, 205, 217, 218, 222, 233, 234, 238–239, 250–251, 255, 257, 260, 263, 264, 265, 280
Copley, James Joseph (convict's grand-son), 280
Copley, Jane (convicts' daughter-in-law), 167, 174, 178, 183, 218, 221–222, 234, 261, 280–281
Copley, Jane (convicts' grand-daughter), 234
Copley, John (convict)
  application for permission to marry, 88, 89, 91
  *Argus* advertisement, 132
  birth, 43
  burial of son William, 130–131
  business problems, 102–107
  conditional pardon, 98, 105, 118–119
  conditional pardon recommendation, 62, 65
  death, 179–181
  description, 59
  Frying Pan Plains selection, 135, 136–137
  hawking nails offence, 60–61
  health problems, 172, 177, 179–180
  house burglary conviction, 65–68
  insolvency proceedings, 108–116
  last will and testament, 179–180
  Launceston depot, 81, 82–83
  living in Stawell, 134, 135
  marriage to Catherine McMahon, 88–89, 91–92
  meets Catherine McMahon, 86, 87–88
  metal trades business, 99–100, 101–107
  move to Hobart Town, 83, 84–85
  Norfolk Island
    punishment, 76–80
    schooling, 71
    time on, 69–81
    whale boat incident, 71–74
  probationary term, 60
  Redman Bluff selections, 165–166, 171–173, 174–177, 178–179
  Rotherham committal, 52–53
  sheep stealing, 50–55
  ticket-of-leave, 61, 99
  time on *Justitia*, 57–58
  Van Diemen's Land convict service, 59–62
  voyage on *Lady Raffles*, 58–59
  voyage to Victoria, 71–74

witness to Denis McMahon marriage, 118
York conviction, 53–54
Copley, John (convict's father), 43, 44, 45, 46, 48, 268–269
Copley, John (convicts' great-grandson), 263
Copley, John (convicts' son), 93, 94, 128, 167, 167–168, 170–171, 174, 178, 180–181, 183, 192, 193, 194–195, 204, 205, 209, 218, 221–222, 233, 234, 238, 254, 256, 280–281
Copley, John Robert (convicts' grandson), 178, 234, 263
Copley, Mary (first wife of convict John), 48, 50–51, 61–62, 88, 89, 268
Copley, Mary (wife of James), 217, 218, 222, 233, 239, 250, 251, 254, 255, 256, 260, 264, 280
Copley, Mary Catherine (convicts' granddaughter), 250, 263–264
Copley – O'Brien 1906 wedding, 263–264
Copley, Stanley, 250, 280
Copley, William (convicts' son), 119, 121, 128, 129, 130–131
Coppard, James, 148
Court cases
   Catherine
      1849 sheep stealing, 24–27
      1851 shoe offence, 36
      1879 failure to pay rates, 198–199
   John
      1840 sheep stealing, 52–56
      1844 hawking nails, 60–61
      1847 house burglary, 65–68
      1855 Court of Requests, 106, 107
      1856 insolvency, 108–116
      Lamplough 1860 sheep stealing, 130 Stawell
      1898 insulting language, 234–236
      Stawell 1881 sheep stealing, 216
   Thomas
      1839 plate stealing, 144
      1841 rabbit stealing, 148–150
      1848 misconduct, 159
Court of Petty Sessions, 130
crops details, 164, 165, 169, 171, 175, 176, 178, 183, 184, 227
Crotty, Bridgett (see Goss, Bridgett)
Cutt, John, 51, 52, 53, 54, 55, 177
Cutt, John (son), 51

Daley, Detective Constable, 64, 65
Darling, Governor, 69
Davis, J., 89

Davis, James (Stawell miner), 235–236
DeMay, Peter, 219
Denison, Governor, 66, 68, 84, 91
Dexter, Thomas, 153
Dix, Anne, 147
Dix, Thomas, 146, 147, 148, 150
Djub Wurrung (Aboriginal people), 136
Dooling, Mrs, 243
Doyle, Annie, 230
Doyle, Martin, 230
Duggan, Thomas, 97
Duke of Kent Hotel, Melbourne, 132
Dwane, police sub-constable, 22
Dwyer, Patrick, 22, 26

education
   Catherine, 29, 33–34
   John, 71
   John (convicts' son), 221–222
   Thomas, 143, 153–154, 156–158
   William O'Callaghan schools achievement, 273
Ennis
   Courthouse, 25
   Gaol, 24
elections
   1859 Victoria, 127
   1903 Stawell, 245–247, 248–250, 251–253
   1906 Stawell, 277
   1910 Stawell, 278–279
   1917 Stawell, 278–279
*Elphinstone*, 154–156
Emmett brothers, 238
Esmond, James, 86
Eureka stockade, 126
*Euryalus* (prison hulk), 152, 152–153, 153–154
Ewers, Agnes, 279
Ewers, W., 243

Fagan, Father, 263, 264
Fawcett, Miss, 252
Fitzgerald, Father, 201, 217
Fitzmaurice, M., 230
Fitzwilliam, Earl, 44, 48
Fletcher, John, 45
Franklin, Benjamin, 249
Franklin, Lady, 13
Franklin, Mary, 263
Fraser, James, 63–68, 69, 75–77, 80, 81, 83–84, 269

Freer, Maurice, 70
Frying Pan Plains, 135, 164
Footscray, 222
Fox, John, 27
Fullerton, Colonel, 52, 53

Galbraith, Doctor, 167
Gates, Ambrose, 150
Gaunson, David, 206–207, 208, 214–215, 274
Geelong, 124, 126
Gibson, sub-constable, 22
gold
　discovery, 83
　Ballaarat return to diggers, 122
Golden Age Hotel, Stawell, 219
Goldfield water pipeline, 258
goldfields
　Ararat, 124–126
　Coolgardie, 234
　Kalgoorlie, 234, 258, 259
　Lamplough, 127, 162, 272
　Londonderry diggings, 131
　Mafeking, 238, 254
　Menzies, 239, 259–260, 284
　Moonambell, 131
　Stawell, 125–126, 134, 135, 164, 179, 225–226, 234, 244
Goldstein, Vida, 245–247, 248–250, 252–253, 277–279
Goss, Bridget, 41, 86, 87, 89, 92
Goss, John, 40–41, 85–86, 87–88, 89, 92, 121
*Governor Phillip* (brig), 71
Graham, Father, 265
Grangegorman prison depot, 28–30, 131
Grano, Mr, 235
Gray, Archibald, 223
Green, Hannah (see Copley, Hannah)
Green, Mervyn, 257
Green, Norman, 257–258
Green, Thomas, 201, 222, 233, 238–239, 279–280
Guilfoyle, Father Thomas, 229

Hadfield, Constable, 216
Hadfield, Daniel, 236, 237, 242
Hadfield, Harry, 237–238, 240, 241, 242, 242–243, 243, 244, 245, 247, 254, 260–261, 267–268, 279
Hadfield, Joseph, 279
Hadfield, Mary, 240, 279

Hadfield, Thomas, 237–238
Hall, Father William, 32
Hall, William, 143, 147
Halliday, William, 149–150
Hampton, J.S., 62, 65
Hannan, Paddy, 259
Hardy, Frank, 274
Hargreaves, Edward, 83
Harriott, George, 200
Hart family, 11
Hart, widow, 21–22, 22, 23, 26
Hayes, Ellen, 237–238
Head, Ellener, 148
Head, Thomas, 146–147, 147–148, 148, 150
Head, William, 147–148
*Hindostan* (see *Justitia*)
Hobart Town, 32
　Supreme Court, 65, 66
Hogan, Mrs, 128
Holberry, Samuel, 50, 55
Hold family, 219
Holy Island, 12
Homebush, 129
Hood Hill, 47–48
Hood, William, 200
Hornibrook, James (Stawell sub-constable), 170
Horwood, Christopher, 64, 65
Horwood, Mary, 64, 67
hot air ballooning, 226
hulks
　*Anson*, 33, 37, 41
　*Euryalus*, 152, 152–153, 153–154
　*Justitia*, 57, 59
Hussey, Doctor D., 264–265
*Hyderabad* (convict transport), 33

Illawarra, 232, 233, 236, 237, 238, 243–244, 256, 261
insolvency case, 108–116
Irish potato famine, 13–19, 22, 23–24, 27, 30, 101, 122, 187–188, 283
Isle of the Dead, 158

Jepson, Mr, 158
Jerusalem Probation Station, 60
Jones, Algernon Burdett, 36
Jones, B., 61
Jones, F., 60
Jones, William H.B., 154–155

Jullukar, 131, 135–136, 165, 176, 194–195, 219, 223, 224, 233, 274–275
*Justitia* (convict hulk), 57, 59

Kalgoorlie, 234, 259
Kane, D., 174
Kanowna, 263
Keane, Mary Anne, 282
Kelly, Ned, 207, 274
Kelsey, John, 61
Kilroy, Alexander, 30, 31, 32
King George IV, 140, 141
Kingston (Ireland), 30
Kingston (Norfolk Island), 71, 72, 79, 81
Klaer brothers, 130
Knowles, Samuel, 134

*Lady Franklin*, 69, 80, 81
*Lady Raffles*, 58, 59
Lake Bolac, 223
Lambert, Mrs, 30–31
Lamplough, 127–131, 162, 272
  Petty Sessions Court, 130
land ownership
  Colony of Victoria 1850s/1860s, 133–134, 135, 136, 136–137
  Ireland first half of nineteenth century, 9–10, 11–12, 18, 25–26
  O'Callaghan Victoria attitude, 186–187
  Thorpe Hesley/Scholes in 1812, 44
Land Selection Act provisions
  1860, 133–134
  1862, 134
  1865, 134, 135
  1869, 176, 179, 182, 203, 206, 226–227
  1880, 206, 207, 208, 211, 214–215, 219–220, 226–227
Launceston, 81, 82–83, 97–98, 123, 124, 167, 167–168
Ledcourt squatting run, 161–162
Lees, Mr, 111–113, 115–116
Lewes, 144
  Courthouse, 144, 148
  prison, 145, 148
Lexington squatting run, 136, 172, 203, 228
Limerick, 25, 28, 29
Lindley, Doctor John, 13
Lion Mill, 257–258
Londonderry diggings, 131, 136
Lymer, Thomas, 181

MacMaster, Ronald, 223, 224, 275
McGee, Mary (see Copley, Mary)
McLean, James, 199–200, 220–221
McMahon, Catherine
  applying for permission of marry, 88–89, 89, 91
  birth, 9–11
  birth of her children, 93–94, 94–95, 99, 119, 128–129
  conditional pardon, 98
  death, 264–266
  description, 12, 32
  Ennis conviction, 25–27
  fight with Ararat Shire Council, 198–200, 208–210, 217–218, 220–221
  free certificate, 122
  grave, 265–266, 284–285
  Illawarra land, 232, 233, 234, 236, 237, 238, 242–243, 244, 244–245, 261–262
  journey to Grangegorman, 28–29
  letter to David Gaunson, 207
  marriage to John Copley, 91–92
  marriage to Thomas May, 229–231, 266
  meets John Copley, 86, 87
  mortgage on selection, 223
  move to Victoria, 119–122, 123, 124
  move to Western Australia, 254–259
  selection lease applications, 185–186, 188–189, 202–203
  selection lease fight, 185–194, 195–197, 202–208, 211–215
  service for John Goss, 41
  sheep stealing, 20–23, 26–27
  ticket-of-leave, 94
  time at Cascades Female Factory, 35–36, 36–40
  time at Grangegorman, 29–30
  time on *Anson*, 33–34
  voyage on *Australasia*, 30–32
McMahon, Catherine (Denis McMahon's daughter), 281
McMahon, Denis, 12, 18, 21, 22–23, 24, 26–27, 28, 33, 97, 99, 101, 109, 117–118, 121, 123, 132, 281
McMahon, James (Catherine's brother), 12, 28, 282
McMahon, James (Catherine's father), 9, 10, 11, 12, 13, 20, 99, 229
McMahon, James (Denis McMahon's son), 281

McMahon, John (Catherine's brother), 12, 28, 282
McMahon, Julia, 18, 117
McMahon Margaret (Peggy), 9, 11, 12, 28, 229, 282
McMahon, Mary, 282
McMahon, Michael, 12, 28, 282
McMahon, Michael (Denis McMahon's son), 12, 28, 282
McMahon, Paddy Joe, 282–283
McMahon, Patrick (Catherine's brother), 12, 28, 282
McMahon, Patrick (son of Michael McMahon who lived at Cappabane), 282
McMahon, Susan, 117, 281
McMahon, Una, 282–283
McMahon, William, 12, 21, 22–23, 24, 26–27, 28, 33, 97, 98, 101, 109, 119, 121, 123, 281, 281–282
McMahon, William Patrick (son of the convict William McMahon), 282
McMinn, Washington, 115–116
McNamara family, 11
Mafeking, 238, 254, 281
Manchester, 45
Marcom family, 219
Marsden, John, 167
Marshall, Joseph, 216
Martin, Mary (see May, Mary Anne)
Mass Rock, 10, 12
Matthews, Marie, 269
Matthews, W., 168
May, Anne (nee Bottrell) (convict's first wife), 160, 161
May, Catherine (see McMahon, Catherine)
May, James (Jallukar selector), 168
May, Mary Anne (convict's mother), 139, 141, 141–142, 229
May, Mr (Superintendent of Cascades Female Factory), 39
May, Richard, 141
May, Thomas
  birth, 139–140
  birth and death of son, 160
  bush fire experience, 228–229
  Caledonian hotel incident, 234–236
  convict service, 158
  death, 240–241
  description, 155
  Egremont Street life, 142

hulk *Euryalus*, 152–154
land selections, 163, 165, 168–170, 173, 216–217, 219–220, 226–228, 230–231, 232–233
last will and testament, 241, 247
living with rabbits, 164–165, 218–219, 227–228
marriage to Anne Bottrell, 160
marriage to Catherine Copley, 229–230
married life in Stawell, 232, 233
misconduct charge and conviction, 159
move to Victoria, 161
Nottingham Street life, 139–140
Patrick Street store, 236–238
stealing a plate, 143–144
stealing a plate conviction, 144
stealing three rabbits, 146–148
stealing three rabbits conviction and sentence, 148–151
Stawell hospital, 162
ticket-of-leave, 158–159
time at Point Puer, 156–158
time at Lamplough, 162
time at Ledcourt, 161–162
transportation on *Elphinstone (4)*, 154–156
May, Thomas (convict's father), 139, 141, 229
May, Thomas Fredrick, 160, 230
Menzies, 239, 258, 259–260, 284
  cemetery, 265, 284–285
  railway, 259
  weather, 255, 260, 264–265
Milner, William, 104, 105, 106–107, 117
Minogue family, 11
Mitchell, Major, 135–136, 166, 224
Moir, Joseph, 106
Mokepilly squatting run, 216, 218
Montague, Justice Algernon, 66, 67–68
Moonambel (see Mountain Creek)
Mount Helena, 258
Mount Wellington, 37
Mount William, 135, 165–166, 175, 200, 204, 207, 223, 238, 254, 261, 276
Mountain Creek, 131
Mountain Hut, 175, 180, 183, 217, 222, 275
Murfin, Charles, 51, 52–53, 55
Murray, Vincent, 125
Mutton Town (Thorpe Hesley), 45

Nairn, W., 118,
Napthine, Councillor, 248

Nelson, Lord, 152
New Town, Hobart Town, 34, 114, 158, 271
New Wharf, Hobart Town, 94, 95, 101, 106, 112
Norfolk Island, 69–81
  school, 71

O'Brien – Copley 1906 wedding, 263–264
O'Brien, Daniel, 263–264
O'Callaghan, Daniel, 212, 214, 215
O'Callaghan, William, 186–188, 189–194, 195–196, 205, 207–208, 215, 222, 272–273
O'Connell, Daniel, 25
O'Connor, Charles Yelverton, 258–259
Old Wharf, Hobart Town, 93, 94
Owen brothers (John and James), 127

Padbury, Mr, 72, 73
Parkhurst Reformatory, 150–151, 152
Parsons, Harriett, 147
Parsons, James, 146, 147, 148, 227
Peel, Robert, 14, 15
Pentlands Creek, 136, 137, 165, 182, 198
Phillips, Henry, 142
Phillips, Mary (see Mary Anne May)
Pleasant Creek (see Stawell)
Point Puer, 155–158, 161, 165, 270–271
Pola, Pietro, 261
Port Adelaide, 256
Port Arthur, 63, 80, 85, 155, 156, 156, 271
Port Fairy, 124
Portland, 135, 245
Portland Bay, 124
Potato famine (see Irish potato famine)
Poynton, Mr, 104
Price, John, 69–70, 74, 75, 76, 77, 78–79, 79, 79–80, 98, 121, 123, 124
Price, Professor, 226
Prisoner Barracks Hobart Town, 59

Quartz Reefs, 134, 135, 164, 201, 225–226, 234, 236, 244
  miners' wage, 179
Queen's Orphan School, 158

rabbits, 16, 20, 146–147, 148, 150, 153, 164–165, 218, 227–228
Ratcliffe, W.H., 129, 130
Redman Bluff, 165–166, 166, 171, 172–173, 174–175, 198, 200, 226, 275–276

*Red Man's Review*, 275
Rex, George, 99–100, 102, 103–104, 105, 106, 111, 112
Richards, Baron, 25–26, 27
right to vote
  1827 Ireland, 11
  1830s England, 47
  1859 Victoria, 127
  1902 Women, 239
Risby, John, 106
Robinson, J., 155
Rogers, Darby, 20–21, 22–23, 26, 122, 177, 188, 265
Rogers, Reverend Thomas, 75–76, 108
Roosevelt, President Theodore, 246
Rotherham, 45, 46, 47, 50, 52
  Courthouse, 51, 52
Rowan, Mr, 235
Rowden, Robert, 118
Royal Pavilion, Brighton, 140–141
*Royal Shepherd* (steamer), 123
Rupel, Mr, 101
Russell, Lord John, 15

St David's Church, Hobart Town, 91–92
St Joseph's Church, Hobart Town, 94, 95, 99, 119
St Mary's Church, Ecclesfield, 44, 45, 46
St Nicholas Church, Brighton, 139
St Patrick's Church, Stawell, 200–201, 201, 217, 236, 240
Sampson, John, 13
Sanders, John, 150
Sargent, Thomas, 146–147, 147, 148, 150, 151, 152, 153
Scarriff, 9, 15, 16–17, 18, 19, 130
  graveyard, 15, 16–17
  police, 22, 23
  work house, 15, 18–19, 20
Shalder family, 174
Shaw, Mr, 60
Sheep stealing
  Copley, 51–53
  Lamplough, 130
  Marsden, John, 167
  McMahon, 20–23
  Mokepilly squatting run, 216
Shirley, James, 132
Shoulder, Emma, 238
Simmons, Mr, 72, 73

*Sirius*, 72
soup kitchen, 17, 34
Spears, Robert, 199
squatters, 133–134, 136, 136–137, 161–162, 169, 170, 172, 187, 200, 202–203, 215, 216, 229
Stanton, Walter, 241, 243, 244, 247, 250, 253
Stawell
 ballooning, 226
 Borough rate records, 225, 233, 234, 236, 242
 hospital, 162, 164, 179–180
 Patrick Street store, 236–237, 243–244, 244–245, 260–261
 Shire rate records, 134, 135, 233, 234, 236, 238, 243
 weather, 255, 260
Stawell, Sir William F., 174
Stone, Reverend, 181
Stonehouse, Jane (see Copley, Jane)
Stonehouse, Robert, 167, 192
Sullivan, Daniel, 203–204, 207, 215, 273–274
Summerford, Jesse, 143, 144, 145, 147
Symes, Doctor William, 228, 232
Symonds, Chief Detective, 64

Taylor, Constable, 23
Thorpe Hesley, 43, 44, 45, 48, 53, 55, 85, 177, 178, 268–269
 The Gate pub, 45
Tonkin, Mr, 110
Trinity Church, Hobart, 59–60

Van Demonian law, 119–122, 124, 132, 134
Van Diemen's Land name change, 108
Victoria Wharf (Kingston, Dublin), 30
Viola, Mdlle Millie, 226

Walker, Elizabeth, 270
Walker, Jane, 72, 270
Walker, Matilda, 270
Walker, Matthew, 72, 74, 75, 98, 270
Walstab, George Arthur, 207, 208
Walter, James, 240
Walter, Mary (see Mary Hadfield)
Watson, Sergeant John, 160
Webster, John, 241, 243, 244, 247, 250, 253
Wesleyan Church, 48–49, 59, 131
West Moyston, 176
White, Inspector George, 150
Whittlesea, 218
Williams, J., 243
Wilmot, John, 85
Wilson, Alexander, 203
Wilson & Co., squatters, 203
Winford, John, 155
Womack, Constable Henry, 52
women's rights
 1827 Ireland, 11
 married women property rights, 193–194
 right to vote, 239
 select land, 273
 Vida Goldstein 1903 election, 245–247, 248–250, 252–253
Woolwich, 57
 Arsenal, 57–58
 Naval dockyard, 58
Wren, John, 274
Wylie, Robert, 58, 59

York
 Castle prison, 53
 Court House, 53, 54

Zala, Remigio, 232, 261